Interpersonal Competence and Organizational Effectiveness

Interpersonal Competence and Organizational Effectiveness

Chris Argyris

Professor of
Industrial Administration
Yale University

with a chapter by

Roger Harrison

Assistant Professor of
Industrial Administration
Yale University

1962

RICHARD D. IRWIN, INC.
HOMEWOOD, ILLINOIS
THE DORSEY PRESS, INC.

First Printing, February, 1962
Second Printing, May, 1965
Third Printing, November, 1966

Library of Congress Catalogue Card No. 62–11287

PRINTED IN THE UNITED STATES OF AMERICA

to
Arthur
and
Arnold

Preface

My deepest concern is to express my appreciation to the president, without whose initiative the study may never have been undertaken, as well as to the total executive group that co-operated magnificently. If there are heroes in this story, they are the ones.

The project was generously assisted through a grant of the National Institutes of Mental Health, 3M–9128C.

Dr. Leland Bradford helped me plan and administer the laboratory. William Lytle and David Peters helped me clarify my thinking as well as conducted research on various aspects of the study. Miss Sally Marchessault worked hard and effectively on getting the manuscript ready for the publisher. My wife, Reneé, as always, helped throughout all the stages of the manuscript in reading it and making important contributions.

This book is dedicated to my two earliest friends. Each in his own way has helped me to value growth and development.

CHRIS ARGYRIS

NEW HAVEN, CONNECTICUT
January 1962

vii

Contents

PART ONE. THEORY AND MODELS

PART TWO. DIAGNOSIS AND FEEDBACK

PART THREE. THE LABORATORY PROGRAM

PART FOUR. EVALUATION AND CONCLUSIONS

INDEX

Introduction

Human organizations are an integral part of our societal existence, a basic resource to its survival, and a living challenge to, as well as a continued opportunity for individual growth. Without human beings, organizations would never be alive. However, human beings also need organizations. They can test their freedom by being in organizations; for as we are beginning to realize, the way man can be free is to be responsible.[1]

The individual and the organization are living organisms, each with its own strategy for survival and growth. The individual's strategy for existence is at crucial points antagonistic to the strategy that guides the formal organization. This may lead to a continual conflict between the individual and the organization. The conflict, however, can be a source for growth as well as a stimulant for disintegration. It is my hypothesis that the present organizational strategies developed and used by administrators (be they industrial, educational, religious, governmental, or trade union) lead to human and organizational decay. It is also my hypothesis that this need not be so.

This hypothesis has support from several sources. If one examines the basic research literature, one finds that both the individual and the organization are fundamentally living organisms. If we strip away the skin surface properties that we have given to both of them, we will find that at their core they

---

[1] Victor E. Frankel, "Dynamics, Existence and Values," *Journal of Existential Psychiatry*, Vol. II, No. 5 (Summer, 1961), pp. 5–16.

are highly similar.[2] The belief that the conflict between the individual and the organization can lead to growth also finds support in much of the thinking in personality theory. Conflict is seen as one of the "levers" for growth and development. Finally, there is a practical reason why the hypothesis may be true. Organizations and individuals have existed side by side for years. And even if this were not the case, one might say that they have little choice but to learn to live with each other. The individual cannot exist without the organization and the organization (at this time) depends tremendously upon the individual.

Much research has been conducted, and much more is needed, regarding the "proper mix" of individual needs and organizational demands. There are two very important trends discernible in the research results. There is a *decreasing* interest in developing individuals who are "happy," "satisfied," and who have "high morale." There is an *increasing* interest in developing individuals with commitment and self-worth, who are fully functioning, productive, and self-responsible. This new interest stems from the increasing evidence in personality research that tension, struggle, and "unhappiness" can all be used "in the service of growth." "Pleasure, in the sense of relief from tension, may be a necessary state of respite. But it is a phenomenon of stand-still." It may be akin to psychological death.[3]

As a result of shifting our views of the causes of problems, there has been a concomitant shift in hypothesis regarding how to resolve them. Briefly, the integration of the individual and the organization may be influenced as follows:

1. The lower one goes down the chain of command, the more the job and the work environment control the individual's behavior; the more important it becomes to change the psycho-socio-technical environment. For example, changes in tech-

---

[2] Chris Argyris, "The Integration of the Individual and the Organization," *Social Science Approaches to Business Behavior* (Homewood, Ill.: Richard D. Irwin, Inc., 1962).

[3] See, for example, the chapters by Maslow, Allport, and Goldstein in A. H. Maslow, *New Knowledge in Human Values* (New York: Harper & Bros., 1960). Also the work of Victor Frankel cited in the first footnote.

nology, job design, incentive systems, budgeting activities, salary systems, and training activities.

2. The higher one goes up the chain of command, the more the individual has control over his work environment and the more important it becomes to change the interpersonal (and then the policy) environment. Examples of the former are the degree of trust, confidence, openness, nonconformity, as well as rivalry, defensiveness within the organization. Examples of the latter are policies in the service of human growth and commitment such as decentralization.[4]

One of the interesting phenomena in recent times is the increasing discouragement (with the results of decentralization) on the part of company officers as well as those below. Not that decentralization has failed to keep organizations alive. There is increasing concern, however, that it has not fulfilled its promise or approximated its potential.

My own experience, and that of my colleagues, confirms this observation. However, I personally believe that it is *not* because decentralization is a faulty concept. Fundamentally, decentralization means pushing down authority and responsibility to the lowest possible level. The aim is to have decisions made at the lowest possible point in the organization. Such a policy is congruent with the basic research about human personality and its potentiality for work.

However, decentralization occurs within the context of the traditional pyramidal structure. This means that people "on top" may not delegate their accountability. If someone below makes a poor decision, the people on top are still held responsible.

For decentralization to work under these conditions one needs, at all levels, technically and professionally competent individuals. One also needs sound policies to map out the highways and byways leading to the goal. Both of these, I believe, are available to most of the large firms undergoing decentralization.

The relatively low effectiveness of decentralization is, I

---

[4] Ralph Cordiner, *New Frontiers for Professional Managers* (New York: McGraw-Hill Book Co., Inc., 1956).

suggest, in the lack of attention to the human dimension. For example, economist Ernest Dale suggests that the lack of free discussion, openness, and trust among management has reached the point where it can be a primary cause for management to lose its claim to legitimacy.[5] "The greatest single bane of management today is its growing absolutism, its refusal to discuss or listen to different opinions. Management must encourage free discussion among its own executives. . . ."[6]

For decentralization to work, open superior-subordinate relationships are required, where trust is high, where conformity, fear, dependence are low, where experimentation and risk taking are prominent. These qualities cannot be issued, ordered, or even delegated because most human beings, if they are to develop them, do so at an early age. These are the *values* at the core of our society and our way of life.

The need is to find ways to uncover, to unfreeze these values wherever they exist. There is also a need to find ways to help man increase and strengthen these values because, lying dormant for years, they have tended to become weak, soft, and seemingly not very effective—especially in the tense, action-packed world of industrial life.

I believe the project described in this book takes a small first step in that direction. As a result of this experience and several others since then, I am encouraged that the development of trust, openness, confidence, and so on, is not only possible, it is also very practical. However, let us wait and see how the executives describe in their own words the experience and the results.

A New Concept of Social Responsibility

In the past, industry has tended to conceive of its social responsibility as being what it can do for the community at large. This has been of value, although as some writers suggest, it places industry in the peculiar position of becoming responsible for more than it should in the community.

---

[5] Ernest Dale, "The Social and Moral Responsibilities of the Executive in the Large Corporation," *American Economic Review*, Vol. LI, No. 2 (May, 1961), pp. 540–48.
[6] *Ibid.*, p. 545.

I should like, if I may, to say that this project suggests another (and in my opinion) more viable concept of social responsibility. Mutual understanding trust, self-esteem, openness, internal commitment, fully functioning human beings who aspire to excellence—all these we as a society say we value. The results of this study suggest that these values can not only be protected, but indeed increased, in an industrial setting. Here lies a great service the industrial world can offer to our society at large. It can show that it is not only possible to believe in these values but to use them in everyday living. If industry can integrate these values, then perhaps schools, churches, governmental organizations, unions, and so on, might re-examine themselves to see how their respective internal systems can begin to integrate, sanction, and strengthen some of the values to which we, as a nation, aspire.

How the Study Began

The conception of the study occurred at one of our country's more respected universities in a top-executive program which the president of the organization concerned was attending. The organization is one of the larger divisions of one of the biggest corporations in America. The division's annual gross sales exceed half a billion dollars. During one of the sessions he participated in some diagnostic role playing. He acted the part of a chief executive who attempted to "diplomatically" (in his eyes) "needle" the "vice-presidents" to tighten up their costs. During a discussion of the role playing some of the "vice-presidents" and part of the audience felt he was excellent. This was in accord with his back-home experience. However, to his surprise the other half described his behavior as "smooth," "sales-oriented," "same old bull s——," "pressure," and so on.

Our president was not the first to be somewhat shocked by this type of experience. And, no doubt, he will not be the last! But what made him different is that he was one of the few who had courage to go further. He wanted to find out if his people held the same range of opinions. Up to this point, they had all kept telling him how good he was. Now he began to wonder. What was his actual impact upon the organization? Is it possible to establish a degree of mutual trust and openness in an executive group where people will really "level" with one another? If so, what difference would it make to the operating effectiveness of the top executive team?

THE OVER-ALL SCHEME FOR THE PROGRAM

When I was asked if it would be possible to obtain insights into these questions, I replied that in my opinion, knowledge and research methods in behavioral science had progressed to the point where it would be worth trying, but success could not be guaranteed.

It is very important to emphasize that this hypothesis could not be held with any relevant (to action) degree of certainty if it had not been for years of research and thinking at Yale and many other universities (which I will discuss in the next chapter). At Yale, for example, there has been an increasing interest in organizational effectiveness and health. After years of diagnosing human problems of organization, we felt we were ready to begin to study how to solve them. This thinking and research led to the development of new models of organizational structures, managerial controls, incentive systems, and so on. When we attempted to find opportunities to try out and test the validity of our ideas in the "real" world, we found great difficulty. Not one case of resistance, however, was due to a disagreement in objectives and principles, to lack of funds, or to fear of research.

The most important reason for resistance was the realization by top administrators that if the ideas were to be tested they tended to require a high degree of trust, confidence, openness, and experimentation, on the part of management as well as the employees. In a sense the same factors which, as I suggested above, make decentralization operate much less effectively, turned out to be the causes for resistance to research. It became clear that we could not test our models in present organizations without first developing a new "human climate" within these organizations.

This awareness plus the realization that changes, if they are to be lasting, need to begin at the top, caused us to focus on the problem of diagnosing top management effectiveness. This lead to the development of a model which will be described in detail in Chapter 2. Briefly it is a model of a system with inputs, outputs, and feedbacks. It attempts to show the probable impact of specific values about "effective human relations" upon the interpersonal relationships among and administrative competence of the executives in the system, and how all of these in turn influence organizational factors such as conformity, lack of trust, confidence, organizational defensiveness, organizational structure, interdepartmental conflict and co-operation, rational decision making, and policy formulation and execution.

One objective of this study was to explore the diagnostic validity of the model as well as its capacity to provide the foundations upon which a change program could be developed and evaluated. If the results were positive, then further research would be conducted. The second and highly interrelated objective was to help a group of top executives develop the insights and understandings they needed to help them enhance their administrative competence as well as to hopefully enhance the competence of other parts of the organization.

The strategy developed was a rather simple one and also was based upon previous thinking and research. The first step was to make a diagnosis of the executive system. Second, the research results were fed back to the executives for their examination. The hope was that, once they became aware of their impact upon one another as well as upon the organization, they would begin to "unfreeze" and to desire to change.

The third step was to plan and execute a "laboratory" program *to begin* the process of increasing their effectiveness. I should like to emphasize that executive and organizational effectiveness is *not* simply a matter of interpersonal and group relationships. The laboratory, therefore, is viewed as but *one* step in the change process. If it is to be effective, then the resulting increasing awareness, mutual trust among the executives, would provide the beginning point to plan changes in the organizational structure, managerial controls, and so on.

The fourth step was to describe the changes, evaluate their impact upon the organization, and to help the executives make whatever corrections they felt were appropriate so the changes hit the desired targets as well as to become an integral part of the executive system and the organization.

The president agreed with the strategy with the understanding that the top 20 executives would have to be offered the same opportunity as he had: to listen to the project and accept or reject it. Two such meetings were held and the vote was unanimous to experiment with the first 10 executives. If, after the laboratory program was over, it seemed useful to the organization, they could recommend it to the next 10 executives.

I do not believe the reader will find in the strategy used methods developed to "sell," "persuade," or "push" the executives into change. The responsibility for changing their values and behavior (or parts of the organization) belongs to the executives and is kept, as much as possible, under their control.[7]

My role was to try to minimize my responsibility in inducing the executives to make changes in their values. I was prepared to do my best to feed accurate information into the system, help the executives clarify their views, assist them in expressing their more latent feelings, help them plan for changes, and help them in carrying out these changes. However, I did not try to move the executives toward change against or in spite of their will. This seemed to me to be not only professionally wrong, but fruitless because it would not work (more of this in Chapter 5 and 6).

THE EXPLORATORY NATURE OF THE RESEARCH

It is important to emphasize the exploratory nature of this research. The theories and models used were up to the time untested. The measuring instruments were and still are (it is hoped not for long) very crude.

Another factor that should be kept in mind is that I was unable to define the research conditions as I wished. A number of opportunities had to be compromised to do the research. For example, in this study I wanted an experimental and a control group. This was a requirement I could not permit to be violated (for the executives' sakes as well as my own). However, I was willing to accept 10 in the experimental and 10 in

---

[7] Chris Argyris, "Explorations in Client-Consulting Relationships," *Human Organization,* Vol. 20, No. 3 (Fall, 1961), pp. 121–33.

the control group, although a higher number would have added materially to the results. Also, I wished that the laboratory program could have included certain individuals who, when it was held, were 3,000 miles away. However, there was a minimum number of people below which I would not have recommended a laboratory (again for the sake of the executives as well as my own). Also, it would have been valuable to administer certain additional measuring instruments. However, because of the somewhat negative impact that our initial "testing" had upon the executives, it seemed wise to reduce them to a minimum. The tests were not completely eliminated.

However, there are limits to which the subjects and the research setting may influence research. There are certain minimum research standards below which a researcher should not tend to go for the clients' sakes as well as his own. In conducting action research, where human lives are continually being influenced, the necessity for valid data is very high. It is not possible to protect human beings from themselves or the researcher without valid data. The higher the research standards, the greater the protection the subjects will tend to receive. I shall always be indebted to the executives for permitting me to conduct this exploratory study with adequate amount of freedom.

To summarize and re-emphasize: Although the results are more optimistic than expected, they neither firmly confirm the models used nor do they provide a final stamp of approval of the laboratory method on organizational development. Much more research is needed. One of the reasons for publishing such a preliminary statement is hopefully to develop more interest on the part of researchers of the potential value in studying these processes. A second reason is to begin to fill the huge void existing today on the laboratory approach and the even bigger void on the relationship of interpersonal competence and laboratory method on the one hand, and organizational effectiveness on the other.

An Important Strength of the Executive System

It is interesting to note that in accepting the program the executives were taking certain risks. They were risking their relationships with one another, especially with the president and the "home office." These risks in turn could have led to negative impacts upon the organization. They were also risking that they would learn something from the program. They were taking these risks when most of them did not clearly understand the program. As one put it after listening to me attempting to describe a laboratory program, "Look, I don't really understand what you're talking about. But, I'd like to experiment with it. If we can increase our own competence, I'm for trying."

The risk-taking capabilities of the president apparently also existed in the subordinates. This is one of the attributes of these executives as a group that impressed me. They were not afraid to experiment and take risks. And, as we shall see, they had the intellectual and interpersonal capacities to develop themselves significantly.

One word of caution: The reader will observe (in the section describing the diagnosis) that the executives report that they experienced conformity, management by crisis and through detail, backed by fear, interdepartmental rivalries, and so on. These experiences are typical of most large organizations. They are, as one man put it, "woven into the very fabric of modern organizational life." Thus, this organization is by no means atypical nor is it necessarily worse than others. (Indeed, I sometimes think universities, churches, and hospitals, suffer more from these problems than do industrial organizations!)

However, the organizations and the executive team *do* differ greatly from many American industrial (and other) enterprises along one important dimension. They stand out by their willingness to take risks, experiment, and learn to develop.

THE ORGANIZATION OF THE BOOK

The book is divided into four parts. Part I contains the theoretical framework and the model. Part II contains the diagnosis of the executive system as well as the feedback session to them. Part III discusses the philosophy behind, the structure of, and provides illustrations of the laboratory program.

Part IV contains the evaluation of the program upon the

experimental and control groups, as well as on other parts of the organization. Dr. Roger Harrison has written Chapter 11, which reports the research he conducted to evaluate the impact of the program. He was completely responsible for the planning, execution, and analysis of this aspect of the research. We purposely did not inform each other about our designs so the projects could be conducted as independently as possible.

There is a final chapter with a summary of findings and some recommendations to those who may want to consider this type of program seriously.

PART ONE

□□

THEORY
AND
MODELS

1

The Nature of Interpersonal Relations and Formal Organizations

The primary action objective of this research project was to help an organization increase its administrative competence. Competence is a difficult and complex concept; and by the end of the book we shall be able, at best, to understand only a small part of it.

Administrative competence is related to the organization's abilities to achieve its objectives, maintain itself internally, and adapt to its external environment. Many factors act to influence the organization's competence. Some of these are the leadership, effectiveness of the groups and intergroup relationships, formal organizational structure, managerial controls, policies and practices, the technology, and last but not least, the people at all levels of the organization.

Some existing studies explore the impact of each of these factors upon the organization. For example, elsewhere I have suggested that formal organizational structure, managerial controls, and directive leadership tend to have some unintended consequences that decrease the human effectiveness of the organization if the participants aspire to work that permits them self-responsibility, self-control, and the use of their intellectual and interpersonal abilities.[1] Whyte[2] has shown the unintended consequences of incentive systems, Walker and Guest,[3] and

---

[1] Chris Argyris, *Personality and Organization* (New York: Harper & Bros., 1957).

[2] William F. Whyte, *Money and Motivation* (New York: Harper & Bros., 1955).

[3] Charles R. Walker and Robert Guest, *Man On The Assembly Line* (Cambridge, Mass.: Harvard University Press, 1952).

15

Walker, Guest, and Turner,[4] of the technology. Shepard[5] and Blake and Mouton,[6] have focused on the impact of intergroup conflicts within organizations.

The present study focuses on the impact of interpersonal relationships and leadership upon the organization. And it should be clear that in stating this focus I am *not* implying that these factors are the only major factors related to organizational competence. They do represent, however, an important segment of the problem.

One way to begin is to hypothesize that the administrative competence of an organization is composed of two interrelated but analytically separable components. They are intellective, rational, technical competence and interpersonal competence. The former deals with things and ideas, the latter with people. Needless to say, they are interrelated and extremely important. It remains for research to make explicit the relationship each of these has to the other and to the organization.

Measures of technical competence have been and continue to be developed. Budgets, profit and loss statements, production controls, inventory controls, and quality controls are but a few examples of the instruments designed to measure how well the organization is doing with its "things." However, few instruments have been developed to measure how well an organization is doing with people and fewer yet to measure the impact of this upon the organization.[7]

The first step in beginning to develop an understanding of interpersonal competence is to examine the nature of interpersonal relationships. To do this, the literature was reviewed intensively and extensively. Only a *summary* report can be given here; for the sake of clarity it will be presented in the form of propositions. These propositions *outline* one point of

---

[4] Charles R. Walker, Robert Guest, and Arthur Turner, *Foreman on the Assembly Line* (Cambridge, Mass.: Harvard University Press, 1956).

[5] Herbert A. Shepard, "An Action Research Approach to Organization Development," *Management Record*, 1960.

[6] Robert R. Blake and Jane S. Mouton, "Developing and Maintaining Corporate Health Through Organic Management Training," The University of Texas.

[7] Recently Likert has taken such a step. See Rensis Likert, *New Patterns of Management* (New York: McGraw-Hill Book Co. Inc., 1961).

view currently held by some scholars conducting basic research on interpersonal relationships.

1. Human behavior in groups or in the individual case is lawful and not random. The behavior of every individual has a continuity or a patterning that gives it some semblance of an underlying unity.[8] Psychologists conceptualize the unity in various ways. One convenient scheme is to think of it as the *self*.[9] The self is the individuals's needs, values, abilities, and defenses integrated into an organized whole or entity that has some meaning to the individual. The self is typically not observable to the untrained watcher, who tends to see the more skin-surface behavior which appears to be random. To understand the unity or patterning, one must be competent in basic psychological theory as well as be an open, minimally defensive individual. Such requirements are not unusual. In music, for example, if one is to understand the unity of a symphony, he must understand musical theory as well as have the capacity to listen to music accurately (for example, not be tone deaf).

2. Even though there are differences in conceptualization of human personality (self, ego, construct system, and so on), there is an underlying agreement that this unity develops largely as a result of interpersonal relationships. Man's personality is essentially an interpersonal phenomenon.[10] (The "external" [to his self] environment is extremely important and its relationship to personality growth very complex.)[11]

3. The *initial* interpersonal relationships that have the greatest effect are those with parents and siblings. Later, the important relationships are extended to include relatives, friends, working associates, and so on. An effective, interpersonal family life may be viewed as one that helps the individual to evolve a self he can use to deal competently first with his family and later with the extended relationships that he will

---

[8] Earnest R. Hilgard and Daniel Lerner, "The Person: Subject and Object of Science and Policy," in D. Lerner and H. D. Lasswell, (ed.) *The Policy Sciences* (Stanford, Calif.: Stanford University Press, 1951), pp. 16–43.

[9] See, for example, the works of Allport, Mead, Rogers, and Sullivan.

[10] For example, see the works of people such as Angyal, Kelly, Lewin, Maslow, Mead, Rogers, Fromm, and Sullivan.

[11] See the excellent work of Barker, Roger, and Herbert F. Wright, *Midwest and Its Children* (Evanston, Ill.: Row, Peterson & Co.).

encounter during the remainder of his life.[12] This implies that the family is composed of members who are relatively healthy and whose culture is not in complete "dissonance" with the larger environmental matrix in which it is embedded. It does not imply, however, that the family or the individual may not develop desires to change the culture. Individuals are not "doomed" to be carbon copies of their culture unless they so desire.

4. As the individual develops a somewhat stable self, it becomes the "filter mechanism" through which he perceives himself and his world and by which he evaluates his and others' effectiveness in it. The individual will tend to accept those experiences consonant with his self; and he will tend to distort, deny, and reject that behavior that is different from, and is not immediately integratable with, his self. The latter is usually described as defensive behavior. Behavior is "defensive" when it is a response to a perceived threat to the self.[13]

One way to minimize the probability of creating defensiveness in self, or in others, is to give feedback that describes a relationship without placing a value judgment on it. We call this *descriptive nonevaluative* feedback because it attempts to describe and not evaluate. For example, there is a significant difference between saying "You shouldn't behave in *x* manner"[14] and "I experience the following feelings when you behave in *x* manner."

Giving and receiving nonevaluative feedback cannot be learned simply by practice. It is an ability that is not learned from practice. It is acquired by developing a basic philosophy

---

[12] Bingham Dai, "A Socio-Psychiatric Approach to Personality Organization," *American Sociological Review*, Vol. 17, No. 1 (February, 1952), pp. 46–49. Otto Allen Will, "Human Relatedness and the Schizophrenic Reaction," *Psychiatry*, Vol. 22, No. 3 (August, 1959), pp. 205–23.

[13] Carl Rogers, a chapter in Vol. III, S. Kock (ed.), *Psychology: A Study of a Science* (New York: McGraw-Hill Book Co., Inc., 1959). Daniel Katz (ed.), "Attitude Change," *Public Opinion Quarterly*, Vol. 24, No. 2 (Summer, 1960); see Dr. Katz's "The Functional Approach to the Study of Attitudes" and Irving Sarmoff's "Psychoanalytic Theory and Social Attitudes" in the same issue.

[14] Positive evaluative feedback does not necessarily lead to growth. Positive feedback could create feelings of obligation and/or dependence by the sender upon the receiver. Also, positive feedback may be used to control individuals.

and a set of values for individual growth. The underlying requirement is that the individual be accepting of his self and of others. As his acceptance of self and others increases, his need to make evaluative feedback tends to decrease. The degree of acceptance an individual has at any given moment varies with each individual and with the same individual under different conditions.[15]

5. The individual will tend to be aware and accepting of his or others' behavior that is not a threat to his self. He will not tend to be aware of and/or accepting of his or others' behavior that is a threat to (that is, nonintegratable with) his self. Stated differently, the individual's capacity to become aware of and accepting of his or others' behavior will be related to the degree that this behavior threatens his self. The greater the threat (that is, the more the behavior threatens central aspects of his self), the less the probability of becoming aware and/or accepting of that behavior. By "being aware," I mean the state of being able to perceive the aspects of one's own or another's behavior.

Acceptance is intimately related to awareness because, as we have shown above, we will not tend to perceive that behavior that threatens our self. Acceptance may be defined as perceiving one's own or others' behavior as the self or others intended it to be perceived. Acceptance implies nothing as to whether one likes or agrees with what one sees. It simply means that the individual is willing to see it, to accept it as existing in the way the person who manifests it wants it perceived. The operational criteria for whether an individual A is accepting of his (or someone else's) behavior x are as follows:

> *a*) In the case where x is A's own behavior, does A permit feedback about x from others without becoming defensive or making them defensive for giving such feedback?
> *b*) In the case where x is someone else's behavior, does A provide feedback to B about x without being defensive or inducing B to be defensive?

---

[15] I believe that some interpersonal abilities are learned more by developing the "correct Gestalt" than by practice. By "correct Gestalt," I mean the cluster of values that act as commands to the individual to behave in specific ways (in this case in ways that assists self and other acceptance).

6. This point of view postulates that a basic need of man is to increase his sense of self-acceptance and acceptance of others.[16] If, in a given case, an individual seems to be behaving in an opposite manner, it is because he has experienced failure in attempting to increase his self-acceptance. The failure is so great, the hurt so strong, that he has become defensive, and uses his defensiveness to protect himself from being hurt further. However, the probability is quite high that his defensiveness will tend to lead to greater failure and consequently deeper feelings of being hurt.

7. The preceding propositions hypothesize an intimate relationship between self and others. Awareness and acceptance of self and others are impossible to separate. Assume A wants to increase his acceptance of self. How does he do it? A has a self with a particular filter mechanism that influences the feedback he receives or gives.

The greater A's defensiveness, the less the probability that he will create conditions where he can receive helpful (descriptive nonevaluative) feedback. However, the greater the defensiveness of B, the greater the probability that he will give distorted feedback to A. Thus, A is in a human bind. He will not learn unless he is willing and capable of learning *and* unless B is willing and capable of helping him learn. He will not tend to be willing and capable unless A helps create the conditions in which B will not be highly defensive. The opposite is also the case. A cannot decrease B's sense of self-acceptance without hurting his own. If A hurts B, B will respond defensively, and the feedback A will receive will either be designed to hurt him or it will be distorted, which may have a negative effect on it.

8. We come to the conclusion that it is impossible for a human being to enhance his awareness and acceptance of (aspects of) his self without simultaneously creating the conditions for others to do the same. Put in another way, an in-

---

[16] An individual's valuation of his self may be related to the self as a whole and/or to various components. Both levels of valuation may be significant in influencing behavior. The exact one to be relevant may vary as of the total situation in which the individual is in between individuals, and with the same individual at different stages of development.

dividual's growth and learning (on the interpersonal level) is inexorably tied up with his fellow man. It is this human bind that makes a relationship of "oneness" imperative in human life.[17] The human condition may be the source of what Buber calls the basic wish to be *confirmed.* He defines confirmation as the "experience of an individual to be confirmed by men as to what he is, even as to what he can become."[18]

9. It is fundamental hypothesis of this viewpoint that a basic drive of human beings is to experience "success" in living and experiencing their "human condition." By "success," I mean that their interpersonal relationships will tend to lead them to become more aware and accepting of their selves and others. Human relationships that lead to self and other awareness and acceptance are the mechanisms by which each one of us develops, maintains, and modifies appropriately that unity called our personality. These human relationships are those in which man originates and becomes increasingly genuine in such a way that his fellow man can also become genuine.

10. Because these human relationships involve increasing self- and other awareness and acceptance, they are hypothesized to be the source of psychological life and human growth; for this reason I should like to call them authentic relationships. *Authentic relationships are, therefore, those relationships in which an individual enhances his sense of self- and other awareness and acceptance in such a way that others can do the same.*

Human authenticity is an interpersonal phenomenon. An individual cannot be authentic independent of the relationships he has with others. His feelings of authenticity will depend as much upon the capacity of others to create authentic relationships as well as upon his own.

In this connection, it is interesting to note that recent developments in the study of the nervous system and thinking

---

[17] See Erich Fromm, *The Art of Loving* (New York: Harper & Bros., Inc., 1956); and Marie Jahoda, *Current Concepts of Positive Mental Health* (New York: Basic Books, Inc.).

[18] Maurice S. Friedman, *Martin Buber: The Life of Dialogue* (Chicago: University of Chicago Press, 1950), p. 81.

suggest that thought is also an interpersonal phenomenon. Shands[19] states that it is misleading to assume that the single nervous system is the mechanism of thought. Cobb points out that the mechanism of thinking can be understood if one conceives of two nervous systems *in relation to each other.*[20] "An isolated nervous system is as functionless as an isolated telephone instrument. . . ."[21] Finally Piaget states that it is precisely by constant interchange of thought with others that we are able to see ourselves in perspective and to conserve the permanent meanings of concepts.[22]

One of the first social psychologists to discuss systematically a concept of authentic relationships is Howard Perlmutter.[23] Although his analysis focuses primarily on the relationships that a visitor is probably seeking or going to experience in a foreign country, the concepts and theory may easily form the basis of a general theory of interpersonal relationships.

Perlmutter's definition of authentic relationships differs somewhat from the one presented in this book. For example, he differentiates between authentic experiences, which if they occur frequently enough, lead to authentic relationships. Also, a genuine relationship and an authentic one are not different from Perlmutter's view. These and other differences, however, should not cloud the similarity of the underlying theme in both views, namely that man seeks deeply satisfying (to quote Buber) "I-Thou" relationships.

Some of the qualities of authentic relationships Perlmutter defines when he discusses the experiences of Americans abroad:

> *a*) A foreigner is seen as another person in his own right with a life history in another culture, with culture-determined drive, attitudes, and values.

---

[19] Harley C. Shands, *Thinking and Psychotherapy* (Cambridge, Mass.: Harvard University Press, 1960).

[20] Italics mine.

[21] Stanley Cobb, *Borderlands of Psychiatry* (Cambridge, Mass.: Harvard University Press, 1943).

[22] Jean Piaget, *The Psychology of Intelligence* (New York: Harcourt, Brace, Inc., 1950).

[23] Howard Perlmutter, "Person to Person: A Psychological Analysis of Cross Cultural Relationships" (mimeographed), Menninger Foundation, October, 1959. Presented at Yale University, New Haven, Connecticut.

b) The other person is distinguished from idealized, feared, models and current stereotypes.

c) There are repeated experiences that the central feelings and dilemmas of life can be discussed.

Later Perlmutter states:

Among those students who have had authentic interpersonal experiences we record memories and/or crystallized images of the country which reflect an *essentially warm emotional tone* as contrasted with anger that some other students retain. The former continued to think of the country or sojourn and its culture with affectionate interest. In short, there appeared a relatively unconflicted "cultural" *empathy* for the ideas and values connected with these people. A sense of basic trust for the motives that "these people" have underlay their appreciation for the complexity of persons from this country.[24]

d) There are experiences of giving and receiving (a *reciprocity* in the relation).

e) There are infrequent experiences of exploitation, submissiveness, dominance of the other.

f) There is acceptance of both the positive and negative feelings the relationship produces.

g) There is acceptance both of the strengths and limitations of the other.

Deutsch has recently shown some experimental evidence that illustrates one aspect of the proposition that one cannot be authentic without others experiencing authenticity. To trust and to be trustworthy are aspects of authentic relationships. Deutsch found that the subjects who were trusting and trustworthy also expected others to be the same. Subjects who tended to be suspicious and untrustworthy predominantly expected an exploitive orientation from others. Deutsch concludes that the personality predispositions such as to trust are *not* simply "one-sided internalized orientations toward another or internalized expectations from another but are instead internalizations of a reciprocal pattern of interrelationships with another." He continues later on to say "what appears to be internalized is a *system* of interrelations between oneself and

---

[24] *Ibid.*, p. 8.

the other including the norms which prescribe *both* what to expect from the other and how to act toward the other.[25]

Deutsch's findings also emphasize the position taken here that authenticity is not a state of affairs internalized in one person. It is the internalization of the *interpersonal relationships* with others. To put this another way, it would be improbable that an individual can *be* authentic. This implies that the operational test of authenticity is not to ask the individual if he is authentic. The test would be to observe the individual's behavior and see if he is able to create conditions under which *his and the other's* authenticity (self-awareness and acceptance) can increase.

By "authenticity," therefore, I do *not* mean simply that an individual is being himself—if, for example, being himself is to be defensive. This defensiveness may *be* the individual at that given moment. Defensiveness may be genuine and real, but it does not tend to lead to authentic human relationships. I would hypothesize that if the layers of defensiveness could be unpeeled through exposures to authentic relationships, one would find at the core of the individual the desire and capability for authentic relationships.[26] I should hasten to point out that I do not know if life can ever be completely authentic. I doubt it. Certainly, in the present state of our culture man may need to be able to hate, to be aggressive, hostile, and nonaccepting. If not, he could experience situations in which he could be destroyed. In war, for example, one cannot be very accepting of a man about ready to kill him. Perhaps such activities as capital punishment can be viewed in the same light. Murderers may have to be killed because we do not know how else to cope with them. Hate and hostility can also be functional in everyday human relationships. In this world of low authenticity we can defend ourselves and others through hate and hostility. However, these *are* defensive, and if our life became saturated with them, then according to this view we would tend to hate ourselves as well as others.

---

[25] Morton Deutsch, "Trust, Trustworthiness, and the F Scale," *Journal of Abnormal and Social Psychology*, Vol. LXI, No. 1 (1960), pp. 138–40.

[26] Carl Rogers was one of the first researchers to suggest that at the core of man is a basic sense of goodness.

11. As individuals succeed in enhancing their sense of self-acceptance (that is, as authentic relationships increase), they create the following new possibilities for growth:

a) The greater the sense of self-acceptance, the greater the probability that one will be one's self and will "*own*" one's ideas, values, and feelings and permit others to do the same should they wish to do so.

b) As the conditions in (*a*) above increase, the probability increases that the individual will be *open* to considering new ideas, values, and feelings.

c) As the conditions in (*a*) and (*b*) increase, the probability increases that the individual will tend to *experiment* and *take risks* with new ideas, values, and feelings, and permit others to do so.

d) As the conditions in (*a*) and (*b*) and (*c*) increase, the probability *decreases* that the opposite conditions will tend to occur.

Examining these propositions, we note that each influences the other in a chain reaction, which in turn leads to a cumulative and circular state of affairs. For example, the greater the awareness of self or other, the more the accurate feedback. But as accurate feedback increases, the probability for awareness of self and others tends to increase. As self-awareness and acceptance increases, "owning" one's feelings and permitting others to do the same tends to increase. But as owning one's feelings and permitting others to do the same increases, the probability of self- and other acceptance increases. We conclude, therefore, that we are dealing with a cluster of variables so interrelated that they form an interacting dynamic system in which the state of any one of the variables is a function of all the others.

In conducting research in a laboratory setting, it may be possible to separate experimentally these variables so they may be dealt with in terms of the dependent-independent model. However, if one desires to test these hypotheses in the field, one is led to deal with these variables as they exist; that is, as a dynamic interrelated system of variables.

12. The probability that growth (self and other awareness and acceptance) will take place in any interpersonal relationship increases as the desire of individuals to enhance

their, and other's, self-awareness and acceptance increases. Given that this basic need has not been so frustrated that the individuals have suppressed it, or constantly expect and create failure in trying to achieve it, then one may generalize that human growth (authentic relationships) will tend to increase as the following increase:

a) Giving and receiving nonevaluative descriptive feedback.
b) Owning and helping others to own to their values, attitudes, ideas, and feelings.
c) Openness to new values, attitudes, and feelings as well as helping others to develop their degree of openness.
d) Experimenting (and helping others to do the same) with new values, attitudes, ideas, and feelings.
e) Taking risks with new values, attitudes, ideas, and feelings.

13. We may now begin to spell out the practical implications of all this to organization. As openness, experimentation, owning ideas and feelings, and nonevaluative feedback increase in an organization, we hypothesize that participants' *interpersonal competence*[27] will tend to increase. Interpersonal competence increases as individuals:

a) Are aware of their impact upon others and others' impact upon them.
b) Solve problems in such a way that the same (or similar) problems remain resolved.

One can readily see, I believe, the value of executives being more aware of their impact upon others. The basic issues of conformity, self-development, organizational flexibility, vitality are deeply intertwined with interpersonal competence. So are the desires to solve issues so they remain solved. This is a vexing and continuing problem in the area of attitudes. For example, any executive who has attempted to change an organization from a centralized to a decentralized posture will attest to the difficulty of changing the basic attitudes of dependence that have built up for years. With every new program, there comes the assurance that "they're now sold." Time

---

[27] Recently Robert White has postulated competence as a basic human need. See his "Competence and the Psycho-Sexual Stages of Development," M. R. Jones (ed.), *Nebraska Symposium on Motivation* (Lincoln, Nebr.: University of Nebraska Press, 1960), pp. 40–97.

tends to bring on a bit of disillusionment as well as increasing awareness of the difficulties involved.

Interpersonal competence has important influence on such organizational factors as decision making, interdepartmental co-operation, and so on. All these factors will be explored in more depth in the next chapter and illustrated with research data throughout the remaining parts of the book.[28]

THE NATURE
OF MODERN ORGANIZATION

In the previous pages we have outlined some of the properties of human beings and the relationships they tend to create. We need to develop one more building block before we can construct a model to help us understand, predict, and perhaps influence human relationships in organizations.

The behavior we are attempting to understand always exists in complex organizations. The hypotheses we intend to develop must, therefore, take into account the impact the organization has upon the behavior. One way to attack this problem is to conceive of organizations as strategies designed to achieve certain objectives. We may then explore the underlying nature of the strategy used to create organizations to see if we can make explicit their basic properties. If such properties can be found, then we may begin to explore the impact these properties have upon the individual and vice versa. Another advantage of exploring the problem through the analysis of the underlying strategy is that it leads to generalizations presumed to hold whenever the strategy is used. Since the organizational structure, managerial controls, technology, incentive systems, and leadership are all defined in reference to the strategy, then our generalizations should be valid for all these factors. To put this another way, when the word

---

[28] Most of the human relationships that concern us are conducted in group and organizational settings. As we shall see in the next four chapters, authentic relationships require specific kinds of group and organizational structure and dynamics. Without these group and organizational structures, it would be difficult to develop authentic relationships. Therefore, it should not be concluded that as receiving and giving accurate nonevaluative feedback, owning feelings, and so on, are developed, authentic relationship will automatically increase.

"organization" is used, it means more than the structure. It includes the managerial controls, leadership, technology, indeed anything in the organization defined in consonance with the strategy. This is one of the values of the approach. If valid, it suggests that one does not have to make detailed studies of every organizational factor. If one were to find an organization which, as a whole, (or whose parts) did not behave according to the predictions we will eventually describe, the reason should be that another strategy is being used or one that is much more potent than the one above. If not, then this point of view is not valid.

Let us turn now to the discussion of the formal strategy used in complex organizations.

I. RATIONALITY IN ORGANIZATION

The process of developing an organization has been, and continues to be, conceived as largely an intellective or rational one.[29] The planners usually begin by defining, as clearly as they believe possible, the objectives of the organization. The definition of the objectives according to the rational theorists is a central activity because, as the late General Somervell states, "To accomplish any extensive task efficiently, we must first have a clear idea of what we are trying to do. The objectives to be reached should be set forth clearly and unambiguously so that all . . . know exactly what is to be done."[30] The emphasis on objectives dovetails with the basic assumption of the "traditional"[31] rational organizational theorists; namely, that the people who will participate in the organization are, or at least can be required to be, intellective, rational beings. If the objectives are clearly defined to the employees, then management can rightly expect them to behave logically and strive to achieve the objective as required.

---

[29] The points in this chapter are discussed in more detail in *Personality and Organization* (New York: Harper & Bros., 1957).

[30] Brehon Somervell, General Management Series, No. 142 (American Management Association, 1948).

[31] The word "traditional" is put in quotation marks to differentiate this approach from the newer and much more systematic intellective approach exemplified by March and Simon. James C. March and Herbert A. Simon, *Organizations* (New York: John Wiley & Sons, Inc., 1958).

In addition to the definition of objectives, and in line with the importance of rationality, there are a number of other variables that the rational organizational theorists believe must be clearly defined if the organization is to be effective. They are (1) organization policies and practices, (2) titles for positions and organization components, (3) organization procedures, (4) responsibility statements, and so on.[32] The concise but comprehensive definition of these variables has, in the rationalists' opinion, many advantages. Some of these are:

a) Helps to develop a sound organization. "How else can a manager know what his job is unless it is in writing?"

b) Furnishes direction for administration because it coerces the company to think through what it is organizing for. If one is not cognitively clear on this matter, confusion is the end result.

c) Encourages balance and stability in the organization. When the policies and practices are available in written form, they provide the manager with specific guides and instruction.

d) Provides standard for control of human behavior. A clearly defined organization manual is an excellent yardstick with which to measure and evaluate changes and to evaluate how effectively each individual is meeting his accountability.

e) Helps improve human relations because it provides a clear basis for selection, promotion. It encourages teamwork because each individual is secure in knowing that his job will not be taken by someone else.[33]

We again note the importance of the assumption of human rationality. For the above to be valid, one must assume that the people hired will react rationally. For example, doing a good job is primarily determined *if* a man *knows* what he is supposed to do. Interpersonal confusion is minimized *if rules* and *regulations* are clearly stated. Balance and stability are assured *if* organizational procedures are *well-written* and easily available. Individuals will fulfill their accountability *if* they are *checked periodically* or if they know they can be checked. Human relations will be at their best *if jobs* are clearly defined so no overlapping exists.

---

[32] *Preparing the Company Organization Manual,* Studies in Personnel Policy, No. 157 (NICB, 1957), p. 18.

[33] NICB, *op. cit.*

The difficulty with these assumptions is not that they are completely false. The difficulty is that as they are stated they are half-truths and incomplete. For example, man may not be able to increase his sense of self-esteem, inner worth, sense of confidence, and commitment to work, all of which are required for outstanding performance, if he is to know exactly what to do. One might hypothesize that a man will do a good job, and afterward feel like doing another good job, to the extent that he is able to fill in the content of, or have some control over, his job.[34] This does not mean man should not be told anything. Such an extreme would be equally frustrating to the individual as well as damaging to the organization. The point is that most jobs are so narrowly defined in scope and require so few human abilities, that they do not tend to motivate man to perform effectively.

Turning to interpersonal relations, it is not necessarily true that if rules are stated clearly, interpersonal confusion is minimized. In the world of the pyramid structure, clearly defined relations can create problems, especially for the subordinates who tend to experience a world full of clearly defined rules and regulations as a world tending toward rigidity and increasingly requiring submissiveness. If their boss is an autocrat, clear rules and regulations may easily serve to make it more difficult for the subordinates to behave effectively. One is reminded of Melville Dalton's law of organization. "There is always a way of getting around a rule—find it."

In assuming man is rational, the traditional rationalists do not deny man is also capable of behaving emotionally. Their hope is that man will voluntarily (and with due reward) suppress his emotions "for the good of the organization." The assumption behind this hope is that man can separate his feeling about his work, goals, relationships with others, rewards, penalties, selection, upgrading, control, and so on, from the intellective cognitive fact that these activities must exist if the organization is to achieve its objective.

But there is much evidence to suggest that man cannot simply decide to be primarily an intellective rational being

---

[34] See the research on "psychological success."

with respect to the variables listed above.[35] In fact, the very decision to separate one's emotions from one's intellective aspects is a deeply emotional one. There is increasing concern that this act of "self-separation" is part of a basic process in modern life which leads man to become alienated from himself and others.[36]

II. IRRATIONALITY IS RECOGNIZED BUT NOT DEALT WITH RATIONALLY

Although rationality is assumed and expected by the organizational rationalist planners, they are not blind to the fact that human beings are not completely rational. Consequently, in their own literature they warn the executive against too rigid adherence to the rules that they define because the individuals "may resent being tied down too closely." The organization can be rigidified, individuals may spend too much time "covering themselves," and this hampers teamwork.[37]

However, these potential disadvantages of rationality are hardly ever discussed as systematically as the advantages. For example, in the excellent monograph quoted frequently above, only one page is taken up with a note on the reported disadvantages of "emphasis on rationality." More important, although one will find cautions against too much emphasis on the charts, definitions, and so on, one never finds a criterion that makes explicit when the point of "too much emphasis" is reached. It seems as if the traditional rationalists assume that people can be paid to behave rationally. It seems that they add the note on the disadvantages of rationality because they realize that most people simply are not rational. Finally it is interesting to note the ironic fact that those who emphasize rationality, planning, and so on, do not seem to follow their advice in handling the dimension of emotionality in human beings. No plans, definitions, rules, or regulations are presented to help the executives deal with the emotional or nonrational

---

[35] Gardner Murphy, *Human Potentialities* (New York: Basic Books, Inc., 1958).

[36] Rollo May, *Existence* (New York: Basic Books, Inc., 1959); and Erich Fromm, *The Sane Society* (New York: Holt, Rinehart, & Winston, Inc., 1955).

[37] NICB, *op. cit.*, pp. 14–15.

aspects of man. To put it another way, the emotional or motivational aspects are not defined rationally.

III. THE IMPORTANCE OF SPECIALIZATION

Along with the assumption of rationality, the organizational planners add another; namely, the assumption that man performs at his best if he performs a specialized task. This assumption is partly based on beliefs (which can be supported by research) that man's abilities are finite and cannot enable him to do everything. It also follows logically from the assumption of rationality. If man is largely a cognitive animal, he will clearly see the logic of doing the same thing all the time.

The principle of specialization is usually defined as "the work of every person in the organization should be confined as far as possible to the performance of a single leading function."[38] In the interests of efficiency, the individual concentrates on one thing—hopefully that which he can do best. If the individual must be given two functions, they should be as similar as possible.

Using the principle of specialization creates the second point where man in an organization is asked to become separated from himself. According to the principle above, man should somehow suppress the desire to express his many and complex abilities, especially those related to interpersonal relations. For example, the farther down one goes in the chain of command, the greater are the demands for the individual to use only a few abilities and primarily the more motoric ones. Almost no use is made of man's cognitive or emotional abilities. Most jobs on the lower levels in American industry can be learned in a very short time. Most of them require some degree of mechanical aptitude and motor aptitude (for example, finger dexterity). Almost none of the employee jobs (high and low skill) require the use of emotional or interpersonal abilities of the individual. For example, low-skill employees in plants X and Y find it very difficult to talk about their self-concept as having rich, meaningful (to them) content. "There is nothing much to me" describes the feelings of the majority

---

[38] NICB, *op. cit.*, p. 34.

eloquently.[39] And there isn't, if one focuses on that part of themselves that they experience while working. The high-skill employees, however, are able to discuss their self, but it is a self primarily composed of mechanical skills. It is not difficult to see why the employee eventually learns to respect himself primarily in terms of how much money he can command. Only those abilities that earn money for the company are valued by the organization. This state of affairs is akin to what Fromm describes as a "market-orientation."

Such a life is not an easy one for the worker to accept. The research suggests that it may take an individual as long as three years to give up his desire not to separate his emotional and interpersonal self from his technical self.[40] Moreover, those that do, may well accomplish the feat by day-dreaming and other ways of psychologically leaving their jobs.[41] As one girl put it, "It's wonderful when you learn my job because then you can operate the machine without thinking. You can be away from work and still be working."[42]

Other adaptive activities employees create are absenteeism, turnover, trade unions, noninvolvement in one's work world, and an increased emphasis on money and other material factors with a concomitant decreased emphasis on human factors.[43]

With the exception of trade unions (and possible exception of absenteeism), these activities *enhance* and reward man's increasing separation from himself. Thus, for an employee to be absent when he is not sick, he must report in as being sick. Those who report in as being sick, but are not, may tend to feel uncomfortable if not guilty about their lying. Many may take elaborate measures not to be discovered. Turnover has the same problems. In a hospital study, for example, nurses could overcome their guilt for leaving a hospital to go to

---

[39] Chris Argyris, *Understanding Organizational Behavior* (Homewood, Ill.: The Dorsey Press, Inc., 1960), chap. iii.

[40] Frederick Herzberg, *et al.*, *Job Attitudes: Review of Research and Opinion* (Pittsburgh, Penn.: Psychological Service of Pittsburgh, 1957).

[41] Chris Argyris, *Organization of a Bank* (New Haven, Conn.: Labor and Management Center, Yale University, 1954).

[42] *Ibid.*, pp. 155–63.

[43] Chris Argyris, *Personality and Organization*, chap. iv.

another hospital by building many distorted attitudes about their present place of work.[44] Living in a world in which one consciously prevents himself from becoming emotionally involved, and in which one de-emphasizes the importance of his own acknowledged psychological needs, will also tend to enhance the market-orientation.

Joining a trade union could theoretically lead to an increased expression of one's self, especially if one becomes an official. Ironically, however, the trade union eventually begins to defeat its purpose because to maintain itself, it organizes according to the same principles of rationality, specialization, and centralization of power! The union, according to this view, eventually may act to compound the separation that is being required of the employee by the formal organization.

IV. THE IMPORTANCE OF POWER

As soon as one creates an organization of specialists working on increasingly molecular tasks all directed at a particular objective, one immediately finds it necessary to co-ordinate and direct these activities so they mesh effectively to achieve the organization's objective.

How are these specialized activities integrated with the organization?

The fundamental assumption made by the organization planners is that human activities are best co-ordinated through the exercise of power and that the power should be given to one individual who can delegate its use but never its obligations or "accountability."

The strategy of power is illustrated by the following "principles" of formal organization:

1. There must be clear lines of authority running from the top to the bottom of the organization.
2. No one in the organization should report to more than one line supervisor. Everyone in the organization should know to whom he reports and who reports to him.
3. The responsibility and authority of each supervisor should be clearly defined in writing.

---

[44] Chris Argyris, *Human Problems in a Large Hospital* (New Haven, Conn.: Labor and Management Center, Yale University, 1954).

4. The accountability of higher authority for the acts of its subordinates is absolute.

As a result of these principles the individual is placed in work situations where he is required to be subordinate, passive, and dependent upon the boss for rewards, penalties, direction, employment, and discharge. The degree of dependence *increases* as one goes down the chain of command and as the job controls the man. The dependence *decreases* as one goes up the lines and as the man controls the job.[45]

The strategy of power creates a fifth way by which the individual is asked to give up aspirations that, in our culture, may be characteristic of mature individuals. The power strategy assumes that man's motivation to produce will be at its highest if he is required to be continually dependent upon someone and to give up his feelings of being responsible for his own future. Many human beings in plant X and Y apparently are willing out of a sense of responsibility to themselves (to keep their job) and the firm to become dependent upon their boss and let him and the company be responsible for his future. This was brought about in the predisposition of nonevolvement.

V. The Importance of Control

If one creates layers of authority and many different but highly interrelated jobs to achieve a goal, one needs in addition to power some mechanisms for "control." By "control," I mean the following activities:

1. Continually sensing what is going on throughout the organization at all levels and "all corners."
2. Continually collecting data on the activities within the firm.
3. Continually analyzing the resulting data.
4. Continually comparing the data with predetermined standards defined to judge whether the firm is doing well or not.
5. Asking line to issue orders (or issuing it themselves) to correct any negative conditions.
6. Sensing the results of the action that starts the control cycle of events over again.[46]

---

[45] Chris Argyris, *Personality and Organization,* chap. iii.

[46] L. Reed Tripp (ed.), *Industrial Productivity,* IRRA Proceedings, December, 1951, pp. 90–91.

Following the principle of specialization, control activities are also separated from other line activities. It is a basic rule in the overwhelming number of organizations to separate at every point possible, the performance of a job from its evaluation. For example, inspectors, quality control experts, and so on, are brought into the organization to perform the task of control.

Here lies the sixth point at which the organization requires man to become separated from important aspects of himself. The control systems above require that man feel deeply responsible to produce a product but not feel responsible for evaluating its quality. The separation of the responsibility for the evaluation of an activity from the man performing the activity leads, as we have seen in plants X and Y, for the individual no longer to feel responsible for the quality of his work. If anything, the opposite occurs. He may feel responsible to keep poor quality at a particular level to keep the inspectors and quality control people at work.

VI. CONCLUSIONS

All formal organizations are "born" with a particular "heredity" or strategy implanted by their creators. This strategy is characterized by the "genes" of intellective rationality, specialization, centralization of power, control, and information. As each of these "genes" influences the growth of the organization, it tends to create a social system that operates by holding some fundamental assumptions about the nature of effective human relationships within organizations. They are:

1. The only relations that matter between people in organizations are those defined by the charts and manuals.
2. The behavior of people is governed by explicit logical thinking.
3. The subordinates will do what the objective and circumstances of the organization require if the rules and regulations are clear and if the incentives reward their logical behavior.
4. Major problem solving and decision making are the responsibility of the administrator. He knows best what should be done.

5. The way to get things done is through the power of the leader's position.
6. Employees will be more efficient if they are not required to be responsible for evaluating the quality of their work.

These assumptions about human beings are in opposition to those stated in the review of interpersonal relationships and human personality. This is one of the basic problems involved in using the pyramidal structure.[47] It assumes a concept of man more consonant with a dependent, subordinate, submissive, individual who suppresses his feelings but can be highly rational.

---

[47] Fritz Roethlisberger was one of the first to study the assumptions administrators held about effective human relations. Fritz Roethlisberger, *Training for Human Relations* (Cambridge, Mass.: Graduate School of Business, Harvard University, 1954).

The importance of assumptions to understanding behavior has a long history in psychology. For an early work see H. Cantril, *The "Why" of Man's Experience* (New York: The Macmillan Co., 1950), p. 87. For a more recent discussion, see Jerome Frank, *Persuasion and Healing* (The Johns Hopkins Press, 1961), chap. ii.

2

Interpersonal Competence and Organizational Effectiveness

□ In the previous chapter we concluded that organizations are developed from, and conceived according to the image of a particular strategy. Implicit in the strategy were certain assumptions about how individuals will behave effectively in an organization. These assumptions were found to be questionable in light of what is known about the nature of human beings (Chapter 1).

The next step is to become more specific so hypotheses can be stated regarding the impact of these assumptions on the individuals and the organization.

Recently there has developed an increasing awareness of the relevance of values to understanding human behavior[1,2] and decision making in organization.[3] Let us define values as commands or directives to which individuals are committed.[4] We may then ask what are the commands or directives (or imperatives) implicit in the formal strategy used to create organizations. If we can discover these organizational commands or directives, we can hypothesize that to the extent the par-

---

[1] Donald W. Taylor, "Toward an Information Processing Theory of Motivation," Marshall R. Jones (ed.), *Nebraska Symposium on Motivation* (Lincoln, Neb.: University of Nebraska Press, 1960), pp. 51–79.

[2] A. H. Maslow (ed.), *New Knowledge in Human Values* (New York: Harper & Bros., 1959).

[3] Herbert Simon, *Administrative Behavior* (New York: The Macmillan Co., 1957).

[4] Henry Margenau, "The Scientific Basis of Value Theory," *New Knowledge in Human Values,* pp. 42–43.

ticipants follow them, their behavior can be understood, predicted, and influenced by knowing these values.

As Margenau suggests, a command may define a value, but it requires a dedication to command if the value is to affect human behavior.[5] The major factor to be evaluated, therefore, is the degree of commitment or dedication to these values. The stronger the dedication, the greater the probability that the behavior can be understood independently of the particular personality of each participant. To test this hypothesis one must not only learn the organizational values, but one must ascertain "the extent to which participants follow" are dedicated to these values as determiners of their behavior. (Indeed, we may find that it is easier for certain personality patterns to be dedicated to these values.[6] Important as this hypothesis is for our theory, we are not going to attempt to test it at this time.) In this study, we are going to ascertain the impact of a specific set of organizational values upon the behavior of the participants on the organization.

We begin to develop a model by asking what would happen if participants followed the organizational values. Once the consequences are spelled out, we can go to the empirical world to see if the predicted consequences do exist when the participants adhere to or are dedicated to the values.

THE VALUES IMPLICIT IN FORMAL ORGANIZATIONS

The basic values outlined in the previous chapter about effective human relationships inherent in the formal organizational strategy can be summarized as follows:

1. The important human relationships are those that are related to achieving the organization's objective. (Getting the job done.)
2. Effectiveness in human relationships increases as behavior is rational, logical, and clearly communicated. Effectiveness decreases as emotionality increases.
3. Human relationships are most effectively influenced through direction, coercion, and control as well as a set of rewards

---

[5] *Ibid.*, p. 45.

[6] This is a hypothesis of men like Fromm, May, and men who worked on several of the research projects stemming from the California studies on the authoritarian personality.

and penalties that serve to emphasize the rational behavior and getting the job done.[7]

We may ask:

a) What would tend to happen to interpersonal competence and to interpersonal human relationships if these values are followed?

b) How do (the resulting) interpersonal relationships feed back to influence such rational activities as decision making, problem exploration, information transmission?

c) How do (the resulting) interpersonal relationships feed back to influence the norms of the organization toward or against such phenomena as dependence, conformity, interexecutive trust, and internal commitment?

d) How are such factors as organizational rigidity, flexibility, and climate influenced by all the factors above?

THE IMPACT OF THE FORMAL VALUES ON INTERPERSONAL COMPETENCE

To the extent that individuals dedicate themselves to the value of rationality and "getting the job done," they will tend to be aware of and emphasize the rational, intellective aspects of the interactions that exist in an organization and suppress the interpersonal and emotional aspects, especially those that do not seem to be relevant to achieving the task. For example, one frequently hears in organizations, "Let's keep feelings out of the discussion," or "Look here, our task today is to achieve objective *x* and not to get emotional."

As the interpersonal and emotional aspects of behavior become suppressed, we may hypothesize that an organizational norm will tend to arise that coerces individuals to hide their feelings. Their interpersonal difficulties will either be suppressed, or disguised and brought up as rational, technical, intellectual problems. In short, receiving or giving feedback about interpersonal relationships will tend to be suppressed.

---

[7] For other studies consonant with these conclusions see Douglas McGregor, *The Human Side of Enterprise* (New York: McGraw-Hill Book Co., Inc., 1960); Robert L. Katz, "Toward a More Effective Enterprise," *Harvard Business Review*, Vol. 38, No. 5 (September–October, 1960), pp. 80–120; James March, and Herbert Simon, *Organizations* (New York: John Wiley & Sons, Inc., 1959).

Under these conditions we may hypothesize that the individuals will find it very difficult to develop competence in dealing with feelings and interpersonal relationships. In a world where the expression of feelings is not permitted, one may hypothesize the individuals will build personal and organizational defenses to help them suppress their own feelings or inhibit others in their attempts to express their feelings.[8] If feelings are suppressed, the tendency will be for the individual not to permit himself or others to *own* their feeling. For example, the individual may say about himself, "No, I didn't mean that," or "Let me start over again. I'm confusing the facts." Equally possible is for one individual to say to another, "No, you shouldn't feel that way," or "That's not effective executive behavior," or "Let's act like mature people and keep feelings out of this."

Another way to prevent individuals from violating the organizational values of rationality and from embarrassing one another, is to block out, refuse to consider (consciously or unconsciously) ideas and values which, if explored, could expose suppressed feelings. Such a defensive reaction in the organization may eventually lead to a barrier of intellectual ideas as well as values. The participants will tend to limit themselves to those ideas and values that are not threatening, and so not violate organizational norms. The individuals in the organization will tend to decrease its capacity to be open to new ideas and values. As the degree of openness decreases, the capacity to experiment will tend to decrease, and the fear to take risks will tend to increase. As the fear to take risks increases, the probability of experimentation is decreased and the range or scope of openness is decreased, which decreases risks. We have a closed circuit that could be an important cause of the loss of vitality in an organization.[9]

To summarize, the extent that participants are dedicated

---

[8] This is a common phenomenon in the opening sessions of T-groups. To tell the "truth" is usually interpreted to mean "Let's clobber one another," "tell each other our faults," "to put me on the table and open me up," and so on.

[9] For a recent student who emphasizes the importance of vitality see Marshall E. Dimock, *A Philosophy of Administration* (New York: Harper & Bros., 1957).

to the values implicit in the formal organization, they will tend to create a social system where the following will tend to *decrease* (see Figure 1):

1. Receiving and giving nonevaluative feedback.
2. Owning and permitting others to own their ideas, feelings, and values.
3. Openness to new ideas, feelings, and values.
4. Experimentation and risk taking with new ideas and values.

As any one of these decreases, it acts to decrease all the others and to increase the opposite states of affairs. In terms of our model (Figure 1) inputs (values) feed into a "black box" composed of highly interrelated variables, where an increase or decrease in any one can set off a chain of reactions that influence all the others.

As the above states of affairs continue, we may hypothesize the following "outputs":

1. Members of this system of relationships will *not* tend to be aware of their interpersonal impact upon others (they may be aware of their rational, intellectual impact).
2. The members of this system of relationships will not tend to solve interpersonal problems in such a way that they (or similar problems) will not tend to occur.

We may conclude that the organizational values, if followed, will tend to create a social system in which the members' interpersonal competence will tend to decrease (see Figure 1). (Up to this point we are not hypothesizing the impact upon rational, intellective competence which presumably should not be so affected by these values.)

The Impact upon the Organization of Decreasing Interpersonal Competence

Let us continue our theoretical analysis with the following question: What may we hypothesize are some of the implications upon the organization of decreasing interpersonal competence?

If individuals are in social systems where they are unable to predict accurately their interpersonal impact upon others, and others' impact upon themselves, they may begin to feel confused. "Why are people behaving that way toward me?"

FIGURE 1

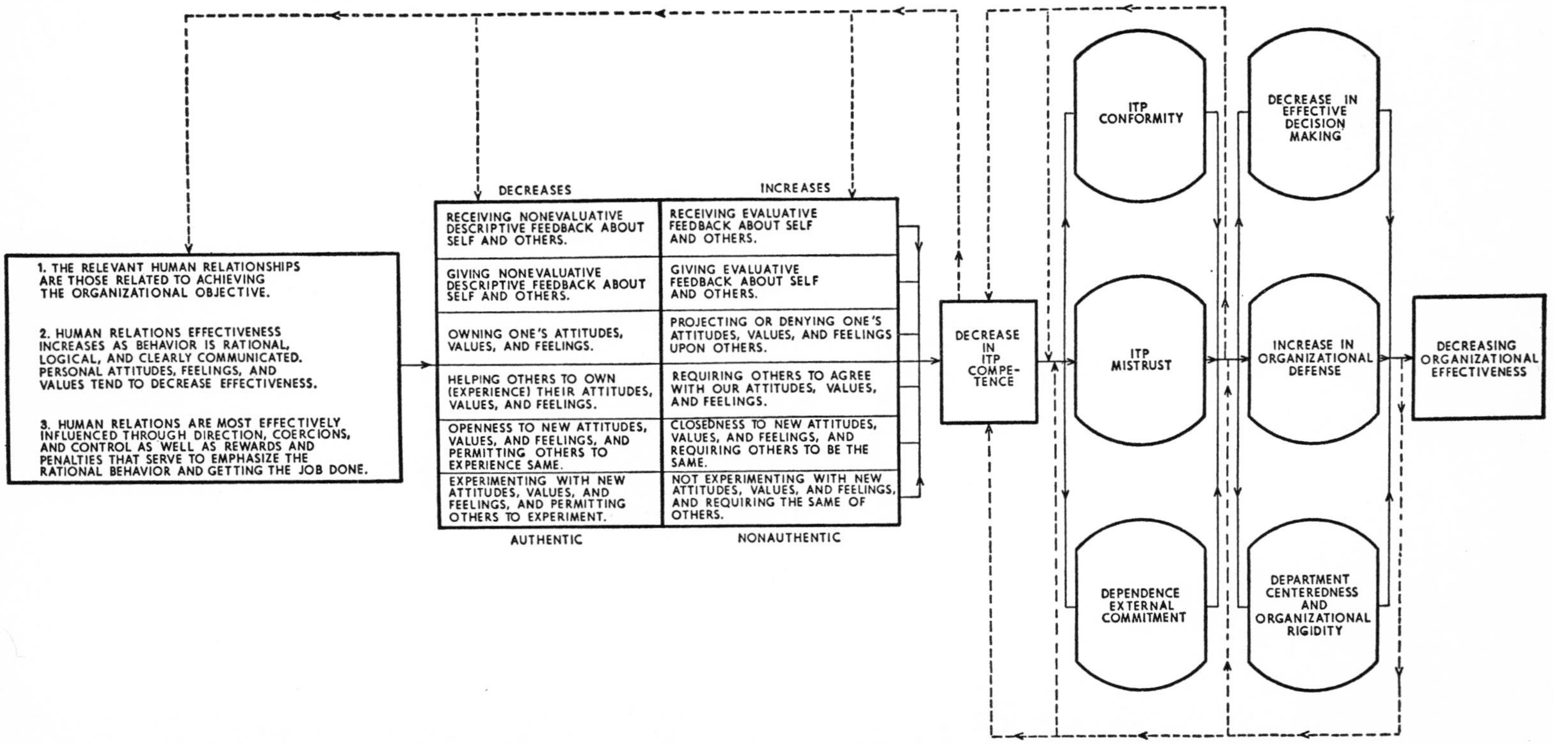

DECREASING ORGANIZATIONAL EFFECTIVENESS

DECREASE IN EFFECTIVE DECISION MAKING

INCREASE IN ORGANIZATIONAL DEFENSE

DEPARTMENT CENTEREDNESS AND ORGANIZATIONAL RIGIDITY

ITP CONFORMITY

ITP MISTRUST

DEPENDENCE EXTERNAL COMMITMENT

DECREASE IN ITP COMPETENCE

DECREASES / INCREASES

AUTHENTIC	NONAUTHENTIC
RECEIVING NONEVALUATIVE DESCRIPTIVE FEEDBACK ABOUT SELF AND OTHERS.	RECEIVING EVALUATIVE FEEDBACK ABOUT SELF AND OTHERS.
GIVING NONEVALUATIVE DESCRIPTIVE FEEDBACK ABOUT SELF AND OTHERS.	GIVING EVALUATIVE FEEDBACK ABOUT SELF AND OTHERS.
OWNING ONE'S ATTITUDES, VALUES, AND FEELINGS.	PROJECTING OR DENYING ONE'S ATTITUDES, VALUES, AND FEELINGS UPON OTHERS.
HELPING OTHERS TO OWN (EXPERIENCE) THEIR ATTITUDES, VALUES, AND FEELINGS.	REQUIRING OTHERS TO AGREE WITH OUR ATTITUDES, VALUES, AND FEELINGS.
OPENNESS TO NEW ATTITUDES, VALUES, AND FEELINGS, PERMITTING OTHERS TO EXPERIENCE SAME.	CLOSEDNESS TO NEW ATTITUDES, VALUES, AND FEELINGS, AND REQUIRING OTHERS TO BE THE SAME.
EXPERIMENTING WITH NEW ATTITUDES, VALUES, AND FEELINGS, AND PERMITTING OTHERS TO EXPERIMENT.	NOT EXPERIMENTING WITH NEW ATTITUDES, VALUES, AND FEELINGS, AND REQUIRING THE SAME OF OTHERS.

1. THE RELEVANT HUMAN RELATIONSHIPS ARE THOSE RELATED TO ACHIEVING THE ORGANIZATIONAL OBJECTIVE.

2. HUMAN RELATIONS EFFECTIVENESS INCREASES AS BEHAVIOR IS RATIONAL, LOGICAL, AND CLEARLY COMMUNICATED. PERSONAL ATTITUDES, FEELINGS, AND VALUES TEND TO DECREASE EFFECTIVENESS.

3. HUMAN RELATIONS ARE MOST EFFECTIVELY INFLUENCED THROUGH DIRECTION, COERCIONS, AND CONTROL AS WELL AS REWARDS AND PENALTIES THAT SERVE TO EMPHASIZE THE RATIONAL BEHAVIOR AND GETTING THE JOB DONE.

"Why do they interpret me incorrectly?" Since such questions are not sanctioned in a rationally dominated system, much less answered, the confusion will tend to turn to frustration and feelings of failure regarding interpersonal relations. In an attempt to maintain their sense of esteem, the members may react by questioning the honesty, and genuineness of the interpersonal behavior of their fellow workers. Simultaneously, they may place an even greater emphasis upon the rational, technical interactions, in which they are probably experiencing a greater degree of success. The increased emphasis upon rationality will act to suppress the feelings even more, which in turn will decrease the probability that the questions of confusion and the mistrust (of self and others) will be explored.

As interpersonal mistrust increases, and as the capacity (individual and organizational) to cope with this mistrust decreases, then the members may tend to adapt by "playing it safe." The predisposition will be to say those things that cannot be misunderstood and to discuss those issues for which there exist clear organizational values and sanctions. The desire "to say the right thing" should be especially strong toward one's superiors, toward one's peers with whom one is competing, and toward one's subordinates, who may be known to bypass their superiors. The result is that conformity begins to develop within an organization. Along with conformity, the interpersonal relationships will tend to be characterized by "conditional acceptance" (to use a Rogerian concept) where the members will tend to feel accepted if they behave in accordance with certain organizational specifications.

Another possible important force acting toward conformity is the predisposition of individuals to bring around them people whose self-concepts are congruent. There is a tendency to hire or upgrade individuals who manifest the accepted image of the system.[10] For example, Ward found that executives prefer subordinates who do not make trouble, are not argumentative, somewhat retiring, meek, and even bashful to the more argumentative, impatient, rebellious types. This

---

[10] E. J. McCormick and R. W. Middaugh, "The Development of a Tailor-Made Scoring for the How-Supervise? Test," *Personnel Psychology*, Vol. IX (1956), pp. 27–37.

would be understandable in terms of our model, since the latter qualities would violate the norms of the executive systems and consequently require a degree of interpersonal competence that may not exist. In the same study Ward showed that another preferred pattern was for the subordinate to be systematic, orderly, precise, and accurate. These qualities are consonant with the "inputs of rationality."[11] Evidence consonant with Ward's findings was published by Freeman and Taylor. They found that while 100 top executives said that they looked for aggressive, energetic applicants, they personally wanted "tactful subordinates." The executives tended to attribute their own success to "brain and character," but they preferred "emotionally controlled and balanced" subordinates rather than overly bright or highly ethical ones.[12]

As we have seen in Chapter 1, basic to the formal strategy is power over and control of the subordinates by the superior. The power is especially related to the capacity to direct, reward, and penalize. If we now add the existence of mistrust and conformity to dependence, we may hypothesize that the members' commitment to the organization will tend to be external as far as interpersonal activities are concerned. By "external commitment," I mean that the source of commitment to work for any given individual lies in the power, rewards, and penalties that some other individual may use to influence the first individual. Internal commitment exists when the motive for a particular behavior resides from within (for example, self-realization). A certain amount of internal commitment restricted to rational activities may be possible in this system, if the rational, intellective aspects of the job are consonant with the individual's abilities and expressed needs.

External commitment will tend to reinforce the conformity with, conditional acceptance of, and especially the dependence upon the leader. The subordinates will tend to look for cues from the leader and will be willing to be influenced and guided by him. In fact, they may develop great skill in

---

[11] Lewis B. Ward, "Do You Want a Weak Subordinate?" *Harvard Business Review,* September–October, 1961, pp. 6–26.

[12] G. L. Freeman and E. K. Taylor, *How to Pick Leaders* (New York: Funk & Wagnalls Co., 1950).

inducing the leader to define the problems, the range of alternatives, and so on. The subordinates will tend to operate within limits that they know to be safe. As the dependence increases, the need for the subordinates to know where they "stand" will also tend to increase.[13]

Thus, interpersonal mistrust, conformity, conditional acceptance, external commitment, and dependence tend to be "outputs" of decreasing interpersonal competence. Each of these feeds back to reinforce itself. All, in turn, feed back upon interpersonal competence to decrease it further or to reinforce it at its existing level.

At some point (to be empirically determined) the consequences above will tend to feed back to influence the rational intellective competence of the executives. For example, in some of the situations to be discussed later we learned that executives (with mathematical and engineering background) dealing with highly technical issues developed strong emotional attachments to these issues. During discussions held to resolve technical rational issues, the emotional involvements tended to block understanding. Since the men did not tend to deal with emotions, their inhibiting effects were never explored. On the contrary, they were covered up by technical, rational arguments. Since these arguments were attempts by people to defend their self or attack others', there was a tendency for the rationality of the arguments to be weak. This in turn troubled the receiver of the argument, who tended to attack obvious rational flows immediately. The attack tended to increase the degree of threat experienced by the first person, and he became even more defensive. Similar impacts upon rational decision making were also discovered in areas such as investment decisions, purchasing policies, quality control standards, product design, and marketing planning.

Similar problems tended to occur with decisions that involved human factors in an organization. They were not explored thoroughly, especially when the values and ideas to be

---

[13] I am perplexed as to how many writers "prove" the importance of "merit ratings" or "evaluation" programs by citing peoples' needs to know. These data may simply show how dependent the subordinates are and how well the programs are institutionalizing the dependence.

explored were not tolerated by the system. Demotions, promotions, reprimands, discipline, and evaluation of ineffectiveness are but a few examples of such decisions. Finally, there were cases on record in which the organization never explored a new product or a new manufacturing process because the "powers that be wouldn't hear of it."

Another crucial area of decision making that could be influenced by interpersonal incompetence would be the area of organizational change. For example, let us consider an organization that desires to go from a highly centralized to a decentralized structure. One may predict that executives operating under the conditions above will not tend to explore or take adequate account of the feelings that subordinates under decentralization would have regarding decentralization. The executives will tend to "sell" decentralization by using rational reasons, largely missing such subordinate's feelings as dependence, conformity, and fear of authority. The subordinate's in turn will tend to suppress such feelings (assuming they are even aware of them) and communicate to their superiors that they understand the meaning of decentralization and that they agree with it. However, one would predict that if the superiors actually did decentralize and give the subordinates authority and responsibility, the latter will tend to seek ways to induce their superiors to make the decisions. The superiors, in turn, will tend to feel perplexed if not irritated. However, since the expression of such feelings is not sanctioned, they will tend to find indirect ways to express their disappointment and/or hold new meetings loaded with new rational reasons "selling" the importance of decentralization. (Examples will be presented in Chapter 4).

When executives perceive that their present leadership is not as effective as they wish it to be, one finds that they tend to take two courses of action. The first is to emphasize even more the values of the formal organizational structure. This means that they tend to place greater emphasis on the use of rationality, direction, control, rewards, and penalties. In practice this tends to mean that they begin to check on other people's work not only to see if it is done but also how it was accomplished. Another activity is to manage through detailed questioning about issues and problems that may exist at levels lower than the man being questioned but for which he is responsible. For example, asking a personnel vice-president the capacity of a parking lot in a plant away from the home office.

The result of such action on the part of the superior is to create a defensiveness in the subordinate. The subordinate now finds himself constantly checking on all details so he will not be "caught" by the superior. However, the activity of the organization is not carried forward with such behavior. The result is simply one of making the subordinates (and usually his subordinates) more defensive. Their response is to build up organizational defenses to protect themselves. For example, in one case where executives were managing by detail, the subordinates created the "JIC" file which stands for "just in case" some superior asks. This file was kept up to date by several lower-level managers who were full time and countless other people working part time. The JIC file is an organizational defense against threat experienced by individuals at various levels.

In short, one may hypothesize that organizational defenses may be developed in an organization to protect various individuals and groups.

These organizational defenses can be used to "needle" people. This tends to occur when the rational methods seem to fail. But since the use of feelings is deviant behavior and since the superior or subordinates do not have much experience in their use, the tendency may be to have feelings "overdetermined." By "overdetermined," I mean that feelings tend to be much stronger than the situation warrants. Their overdeterminedness is compounded by the fact that subordinates do not tend to be accustomed to dealing with feelings.

Executives may speak of "needling the boys," "once in a while, 'raising hell' to keep them on their toes," and so on. If these conditions continue, it is not long before the "hot" decisions of the organization are administered by using emotions. This is commonly known in industry as "management by crisis."

As management by crisis increases, the subordinate's defensive reaction to these crises will tend to increase. One way to protect himself is to make certain that his area of responsibility is administered competently and that no other peer executive "throws a dead cat into his yard." The subordinate's predisposition will tend to be centered toward the interests of his department. As the department centeredness increases, the interdepartmental rivalries will tend to increase. All these decrease the organization's flexibility for change as well as the co-operation among departments. This decrease, in turn, will tend to be adapted to by the top management by increasing their directives, which in turn begins to recentralize the organization.

The external commitment, conformity, interpersonal mistrust, ineffective decision making, management by crisis, and organizational rigidity will tend to feed back to reinforce each other and to decrease interpersonal competence (see Figure 1). Moreover, each will feed upon all the others to reinforce itself. We would conclude that under these conditions the tendency will be to increase the energy required to produce the same input, or some day it may even decrease the output, although the input remains constant. When this state of affairs occurs, the organization may be said to have begun to be ineffective.

This analysis may help us to understand some of the findings of Guetzkow and Cyr and March and his associates. Guetzkow and Cyr[14] found that groups in industry tend to postpone (withdraw from) complex problems. They prefer to play it safe and deal with the easier problems. In an interesting paper March concludes that rationality in an organization is qualified and constrained. Consequently, organizational decision-making behavior is primarily adaptive rather than rational. March mentions four critical activities that can constrain rationality, three of which would be predicted by our model. They are: (1) conflict among parties within the firm (intergroup competition in our terms), (2) avoidance of uncertainty, (3) searching "in the neighborhood" of the problem symptom current alternative, and (4) organizational learning.[15]

---

[14] H. Guetzkow and J. Cyr, "An Analysis of Conflict in Decision-Making Groups," *Human Relations,* Vol. VII (1954), pp. 367–82.

[15] James March, "Some Models of Organizational Decision Making," symposium at American Psychological Association, Sept. 5, 1961 (mimeographed, Carnegie Institute of Technology).

We have suggested that intergroup conflict is inherent in the pyramidal structure, managerial controls, directive leadership.[16] In this study we suggest that it is also inherent in the emphasis upon rationality and suppression of emotionality. If the above is valid, in a world where interpersonal mistrust, dependence, conformity, management by crisis, through detail, and fear are prevalent, then playing it safe and not getting hurt would be predictable. Under these conditions avoiding uncertainty, searching for solutions close to the problem, and looking primarily at the available alternatives would be adaptive. In other words, the conditions March accepts as independent variables or "givens," we view as dependent and changeable. It is hoped that this study (plus the already mentioned work by Blake and Shepard) will suggest that changes can be made in organizations so that at least the first three conditions can be modified. If we learn to modify them to a considerable degree, we may even be able to change the degree to which, as well as the activities through which, an organization learns.

Some Forces Inhibiting Organizational Ineffectiveness

The reader may wonder if we mean to imply that when interpersonal competence is low, the organization is automatically doomed to failure. The answer is obviously, "No."

First, in any organization a large proportion of the decision making is related to "getting the widgets out." There are many technical, professional decisions that must be made if an organization is to achieve its objective. The more the organization requires intellective rational competence, and the more it has such competence, the *less* the probability up to a point (to be empirically determined) that a low interpersonal competence will tend to have negative impact of great significance. However, as we shall show, there is a point at which interpersonal competence becomes so crucial that it can significantly affect the rational (as well as the interpersonal) ac-

---

[16] Chris Argyris, *Personality and Organization.*

tivities of the organization. Competing organizations are able to obtain the finest minds and the best equipment that they need then. In a competitive world, the one that is able to support these resources with effective human relationships may well increase its opportunity for survival.

Another important consideration is that the above state of affairs is consonant with the formal organizational values about effective human relationships. Thus, although the consequences (decreasing interpersonal trust, competence; increasing management by crisis, and so on) may be unintended, and even not desired, they flow naturally from the kind of organizational world in which men are placed. The unintended consequences are, therefore, functional. They are necessary if the executives are to survive in a world of organizational stress. In other words the values about effective human relationships held by the executives, and implicit in the formal organizational structure and managerial controls, lead to a stressful world where a subordinate is dependent upon a superior. To adapt to and operate within this dependence and stress, the subordinates adhere to the same values. The values will probably be maintained as long as their "maintenance cost" does not exceed the cost of their negative impact upon the executive system, the decision making, and the relationship throughout the entire organization.

A third moderating influence is the degree with which interpersonal feelings are openly discussed. One might hypothesize that in an organization feelings are never completely blocked. Our analysis above has been a theoretical one. We have purposely not considered the possibility that feelings may be discussed at times, even if they violate the organizational values. There are examples on record where executives describe a meeting as one in which "the lid blew off" or an interview situation where "we had it out." In studying a specific organization, the degree to which these meetings occur will be determined. If they occur frequently, we should find that (1) they are perceived as violating the organizational values and/or (2) the organization had, in addition to the values listed above, another set that sanctioned such behavior.

A fourth possibility is that after many years in such a system the members will tend to decrease their expectation that feelings are important and relevant in their everyday activities. Given such expectations, the "emotional apathy and noninvolvement" and the frustration of suppressed feelings will not tend to be as great. However, the organizational consequences of conformity, and so on, will still tend to arise.

Finally, although I know of no existing data, it may be that there are "threshold" points which prevent a system from increasing its interpersonal ineffectiveness indefinitely. Similarly there may exist threshold points which will tend to make it increasingly difficult to increase effectiveness indefinitely. One may also hypothesize that at some point and under certain conditions (at the moment unknown) the degree of effectiveness or ineffectiveness will not tend to increase or decrease but tend to remain constant. Any activity continuing in the direction of the dominant state of affairs (effectiveness or ineffectiveness) will only tend to reinforce these states of affairs.

A Note on the Nature of Our Predictions

If one examines the model that we have presented, one will find that it contains certain assumptions about the behavior that it purports to understand. They are:

1. Some human behavior in organization can be understood as caused by individuals adhering or dedicating themselves to organizational values. The greater the commitment to the values, the less one needs to include personality factors to explain the behavior. For example, people with psychologically different personalities (as measured by a test of one's choosing) would still tend to behave in the direction and manner specified by the model. Thus, our focus is on the study of *systems of behavior* which, once in operation, are independent of the particular individuals that composed them.

This does not mean that personality factors are completely irrelevant. The individuals must be capable of perceiving the values and becoming dedicated to them. The system would never be able to influence the behavior of the members, if the members were simply unable to recognize or have the values communicated to them. Nor could the system operate if one attempted to populate it with personality types who simply could not dedicate themselves to these values. One reason why the second condition tends to occur rarely in our society is that our schools, churches, recreational groups, and even some aspects of family life are also based upon formal organizational values. Thus, in our culture, individuals are prepared to live more or less in accordance with formal organization values.

2. The second assumption is that the system, with its inputs, outputs, and feedback processes will tend to remain relatively stable. The stability occurs as the individuals act within the values of the system, thereby keeping out disturbing influences.

Change may be induced in this system through external pressures (that is, environment) or through the "seeding" of the system with enough individuals who are capable of, indeed need to behave in accordance with, other values and have the necessary power to do so.

3. Any change attempted in the outputs (for example, through new policies) designed to be superimposed upon the individuals, will tend to be resisted. Changes that do not or are not permitted to influence the inputs (values) will tend to fail. One can make, for example, changes in organization structure policies require a decrease in interdepartmental conflicts, and so on. None of these changes will have lasting effects unless the inputs are appropriately influenced. The appropriate influence is in the direction of increasing interpersonal competence.

Although increasing interpersonal competence is a necessary first step, *it is not enough.* We may recall that the structure of the organization, its technology, job design, controls, incentive systems, and so on, are all based on the same set of values. Consequently these factors must eventually be modified or else one can negate the changes that may occur through an increase in interpersonal competence. To summarize, the basic changes will require a modification or addition to the present values. To effect changes, organizational, technological, and interpersonal factors will require alteration. The interpersonal factors, however, should come first, closely followed by the others.[17]

---

[17] This assertion has implications for planning laboratories. For example, one would not tend to focus on intergroup problems until interpersonal competence will not tend to be enough, if the organization is characterized by built-in "win-lose" battles among departments.

PART TWO

DIAGNOSIS
AND
FEEDBACK

3

The Diagnosis of the Top
Executive System: Interviews

We now turn to a description of the
interview and observation diagnosis
of the top executive system of the divisional "home office" of a
very large corporation located in the Midwest. There are 18
executives in the system. All have completed the bachelor's degree with 40 per cent having completed the master's degree.
Although detailed official records are not available for publication, the level of intelligence and intellective competence is extremely high. The range of the I. Q. is from 130–170, with
130–140 the predominant pattern. It is the highest that this
writer has experienced in one top management group.

The reader may recall that the president asked if the
writer could develop a diagnosis of the executives as a system
from which a program could be developed to overcome any
deficiencies, if any were found. It was made clear by the president and myself that the diagnosis was not to focus on any individual. And, needless to say, the president was not to receive any information that the rest of the group did not receive.

The first step in the diagnosis was a personal interview
with each executive. The interviews ranged from one and a half
to three hours. Each executive was interviewed at least once.
The questions asked the executives were based upon the model
presented in Chapter 2. There were questions asked to ascertain:

1. The degree to which the executives adhere to the organizational values.
2. The degree of interpersonal competence of the executives
   as a system.

57

3. The degree to which the executive system may be said to have interpersonal mistrust, conformity, and external commitment.
4. The degree to which such organizational defenses exist as management by crisis, interdepartmental conflicts, and rivalries.
5. The effectiveness with which rational decisions are made.

A. THE EMPHASIS UPON RATIONALITY

The results of the diagnosis based upon the interviews are presented below. The major hypothesis is that in all the questions asked regarding the values, the intellective, rational activities will be described as "frequent" and "effective" or "good." Interpersonal or emotional activities will not tend to be described as "frequent" or "effective" or "good." Put in another way, a major hypothesis is that the executives will tend to report that their system sanctions and rewards the intellective, rational factors and tends to penalize and suppress the interpersonal and emotional factors.

Hypothesis I: *The majority of disagreements reported in the system should be rational, intellective in character. Interpersonal disagreements should occur significantly less frequently than intellectual ones or deep intellectual ones.*

Evidence for Hypothesis I

1. Seventy-eight per cent report that intellectual, rational disagreements regarding professional, technical questions are "frequent" and "happen all the time." Twenty-two per cent report that they rarely occur. None report that they never occur.
2. Thirty-nine per cent report that long deep disagreements do occur frequently; and, as predicted, 50 per cent report that they rarely occur or never occur.
3. More significantly 72 per cent of the executives state that interpersonal clashes rarely or never occur. Twenty-two per cent report that they do occur.

Hypothesis II: *The executives will report that they will attempt to inhibit themselves and others from expressing feelings and views of interpersonal relationships at meetings.*

Evidence for Hypothesis II

1. The executives were asked how they would cope with deep disagreements if they were to occur in a meeting. The prediction is that the solutions would emphasize rational solutions and not solutions dealing with feelings. In Table 1 below, we find that this is the case. One hundred per cent of the solutions were of a rational character. No solutions were reported that attempted to cope with feelings.

TABLE 1

SUGGESTED SOLUTION TO DEEP DISAGREEMENT
(Per Cent)

N = 18

a) Tell the group that they are off the facts and then direct them back to the facts.. 50
b) Stop the disagreement by redefining the purpose of the meeting.. 39
c) Get them to talk about the facts or else call off the meeting...... 11
    Rational-oriented solution..............................100
    Solution that copes with admitted feelings................. 0

Some Typical Comments

I never really experienced a deep disagreement among people since I have been here. It's usually a disagreement as a matter of dispute over ideas.

The way I would handle it would partially depend on the solution to be reached. If time were available, of course, the best thing to do would be to postpone the meeting so that we cooled off a bit— time for reflections. I believe that time can help people see things more clearly.

Yes, I think this occurs once in a while, but I don't think the deep disagreements come out. I think people hold back.

Well, I reflect myself, check on the balances; I'd call some other people over the phone and get some neutral opinions.

Well, I'd say I hadn't been in any management meetings where meetings are that strong. Disagreement, but I think that when there was disagreement, people sat on it rather than opened up on it. You could feel that people disagreed, but they usually sat on their hands.

2. In another question, the executives were asked how they would handle an emotional outburst in the meeting. The hypothesis is that the executives would tend to cope with

feelings by rejecting them or by transforming them into intellectual, rational problems. The data confirm the hypothesis.

TABLE 2

SUGGESTED SOLUTION TO EMOTIONAL OUTBURST
(Per Cent)

N = 18

a) If possible, stop the meeting. Calm the people down by saying that they are not prepared to discuss the subject. More groundwork is needed. Call off the meeting..................89
b) Let the feelings be expressed. You might learn something about the individual.. 6
 Total solutions of "leaving the field.".....................95
 Solutions of dealing with feelings........................ 0

Illustrative Comments

Well, what would I do? I guess the first thing I'd do is I'd hope that it was near 5:15. I'd close the meeting before there was damage done, before feelings are put on the table and hurt. Then I'd make some personal appointments and deal with it that way.

―――――――――

Well, that's very clear. I would call it off. If it looked like we weren't getting an answer, I'd call it off. Then I think I'd say, "Maybe it should be done. Why don't you guys give me in writing what you want to do, and then we'll make a decision."

―――――――――

Not here—that's one thing that wouldn't come up. In fact, I wonder if people would really be free to be open, especially with hostility? You know there are a few people with whom you just don't do this.

―――――――――

He is the leader and therefore will decide and take the responsibility. He squares things with the loser later on.
Q: How does he square them?
He can't apologize to him, that's certain. The best he can do is make sure that the loser understands the issues, the facts. It's better done by letter, of course, because that will prevent people from getting further into feelings.

B. INTERPERSONAL COMPETENCE IN THE EXECUTIVE SYSTEM

So far, the data support the hypothesis that the executive system is dominated by the organizational values of rationality, intellective clarity, and the suppression of feelings.

According to our model, the executives should manifest less interpersonal competence than intellective, rational competence. No such data were obtained through the interview. All of the executives characterized themselves as "relatvely" competent or "satisfactorily" competent in both areas. None of them reported that interpersonal competence was a problem in the division.

In the next section this apparent lack of fit between the model and reality will be explained. We shall see that our observations of actual meetings plus interviews afterward suggest that (1) the executives' interpersonal competence is significantly lower than their rational competence and (2) the executives are unaware of this. Their lack of awareness is partially due to their lack of sensitivity in this area and partially due to the defenses in the system that prevent them from becoming aware. More of this later.

C. INTERPERSONAL MISTRUST OR LACK OF CONFIDENCE

This is another factor that was not picked up through interviews. The executives reported that there was "adequate," "high" degree of confidence and trust within the system. As in interpersonal competence, we will see that lack of confidence in one another does exist. Also, as in the case above, the system has defenses developed within it which either prevent the executives from reporting it and/or even being aware of the extent to which it exists. The degree to which the latter is the case may be best ascertained by examining the chapters that describe what occurred during the laboratory (Part III) as well as the executives' evaluations of the laboratory one month after it was held (Chapter 10).

There is one set of data that is related to trust. It is interesting to note that the executives perceive trust in terms of the rational, technical dimension. If an individual can feel free to deviate from the formal policies and practices, then this is a sign of trust. Few, however, added that the expression of feelings could be a sign of trust. Indeed, 60 per cent of the executives responded that the eruption of feelings in a group is a sign of *"too much* openness." It is also interesting to note in the comments that trust exists when problems can be discussed unemotionally, that people should always put things in writing, and it helps to be "thick-skinned" and "roll with the punches."

TABLE 3

CHARACTERISTICS OF TRUST AND OPENNESS IN A GROUP
(Per Cent)

N = 18

a) Freedom to express views that deviate from the formal policies and practice...72
b) Freedom to do the above and to express one's feelings........11
  Total...83

Illustrative Comments

The key to trust and respect is to be able to discuss a problem in unemotional terms and state it tactfully without letting your feelings get in the way.

I don't think they should trust one another. It seems to me the real business approach is to put things in writing.

Is it possible to be too open?

Yes, I think when it leaves the subject matter and gets to personalities. When each individual feels so strongly about his own viewpoint that he can't see the other person's. In either of those two cases I'd say the group was too open.

————

Ability to deal with people, it seems to me not to be too aggressive but not to establish a personality where there's conflict. The job background is important. It seems to me you should be firm and direct but still leave people with the feeling that you're a good guy.

————

Also, I think they are able to roll with the punches. You slap them down, and they come up smiling. These are good men.

————

He has to be a little thick-skinned so that if people don't like what he's doing, then he's not going to feel badly inside. Or, to put it another way, he can't be torn up inside. Or, to put it another way, he can't be sensitive in an output way.

D. DEPENDENCE
IN THE EXECUTIVE SYSTEM

There are several kinds of data obtained to suggest that the relationship between any given superior and subordinate is characterized by dependence. It is important to keep in mind that we are predicting a degree of dependence beyond that which one might attribute to the very nature of organization (that is, the usual reporting relationships).

Hypothesis III: *Since the expression of feelings is deviant activity, the responsibility for dealing with them in an administrative situation will tend to be delegated to the individual with the highest organizational power, regardless of his competence in these matters.*

The corollary is that the person with the highest organizational power will tend to feel that delegating this function (dealing with feelings) is "wrong" or a "sign of weakness," regardless of his perceived degree of competence to deal with feelings.

Evidence for Hypothesis III

1. In response to the question on who should be responsible for handling emotional outbursts, 100 per cent of the executives responded "the leader in that situation," or "the man with the highest position at the meeting should always be responsible for dealing with these matters." No one felt that subordinates or peers should deal with these experiences as long as the superior is present, even though he is not being the most competent in dealing with feelings.

2. Twelve men volunteered that they may not be very effective in dealing with feelings. All of them, however, would agree with one who said, "Even if I stumble, it's my responsibility to bring things back on the track."

Further evidence of the dependence of the subordinates in a group meeting is obtained when asked how "difficult" individuals are coped with during the meetings. The majority of the executives reported that this task should be delegated to the leader. If possible he should cope with the difficult person in such a way that feelings are not brought out into the open.

3. When asked who is responsible for coping with the persons, "who talks too much," "who keeps the group off its target," "who talks too little," 100 per cent of the executives report that it is the leader's responsibility to cope with such difficult individuals. None of them reported that such "leadership func-

tions" might be shared according to the competence of the members.

4. Ninety-four per cent reported that they would cope with difficult members "diplomatically" and without referring to the problem directly. Only 6 per cent reported that they would deal with the feelings that difficult individuals tend to arouse in the group. For example 94 per cent believe that if a man keeps the group "off target," they would, if possible "without being noticed, ask the man to restate his position and carefully take the initiative away from him." One hundred per cent would involve the "quiet individual" who should be participating in the discussion by "asking a leading question." Not one would explore, in either case, the impact of each of the difficult individual's behavior upon the group.

Some Typical Comments

Of course, if it is a chronic matter that the individual keeps blocking the group's progress all the time, then I think it is another story. I think it should be handled outside the meeting and not inside the meeting. The leader should, with the person privately, tell where he is wrong.

Well, I would say I would take a 10-minute coffee break and chat with him and politely tell him he is blocking the group. This is the job of the leader.

5. Finally, we find that all the executives report that it is the main task of the leader to make certain that a group meeting achieves its objectives. One hundred per cent of the respondents report that the major role of an executive leading the group is to make sure that all points are discussed and that the group achieves its objective. None report that "process" functions are important or relevant in leading decision-making groups in business.

Illustrative Comments

The biggest job is to keep the group from wandering from the agenda. It seems to me that you have to help them reach their objective. That's the big job of the meeting. You, meaning the leader, have to keep the meeting running smoothly and right on target.

He must also, without brainwashing, make sure that the employees and the managers follow the party line. For example, they can say, "Now look, this is the way we're going to do it because I say so and the boss says so." Then, if he were a good man, he'd explain why this is so and why he's a firm believer in this method. Then he should try to sell the people this idea.

Principally, I would say if the group is staying on the subject, if they are going toward the goal, then there is progress. Of course, it is not as easy as all this because there are times when it is. If there isn't sufficient data, then the time isn't ripe.

The point to these five sets of data is that in this system, meetings will tend to be directed by the formal leader. Since the control of the leadership functions is placed in the formal leader's hands, the result will be an increasing dependence of the subordinates upon the superior for the successful running of information sessions as well as decision-making meetings. In the next chapter we will see that the leader tends to run meetings in such a way that they are highly controlled. It becomes a bit ironic to observe, for example, a tightly controlled centralized meeting whose objective it is to induce the participants to take on more responsibility and be less dependent!

E. CONFORMITY
IN THE EXECUTIVE SYSTEM

It is our hypothesis that the executive system will tend to manifest a high degree of conformity as far as interpersonal factors are concerned. The men in the system will tend to manifest similar values regarding feelings and interpersonal relationships. The conformity is *not* predicted to exist on the intellective, rational level since the system rewards (up to a point) differences on the rational level. If conformity does occur on the rational level, it should be traceable to interpersonal factors. For example, a subordinate may not say what he knows to be true about a particular administrative or technical problem because he may fear the response of his superior.

Hypothesis IV: *Conformity will tend to exist in the executive system in terms of the organizational values. Behavior that is rational and intellective as well as that which is directive and controlling will tend to be rewarded.*

Evidence for Hypothesis IV

1. One way to disagnose the degree of conformity in a system is to ask the men to report what they feel is effective behavior within the system. The replies are given in Table 4. They are all in agreement with our predictions.

TABLE 4

CHARACTERISTICS OF EFFECTIVE LEADERSHIP
(Per Cent)

N = 18[1]

a) Ability to articulate one's ideas..............................89
b) Ability to direct, to be aggressive..........................72
c) Ability to think quickly; high intelligence..................50
d) Interpersonal abilities.......................................0

Some Typical Comments

A person who can talk, who can be articulate. I think, as far as I can see, talking here is more important than writing. If he can make himself heard, this is important.

I think there is a little too much emphasis placed on articulateness; put it another way, still waters *can* run deep.

———

Well, I would say that the main characteristic is the drive, enthusiasm for the job, ability to communicate. In this organization, at least in the past, it's the selling-oriented guy that really gets somewhere.

Another area, I think, is technical know-how.

It seems to me that both of these have a place. I don't think that the technical know-how is always appreciated.

———

Gives the impression that he knows the subject whether he knows it or not.

Shows a willingness to do more than is required and to improvise.

Aggressive, glib, good communicator, the man has to be soft-spoken, not shout, but he should be able to make his ideas heard.

2. Further evidence is obtained by analyzing the responses to the question regarding what leadership characteristics tend to help people "get ahead" in the company.

———

[1] The respondents were asked more than one question; thus, the total equals more than 100 per cent.

TABLE 5

LEADERSHIP FACTORS THAT INFLUENCE PROMOTIONS
(Per Cent)

N = 18[2]

a) Technical, professional competence.........................89
b) Persuasive, "seller of ideas."..............................72
c) High intellectual capacity.................................61
d) Interpersonal abilities.................................... 0

3. The above is corroborated by the subordinates' perceptions of their superiors' leadership strengths. Note how the
rational, directive qualities are emphasized.

TABLE 6

SUBORDINATES' PERCEPTIONS OF SUPERIORS' LEADERSHIP STRENGTHS
(Per Cent)

N = 17

Behavior Consonant with the System
   a) Decisive, intelligent, articulate.
     Professionally competent................................60
   b) Never shows his feelings: holds feelings back..............28
Behavior not Consonant with the System
   a) He takes plenty of time to think........................ 6
   b) He emphasizes trust.................................... 6
     Total..100

4. The superiors' views of their subordinates' responses
also confirm the pattern.

TABLE 7

SUPERIOR'S PREDICTIONS OF SUBORDINATE RESPONSES ABOUT
SUPERIOR'S LEADERSHIP STRENGTH
(Per Cent)

N = 17

a) My professional, technical competence.....................47
b) My commitment to work hard............................35
     Total...82
c) My interpersonal competence............................12

When asked to predict what their subordinates would describe as "things they ought to work on in the leadership style,"
the superiors tended to respond in terms of their inability to
fulfill adequately certain leadership behavior idealized by the

---

[2] The respondents were asked more than one question; thus, the total
equals more than 100 per cent.

system. For example, some believed that their subordinates would report that they, too, are not directive enough or are not articulate enough or do not communicate enough about their job. Although these replies are in line with the predictions, there were an unexpected number of replies that discussed the superior's lack of interpersonal competence.

5. It is interesting to note that when the superiors were asked to predict what their subordinates will report as being their (superiors') limitations, they focus primarily on the behavior sanctioned by the system.

TABLE 8

SUPERIOR'S PREDICTIONS OF SUBORDINATE RESPONSES ABOUT
SUPERIOR'S LEADERSHIP LIMITATIONS
(Per Cent)

N = 17

a) Rational behavior. I am not directive enough or articulate
enough..71
b) Interpersonal behavior. I am not friendly enough or patient
enough, too directive......................................35

6. Next we present the executives' perceptions of an effective development program. Their concept of executive development, we see in Table 9, is limited to and influenced by the values of the system.

TABLE 9

CHARACTERISTIC OF EFFECTIVE EXECUTIVE DEVELOPMENT
(Per Cent)

N = 18

a) Give individual a job that challenges his rational, technical
competence..72
b) Give individual a job that provides challenging, interpersonal
as well as the intellectual rational experiences................ 6

Finally, further insight can be obtained on conformity by noting how the men deal with the "creative" or "wild duck" in the system. We note that they would permit an individual to deviate as long as he does not go beyond the limits of the system.

Creativity

7. When the executives are asked if a man can be "too creative" 41 per cent represent that creativity becomes "too

much" when the behavior of the individual goes past the corporate image and mission. Thirty-four per cent define as a creative person being unacceptable to the system when "he refuses to listen to others," "feels he has a monopoly of ideas," or "when he is being creative just for the sake of being a wild duck."[3]

8. When asked to describe examples of creativity, 100 per cent of the executives responded in terms of creative effort in the professional, rational, technical areas. None suggested examples of interpersonal creativity. Yet it is interesting to note that the executives previously reported that some of their most important problem areas lie in "trust," "co-operation," and "understanding."

The executives were also asked, if they felt it was necessary, how would they protect the creative person in this system. Fifty-three per cent reported that a creative person needs no protection as long as he is creative in the professional, rational areas. However, those executives who consider themselves creative individuals definitely require protection. The protection they suggest is (1) to really be listened to, and (2) to create a situation in which he does not have to fight constantly the emotional resistances of others.

Some Illustrative Comments

The wild duck has energy sapped because he has to fight all of them.

All of our people, it seems to me, are ingrained to take it easy. Even the wild duck has to use too much energy.

Here we don't respect differences. We clobber them. Let's say we're in a meeting, the agenda is full, and time is running out. So the boys begin to get edgy. Finally the boss says, "Okay, it'll be this way and that's it." Here you shut up, say, "yes, sure," and even, if you're smart, add, "That's a good idea."

How to protect the deviant? Well, that's a tough one because the essence in a black and white philosophy is to try to clobber him. You know the real problem of protecting a wild duck is to protect him before the facts are known, not after. I would say a balanced

---

[3] $N = 17$.

orientation and reflection are especially important in this society. The really creative guy is the guy who can deal with the balance.

Well, I guess the best way to protect him is to put him off in a room somewhere so he doesn't upset too many people.

F. MANAGEMENT BY CRISIS, INTERDEPARTMENTAL RIVALRIES, AND RATIONAL DECISION MAKING

Although, as we shall see in subsequent sections, there was frequent use of management by crisis and rational decisions were delayed or made less effective by interpersonal problems, none of these was mentioned in the interviews.

Interdepartmental rivalries were mentioned by a few people as a major problem of the division. It is interesting to note that the major future problems identified were the domination by corporate headquarters and the interdivisional conflicts. During the observations and the laboratory, the conflicts and rivalries among departments within the division became major problems. Also, it is interesting to note that in a subsequent study of the lower-level subordinates of these men, they stated that one of their biggest problems was the domination from their superiors.

TABLE 10

MAJOR FUTURE PROBLEM AREAS FOR DIVISIONAL MANAGEMENT
(Per Cent)

N = 18[4]

a) Dominated by headquarters.............................39
b) Interdivisional conflicts..................................33
c) Dominated by headquarters and at times from within.......22
d) Intradivisional conflicts.................................11
e) To really get to know each other.........................11
f) To stay on the job long enough to know it................ 6

Illustrative Comments

There are times when the corporation, however, is not sure whether we are centralized or decentralized. Sometimes I think the corporation wants us to do things that we don't want to do. We don't know how to stand up as much as we should to the corporation. I

---

[4] The respondents were asked more than one question; thus, the total equals more than 100 per cent.

feel very strongly about this. I would say sometimes we're black-mailed by them.

Well, I'd say no more than we have today. Sometimes I feel that we are overmanaged. We're fairly well-balanced; and, of course, the older we get, we tend to become more and more balanced, and hopefully we'll see each others' mistakes and needs.

I think one of the biggest problems we're going to have is to get all the people involved in a particular problem to be present. And right now we are having constant battles to fight the fire, and when things are ready to move, everyone who should be there isn't available.

One of our real problems is that each of us is beginning to develop an interest in what is best for our division rather than what is best for organization. I think we may lose the singleness of purpose of our corporation.

The executives' diagnosis of the major problem that they felt the company was going to have implementing decentralization was the rivalry and lack of trust among divisions and the pressure from headquarters.

TABLE 11

POSSIBLE DIFFICULTIES WITH DECENTRALIZATION
(Per Cent)

N = 18[5]

a) Interdivisional competition and rivalry. Lack of trust among divisions. 66
b) Too much pressure from corporate. Do they really trust our capacity?. 44
c) Too many new people added at the divisional level. 11

Some Typical Comments

One is to believe in decentralization. I really wonder whether people really believe in it. It's not enough to say, "Let's go ahead." You must really believe in it.

I think that the most important problem we are going to have will be in the interdependent decisions, especially when we lack information. People aren't so ready to balance things out and compromise. They try to work on a black and white. It's all dynamic, it

---

[5] Respondents were asked more than one question; thus, total equals more than 100 per cent.

seems to me, and there's not enough time to recognize the value of reflection. Too much emphasis on black or white and make up your mind quick.

I think there is unnecessary competition between the divisions. There is too much feeling that we have to strike a good bargain. Sometimes one division takes advantage of another division. But at times I think because of this there is an awful lot of wasted time.

Perhaps in some cases the corporation has laid down too many rules, and time is spent worrying about what we should do or what we should not do. Not in terms of the effectiveness of the division, but in terms of whether there will be a negative impact if we break and violate the rules. It seems to me that there ought to be rules—we certainly need them—but there will be a negative impact if we break and violate the rules. But there ought to be flexibility in the rules so that if one feels that in a particular case a divergence from the rules is justified, then it seems to me we should be able to get such a ruling. Right now I would say certainly that there is a lot of reluctance to go back and to break the rules. It seems to me we tie ourselves up in knots.

In other words, I would say that the real problem that we have had has to do with the relationship with headquarters.

One may wonder about the degree of fulfillment and satisfaction the executives tend to obtain in the system. Their answer is that it is very high. As one might predict, the overwhelming number of executives report needs that are consonant with the values of the executive system. They, as individuals, value rationality, essentiality in important decisions, and tend to suppress their own and others' emotions. They do not tend to consider interpersonal factors as central to their conception of self.

TABLE 12
Reasons for Job Satisfaction
(Per Cent)

N = 18

1. Important role in important decisions requiring high rational, intellective, technical competence.............................83
2. Important role in facilitating interpersonal relationships....... 6

Some Typical Comments

Prestige, substantial influence in the real important dollar decisions of an important division in a very large corporation. These are decisions that are really important. There's an attractiveness with the responsibility and the power of making decisions. It's immensely satisfying when you have managers who have a real positive substance to the job and they're really first-class competent people.

Well, I think I understand the objective, and I really find it very satisfying in accomplishing it, seeing that long-range jobs get done well.

CONCLUSIONS

We found, as predicted by the model in Chapter 2, the executive system regards as worthwhile the values implicit in the formal organization, its technology, and the managerial controls. Also, in line with the model, we found evidence of lack of confidence, conformity, and external commitment, as well as interdepartmental conflicts and rivalries.

The executives did not report low interpersonal competence (as we would predict from the model). We will present evidence that their interpersonal competence (relative to their intellectual competence) was low and that they were unaware of this. We also found a high intellective, technical competence. These are also in keeping with the predictions from the model.

It is important to emphasize that the predictions from the model are supposed to apply in varying degrees to any formal organization. The fact that we find the predictions are confirmed in this company does not make it atypical or somehow "bad." The results obtained in this company, I would hypothesize, could be replicated in most other industrial organizations. I should predict that the only major differences would tend to be one of the degree to which each factor is operating in a particular company. Therefore, one may not conclude that the company is in serious difficulties. Indeed, as we shall show, underneath these problems lay a sound and deep human potential striving to be released.

4

The Diagnosis of the Executive
System: Observations

The second kind of diagnosis made of the executives was to observe them while "in action" holding meetings and making decisions. The executives granted me permission to attend any meetings I wished. They placed "off limits" upon a few meetings that dealt with pricing of new products, profits, and other confidential financial information. In turn, I also suggested that they feel free to ask me not to come in or to leave, if a meeting took an unexpected turn and they felt that for the sake of the company's interest an outsider should not be present.

I attended 51 meetings ranging in number from one to 30 individuals and in time from 10 minutes to seven hours. Because of my university schedule, I was able to observe only on certain days of the week. Whenever it was possible, the executives shifted meetings so I could observe as many different meetings as possible. One concern that I had was that the executives might resist the research by simply scheduling difficult meetings during the days that I could not attend. With the exception of two instances in the early days of the research, to my knowledge this was not done. Indeed, the opposite occurred. The men co-operated fully and made conscious efforts to schedule "hot" ones on the days that they knew I would be present. Another bit of evidence to support this conclusion is that on four days I arrived unannounced. The quality of meetings on those days was not any different. A third bit of evidence comes from the interviews that I held with the executives in which they freely discussed meetings that I was not able to attend. Several kept copious notes, and all opened up their files that contained memoranda or notes on the meetings. The last validity check available was to compare the observations with the problems explored during the feedback sessions and the laboratory. If the discrepancy was great in either instance, it would have raised serious questions. As we shall see, no discrepancy arose. Indeed, during the feedback session and the laboratory the men added to and deepened the diagnosis.

My role at the meetings was one of an observer. I made no comments whatsoever, although as one might predict there were moments when I was bursting to intervene. On several occasions, the executives asked to meet with me so I might give them a critique of their behavior.

I agreed, although as a researcher I had some qualms. How much would I alter the situation by my feedback? My solution to the problem was as follows: I resisted giving any feedback to an executive until I had observed him several times. The reason that I gave was that I had to have more data, which was a genuine need on my part. As I developed a conception of the individual's leadership pattern, I felt free to meet with him to discuss it.

My objective during the discussion was not to help him become more aware of himself in the way that I believed was necessary if changes were to occur. I knew that this would require time that was unavailable and motivation for change on the part of the executives that was not as yet evident. I gave a straight-forward description of his impact as I saw it upon the group. I attempted to keep out any evaluations of good or bad, right or wrong. I usually began by asking the executive about his objectives for the meeting and how well he felt he had achieved them. Typically, I would then give my perceptions. Although, I had data from interviews regarding the others' feelings, I never disclosed these data. To do so would have violated professional confidences, because the individuals could be easily identified. However, I freely told the executive how I would have felt if I were in the subordinates' position, making it very clear that I was not reporting their position.

The impact of my interventions was to create a feeling of dissonance or disequilibrium in the minds of the executives. As one said, "I used to think that I knew exactly what was going on, but now I'm beginning to wonder." Interestingly, *most of the executives attempted no immediate changes.* On the contrary, they asked that I observe them at greater length so that I could, in my own mind, develop an increased degree of confidence in my diagnoses. Their way of resolving the dissonance was to hope that after careful observation I would conclude that I had misperceived the situation. Apparently, this mode of resolution helped these executives to make certain that they did *not* change their behavior. They wanted to be certain that I observed them as they "really act" in meetings.

A smaller group of men did attempt to change their behavior. As one might predict, the attempts were more on the gimmick or technique level. For example, one man decided he dominated too much. During the next meeting he would remain silent. According to my observations he remained silent for 93 seconds. In the heat of discussion he returned to his usual leadership style. Another executive decided that he would ask more questions and "draw people out more." He did do just that. He asked one question which led to his getting feedback to which he was not accustomed. He immediately responded by returning to his usual leadership behavior, the only way he had to cope with the situation. Indeed, I concluded after observing many such instances that the best way for a consultant to prevent changes is to report honestly (and without evaluation) exactly what he perceives. The probability that the client with a certain degree of self-confidence will either desire to change or change successfully is so low that it will not alter the situation significantly.[1] In a later chapter, I will present another reason why changes will probably not occur by such interventions from consultants. Even if the client "learned" in one session and even if he changed his behavior significantly, the probability is quite high that the subordinates will not trust the change (or know how to cope with it). Consequently, they will continue their usual response, which will "prove" to

---

[1] In my experience it is the less secure (personally and/or organizationally) individual who is willing to change his behavior quickly.

the "changed" executives that these new ways of behaving are not very effective.

DATA OBTAINED FROM OBSERVATIONS

A comment seems appropriate about how we are going to present our data. As in the interviews, the model in Chapter 2 served as the guide for the analysis of the data. However, as much as one can consciously control his observations, the model did not serve as a guide to the notes taken at the meetings. My objective was to obtain as many notes as possible that were "independent" of the model. I place quotations around "independent" because I realize that strictly speaking this is impossible. The fact that I developed the model most certainly influenced my observations.

The best control that I could use was to be constantly aware of the limitations that my model placed upon me. I interviewed people after meetings to obtain as many different perceptions as possible as well as to check my own. Also, the method used to observe helped somewhat. I struggled to take on the role of a stenographer taking down as much as I could, regardless of whether or not it made sense. Only after the raw data were typed, did I "cut them up" according to the model. My objective in all these precautions was to do my best to obtain data that might contradict the model.[2]

One final word. Reality does not come "cut up" according to one's model. Consequently, the data I will present tend to illustrate more than one hypothesis.

RATIONAL ATTEMPTS TO INFLUENCE ATTITUDES AND FEELINGS

Hypothesis I: *Since the executive system sanctions and rewards rationality, when influence attempts are made to change the subordinates' attitudes and feelings, they will be primarily rational, intellective ones.*

Hypothesis II: *Since the executive system sanctions and rewards directiveness, dependence, and external commitment,*

---

[2] A stronger test of whether or not I distorted reality comes during the feedback session and the laboratory discussed in Chapters 5 and 8 respectively.

the influence attempts made by the superiors will not tend to include opportunities for the subordinates to diagnose the situation (problems) as they see it and to present their views.

Evidence for Hypothesis I and II

1. A two-day meeting was held at division headquarters for the plant managers. The primary objective was to influence the plant managers to realize even more clearly their roles, responsibilities, and challenges under the new concept of decentralization. The home-office executive, whom we shall designate as the Leader, was especially interested in influencing the plant managers to think of their long-range plans as well as to come to see decentralization as a way of life. Part of his reason for holding the meeting was to suggest that the plant managers weren't taking hold of enough responsibility from division headquarters and that they, in turn, were not delegating adequately in some crucial areas within their plants.

As was predicted, the strategy chosen was to expose the plant managers to a series of rapid-fire presentations, each "selling" some aspect of decentralization and long-range planning. In a two-day period 24 separate "pitches" were made in such areas as "advanced program risks," "new product commitments," "manufacturing research," "delegating," "performance objectives," "systems engineering," and so on. Each presentation was made by an expert staff specialist with liberal use of charts and quantitative data.

Upon questioning the plant managers, they reported that the presentation was excellent, meaty, and raised many unanswered questions. When asked why they did not raise these questions, they replied that they hesitated because "if I raised all the questions that I thought of, we could have been there for a few weeks and certainly we would have never finished the agenda." It is interesting to note that since the plant managers also tend to be rationally oriented, they felt some internal commitment to see that the agenda was completed before they left.

The meeting tended to place the plant managers in a very difficult if not incongruous situation. A primary objective of the meeting was "to sell the attitude of decentralization to the plant managers" yet the "selling" was done under highly centralized conditions. The plant managers *heard* that they ought to accept more responsibility and to think more in terms of long-range planning. However, they experienced very little control over their meeting and equally short opportunities to explore the long-range planning fully. No sooner had they begun to dig into a particular subject than, as one man put it, "The next guy came in with the next act, and we had our cue to move on." How much can the plant managers believe in decentralization, if the entire two days are highly centralized? As one suggested, "The best way out is to listen, to agree as long as it isn't too bad, and then go back and do what you think you ought to do." An illustration may serve to present the reader with a clearer view of some of the problems.

During the meeting a discussion arose about a basic policy of paying for increased production. Plant Manager No. 1 felt that people should be paid more, even though with the increased production standards they are below the new company standards. Plant Managers 2 and 3 did not agree and said so. But because of the lack of time, which in turn was due to planning by people with a rational bias, the discussion had to be terminated by the Leader and the implications for policy were never fully explored.

No. 1:[3] But they are working, and it is important that they should be paid.

No. 2: No, I don't think they should be paid extra money. They're still below standard.

No. 1: You have to. I feel strongly about this. If you don't, you better damn well have a good answer.

No. 3: And we do; we can come up with good answers if they [employees] ask for them. (He laughs and smiles.)

LEADER:[4] Well, let's go to the next point.

Here we find an important policy problem upon which strong feelings exist in opposite directions, and yet they are not explored. The only answer No. 1 received was that No. 3 was not worried about the problem, presumably because No. 3 felt he could "provide the right answers."

---

[3] Plant manager.

[4] "Leader" means the formal leader of the meeting.

2. In another session during the same meeting the Leader was attempting to induce the plant managers to decrease the number of people holding positions along the lines of authority and decision making to provide real opportunity for people to be creative. The overstaffing, he felt, only cluttered up the decision-making processes, inhibiting the good men and protecting poor ones. Note how he "sells" his point and how he explores the plant managers' view with the objective of getting each of them at various times admit that his (leader's) view is the correct one.

LEADER: I think I wondered if all this was necessary. Again, he didn't keep in mind the requirements of the personnel program which make it mandatory for a man to review the ratings of the boss. It seems to me that you say that we are not getting enough done. And one reason why we cut it too close is we don't have strong enough men to do the job.

No. 2: Yes, I would agree with you that if we had better men, then I think I could reduce the levels of management.

LEADER: But then is that the structure's fault?

No. 2: No, a structure, seems to me, represents realistically the company. It must take into account the existing poor people; and if our people are not capable of doing these things, then it's kind of academic to talk about a structure that assumes first-rate people. I might add, however, that in purchasing it's working very well. I would say that it works very well in the less complex jobs. Frankly though, I think one of the reasons that we will have trouble in working this is that I can't find strong enough guys.

LEADER: Wait a minute, that's a good statement; let's keep at it. It seems to me that you are saying that we have some poor managers, and we ought to do something about it.

No. 2: Well, there is no point in talking about a theoretical structure without the people necessary to fill it

No. 1: But that's the way our business has been.

LEADER: But is this effective?

No. 3 (to No. 1): I think what you are saying is the managers are not reliable.

LEADER: Partly right, but the structure protects the manager.

No. 3: Maybe that is a good point; maybe that is a damn good point.

No. 2: Well, I agree with that, too. I'm just saying that I'm not going to let an organization crumble because we have a good idea and we haven't got the people to implement the good idea. We have to find someone, and when we find the people we will be able to do it.

A discussion continued on the problem of "cleaning out" the decision-making structure; because of time, the Leader had to cut it off. He said, "I want everyone to know that every staff should be made line under any conditions. I'm going to order this. If you have got 100 staffmen, I'm going to pick out 20 and I'm going to check to see if they are disturbing the line of authority." No. 3 and No. 2 immediately agreed with the Leader that this was an important point.

LEADER: If you have a broken-down line man, I warn you don't make him a staffman, because we are going to find out.

No. 1: But I have some old line men that can make very good staffmen, but they are not very good line men. Are you telling me that I'm going in a direction that is diametrically opposed.

LEADER: No, no, not at all; you're okay as long as you have a job for them and you have defined it clearly and they are not getting mixed up in the line of authority.

No. 1 (to Leader): Look, we've got five levels at Plant A and Plant B. Now, are you going to say this is wrong!

LEADER: Well, I'm saying we'd better take a close look at it; I'm saying you can't have effective decision making under this condition.

There are several points where the Leader's "hidden agenda" came through and the plant managers learned the Leader's theories plus how he intended to "check up on them." After the session the Leader stated that he could get the plant managers to come up with the conclusions, but because of time he was unable to succeed. Again, we see how the shortage of time and a hurried agenda "centralizes" the meeting and tends to increase the dependence of the subordinates upon the superiors. These are the very conditions the divisional leadership desires to reduce. The hypothesis is that the division executives are not aware of the impact above and that by themselves they will not tend to become more aware. However, such "consulting advice" would only tend to enhance the dependency problem. A solution suggested by the model is that the executives would have to become more aware of the "rational" emphasis of their system, its impact upon them, and to develop a greater interpersonal competence. More of this later.

Hypothesis III: *Since the executive system sanctions the inhibition of feelings and since it requires dependence and* *develops fear of the superior's feelings and reaction, if the subordinates develop negative feelings toward presentations that attempt to influence them, they will not tend to express these feelings.*

Evidence for Hypothesis III

1. Mr. A was sent to Plant X by the Leader[5] to describe to the manufacturing people the possible use of new technology in planning their production. The Leader reviewed reports from the plant suggesting that Mr. A's presentation was excellent and well-received. However, at another divisional meeting, at a moment when feelings were rising and the plant manager was attempting to prove a point, he let it be known that the real impact of Mr. A was that most people thought he was selling "warmed-over toast." "He wasn't able to solve our job-lots problem."

I learned after the meeting that the reason the Leader sent Mr. A was not to solve any specific problem but was that he had hoped that someone at the plant level would get excited about the presentation and take the initiative to solve the "jobs-lots" problem by himself. The Leader never explored this with the plant managers even though it provided an ideal opportunity to discuss the basic differences in managerial philosophy between the Leader and the plant managers.

2. In another session the Leader (of that meeting) was attempting to convince the plant managers that they ought to demote supervisory personnel to nonsupervisory positions if they were surplus. It is interesting to note how he attempted to "sell" his view rationally ("If the supervisors realize the demotion is not a reflection on them personally, they will accept it.") and how he expected the plant managers to do the same. The meeting ended with an apparent agreement by the plant managers and a final word by the Leader.

The Leader had just enunciated the policy described above and had received some "we agree" from the plant managers.

LEADER: I want to say that I really appreciate the fact that you fellows are buying this, because I think it's going to be more efficient and cheaper.

---

[5] This is a different individual.

No. 4: I still don't think we have faced the negative aspect of this; okay, so we have a few free managers, but what happens when we don't have any place or anybody to whom we can make him available, what do we do with him when there isn't any absorption?

No. 2: Well, we will have to face it up and just push him down. That's all there is to it.

No. 1: Another thing is patience; we need time.

No. 4: Well, I'm not sure it is going to be that easy to pull these fellows down.

No. 1: I'll go further than that; I think if the fellows are qualified, we can give them a chance to do something else. My approach is if there are any really meaningful problems, we can take these extra men and have them do these other jobs.

No. 2: Well, I agree.

No. 3: I do, too. If there is an important place where they could be utilized, fine.

LEADER: Well, this is fine. Let's take the really tragic part, the really rough part. Let's assume for a moment that you have to reduce managers by four and you cannot move these men in any other function. Now what are you going to do? It seems to me you have to say to Joe, Dick, and Harry that because we are trying to streamline the organization—this is no criticism of you and no reflection on you —we are going to have to demote you and we may have to demote department managers to managers, and managers right back to the hourly rate people.

No. 2: Sure, that's right.

LEADER: Wait a minute, wait a minute, I see No. 1 wondering here.

(No. 1 cautiously expresses doubts.)

LEADER: Well, I don't think I made myself clear, and I want you to be clear. What if you decided to release these three men in the same area because there is no place else to go? It seems to me these three men may have to be demoted, and this is not a criticism of the men. But it may be that we cannot just wait for this osmosis to take care of all these people. This is a drastic step, and it has to be faced. If a first line manager goes back to the hourly rate it is no reflection on the men.

(The Leader continues his "selling.")

No. 1: Let's just assume if we took your big money and my small money [a laugh on this], I suspect, if we really owned the plant, I suspect, we would not really hold on to the people. I know that we do it, but we must not wait and we must not have this attitude that time will take care of this.

No. 2: In the interest of time I want to make it clear, there is another way of going at this, and that is if you release some men by cleaning up the line of authority, they can be utilized as managers or as consultants with the new technology in the expanded industry.

LEADER: Okay, I appreciate your comments, and I know that you can do an awful lot. It's going to be tough, but please keep it in mind.

The Leader left the meeting, went to his office, and said to Leader No. 2, "I doubt if they really bought what I was saying. We've got to hit them again with this. It is important." This is another example of the lack of discussion of negative feelings which, if explored properly, could decrease centralization and dependence and prevent the necessity for further meetings.

Note also that the rational approach again leads to a climate of centralization and dependence. However, the Leaders stated that they want to decrease dependence and increase the feelings of decentralization. This illustrates how the executives, without realizing it, are utilizing ways to resolve their problems which tend to reinforce and activate the problems. This is a predicted outcome of a low level of interpersonal competence.

3. One day a serious crisis occurred at the division headquarters. The division head was closeted in his office, with various people streaming in and out of his office bringing data or leaving to seek new information. The entire headquarters had the atmosphere of crisis with all sorts of rumors on the nature of the crisis. I obtained the feeling that the staffs almost enjoyed the crisis.

A staff luncheon was scheduled with the top 12 executives which the division head was tempted to cancel. He decided, however, that it should be held. When I arrived at the luncheon, the conversation was almost nonexistent and it seemed that the little talk manifested was strained and quiet. When the division head walked into the room, his face was flushed and he was obviously in deep thought. Everyone looked at him, but no one spoke to him, except one executive who had walked into the room with him. The crisis climate remained until the end of the luncheon when the division head called it off.

When I interviewed the division head two days later, I asked him if he was aware of the emotional tone of the luncheon. He said that he was not. I described my impressions and asked him to react. He said that he could realize how it would be so, since he has been in similar situations before. He reminded me that during the early years crisis became so much a part of their life that he found it quite natural to be in one. He wondered, however, if there was a way he could have helped the others be more at ease and enjoy themselves.

I asked him how he felt upon walking in the room. He replied by describing the pressures, thoughts, and especially his feelings about the problems creating the crisis. I then remarked that his description certainly helped me understand his behavior at the luncheon and wondered if it would not have helped the others who were very much in the dark. As one might predict, the division head smiled and said, "Oh, no—I wouldn't say that. Not that that's not the kind of thing I would say. I don't think any of us would say that!"

Hypothesis IV: *Since subordinates do not tend to express their negative feelings openly, they will, at meetings, tend to "accept" influence attempts that they dislike and resist them covertly at a later time.*

Evidence for Hypothesis IV

Evidence for this hypothesis came from some interviews I conducted after a meeting. A high-level executive, whom we shall designate as the Leader, had staff responsibility to inaugurate a new program throughout all the plants to increase productivity. The program was planned at headquarters. However, the local plant people "were kept informed at all times and expressed enthusiasm." Yet, continued the Leader, when we visited the plants we found many aspects of the program were simply not being used according to plan. When we asked why, we were told by the plant people that they had misinterpreted the presentation, although they had agreed to follow the plans as outlined by the headquarter's group.

During this discussion another example of how the inhibition of negative feelings can lead to organizational difficulties was observed. The headquarters' staff placed rigid rules on how much the first line manager could communicate to his employees about the workings of the program. All sorts of excuses, except the actual reason, were given to the first line managers. Apparently, the headquarters people did not really trust the line manager with all the information and with how they might use it. The irony, of course, is that the line managers sensed the real reason, resented it, and many found ways to fight and inhibit the new program. (Further data will be presented under hypothesis VII.)

Hypothesis V: *In a system in which directiveness and control are rewarded, when the rational approach fails, the tendency will be to utilize emotions. However, since feelings are not often used, they will probably be perceived by the subordinates as being "the last resort" or "needling." This would lead to management by crisis.*

Before the data are presented a comment seems in order. The reader may recall that we obtained little, if any, evidence regarding management by crisis during the interviews. However, the observations turned up many cases of the practice. Indeed, it was the single most frequently repeated phenomenon that I observed. It is interesting to ponder why this is the case. One might hypothesize that the executives were embarrassed to discuss it. However, no such evidence was obtained. Once I observed it and mentioned it, the discussions were free and quite animated. Many of the men volunteered that this practice was part of "the bone" or "fabric" of the company. It would be interesting to conduct a study in depth regarding management by crisis. I believe that the apparent denial that it exists is not so much a denial as an internalization of the practice. As one individual said, "This is so much a fabric of the company that it's like making a point that I have a suit on."

Another interesting aspect is that once the executives began to discuss management by crisis they increasingly described it as a "problem," one of the "thorns in the company's growth." However, at the same time most of the executives admitted that they used the practice frequently "to get the job done." The ambivalence is well illustrated by one executive as follows:

After a day at headquarters, I am glad to leave. I like to think we are not doing the same thing at our place as they are at headquarters. You get the feeling when at headquarters that everybody is rushing around.

I don't think that we're a lot different; however, I am trying to instill a sense of urgency in people. Sometimes I tend to exaggerate when there is pressure. When someone calls to tell me to get the God damn thing out, I don't question it. I turn to my people and say, "We need this thing; let's go, go, go!"

Let us now turn to some of the observational data illustrating the use and impact of management by crisis.

Evidence for Hypothesis V

1. A meeting was called to inform the division head that a certain new product (x) would not be announced as scheduled. Expecting a "blow up" each man who might be called on the carpet was well prepared with notes to defend his position the best that he could.

No. 2 began by saying that they were going to have to delay model x. He gave the reasons.

No. 1: *No, no, no!!!*
No. 2: That's right, and there's more.
No. 1: Jesus! You can't have that! Let's call the program to a halt. This is a national crisis! How are we going to get out of it? Test all new ones?
No. 2: In terms of what's going on, I'd say we're doing the following thing—
No. 1: Tell me something for my own clarification. We knew that we were going to use this product in '58. Why didn't we test that model then?
No. 3 (picks up a pad where he apparently has a lot of notes): I have a thoroughly complete story here.
No. 1: Fine. Okay, go ahead.
No. 3: Well, we do have a very serious problem. [Outlines the problem and concludes.] The significant thing is that the product is not good.
No. 2: Agreed.
No. 3: It's clear, however, that the product is on its back. We need a week or two to decide if it is good or not. And, also it's clear that this is the wrong time to say we need such a check.
No. 3: I would say the engineering judgment here is poor. If you ask me if this is an engineering failure, the answer is, "Yes."
No. 1: We're here now. All right. We're supposed to announce this in November. Now I gather you're telling me that you doubt that we'll make it. It's doubtful that we can make it with any other similar product.

No. 3: Yes, but look, the product wasn't selected callously. I think I feel I have to defend it.

No. 1: But why didn't we find this out months ago?

No. 3: It's easy to come to the conclusion that we didn't have it analyzed enough. This is true. We can't afford, however, to analyze all possible things.

(No. 2 tries to defend No. 3, pointing out that the engineer who was testing this was under pressure.)

No. 3: Well, that's true, but that's an excuse and not a reason. We've struck out.

No. 1: And, we've got to go on record that we've failed. We can't give date. Is that right? Well, what's our corrective? What are going to be our corrective actions? You'll start immediately, tomorrow.

(No. 3 suggests action.)

No. 1: Well, let me take another approach to this. You must have some pretty poor people here, don't you think so?

No. 3: Well, I prefer not to go into this at this time and go into the gory details at another meeting perhaps.

No. 1: Well, we've got to take fast, Fast, FAST, serious action!! People are going to lose their jobs, it seems to me.

No. 2: Now wait a minute, No. 1; before you pull the gun, you better make sure that it's aimed in the right direction.

No. 1: Well, what do you mean?

No. 2: Well, it seems to me they've all worked under a very rigorous schedule.

No. 1: Yeah, look, No. 2, sure, we did give them six months, but we didn't expect a failure with six months. Should we tell them that it's okay for failing?

No. 2: Well, I don't know if the guy ever really thought that he could make it.

No. 4: It seems to me we're going to have to be careful if we're going to throw somebody out, because maybe the guy took a chance, and we're clobbering him now for taking a risk.

No. 1: No. 4 is also implying, however, that the schedule was set against the best engineering advice.

No. 3: Well, time and time again we have these problems. We have for example, dynamited the A, B, C, and then through. "Yes, sir, I'll try." He digs in. And maybe November should not have been the date, whether he fails or not. But it seems to me the important thing to see is not whether he fails or not, but whether he did a good engineering job. If it's clear that a poor engineering job was done, then it seems to me that we've got to take action.

No. 1: I buy that. It sounds like poor engineering to me. Believe me, gentlemen, this is serious.

It is interesting to consider that the rational goal of communicating to the division head the bad views could have been done in relatively few minutes. No new decision was made or could be made because of the pending investigations. Yet the meeting continued for over an hour. It is somewhat ironic that the emotional approach was used to "needle" and "impress the men of the seriousness of the problem" by the individual who in his interviews believed in the rational approach to decision making.

2. In another meeting there was a discussion as to why the forecasts were not as accurate as they desired. Various suggestions are explored with none of them receiving complete agreement. Then one of the executives said:

No. 1: My point is this. If you want to put it in a nut shell, it seems to me that we need enough time to think it through in order to boil it down and for it to be accurate. What we're doing now is trying to write something down very quickly without thinking it through.

(Several others nod heads in agreement.)

No. 2: I agree this is a problem, but we've got to put things in a nut shell if these busy people are going to get their arms around them.

No. 1: Of course, that's obvious. All I am saying is that we need more time so that when we put forecasts in a nut shell, they are accurate.

No. 2: I think you're saying that we should have no more crises. Give us time to think!

(No. 1 and four others say "Yes" and nod their heads in agreement.)

No. 3: Well, we could go on this all day. It doesn't seem to me that we are making progress. I suppose that we should get an opportunity to discuss this more fully.

3. The division's relationships with other divisions was discussed during one meeting. The executive's complained that the other division creates crisis situations. However, the suggestion to solve the problem is for this division to "beat them to the punch" and "be heard first."

No. 1: Well, I think our division rates up high in quality. Now, it seems to me, lets be sensitive a little more about our position.

No. 2: Does it help? Have we told them that they're very hard to deal with? Maybe that would be a good idea.

No. 1: No, maybe we haven't done enough. Maybe this is one reason, because in our position we're not aggressive enough. We don't tell them how they make problems for us. They view us as their problem, but since we don't tell them problems that they cause, all they experience is that we are a problem for them.

No. 2: The point I'm making is that the magnification, the whim becomes the immediate requirement.

(Very strong consensus on the management by crisis comment that No. 2 made.)

No. 1: Okay, then we've got to go back and show these fellows.

No. 2: Well, let me give you another example. We tend to resist the extremes.

No. 3: We must.

No. 1: Well, we must resist with justification.

No. 2: I don't know how to do it when he's yelling that we're going to lose a customer.

No. 1: Maybe one of the ways is to go back to the organization and to the original scene of the situation.

No. 2: I don't kid myself. They're going to come back, and we're going to have to give up because they're not motivated to sell a decent, to sell a reasonable course of action.

No. 5: Mr. —————— gave several illustrations where the other division put up a lot of fuss.

No. 4: They do it as a tactic, it seems to me. I ride in with one of the fellows, and he said to me in the car, "Well, you might as well come across with the information or I'll get you later on." I then said to him, "Well, what do you mean?" He said to me, "I'll start a crisis. I'll get you boys moving."

No. 1: What we're saying is that the other division is using the whipsaw. We all have to be alert to see our position.

No. 5: Yes, yes. But what are we going to do when they say we're going to lose a contract and it's going to lose dollars, prestige, what do you do? How do you sell that?

No. 2: Let's take a case point. The facts are that they panicked on product x, and they told us that they have to have it right away, and they didn't get any orders for three months, but top management accepts these panic speeches.

No. 1: Well, let me take the other side. To me the fact that we didn't have an order the first months is not as bad as the projected price. We're weak as a division to get the other division to accept our forecasts. We should push harder.

No. 2 (argues that the division was closer to being right): The reason that our forecasts were off was that there was not time. All we heard was that there was panic, and we had to get this thing out right away.

No. 4: I bet one reason that they had this panic is that they wanted to plan this for the sales campaign in the fall.

No. 2: No, no, that's dying.

No. 4: Well, I'm not sure. I doubt that.

No. 2: No, I can tell you that that's really in the past. We're thinking of changing these things.

No. 2: Now, I love this. [meaning the crisis] It's the right way to do business, but I'd do it in the product that's not so important.

No. 5: But top management crisis also makes the lower level jump.

No. 2: Well, we've got to live with it.

No. 4: But do we, do we really have to live with it?

No. 2: I doubt it. Sure, we've got to do some softening, but the right answer is for us to do some of our own advertising.

No. 2: They won't buy our selling.

No. 1: Well, I'm sure that Mr. ———— has not listened to our side. You've got to sell harder.

No. 4: Well, I submit that we have to find ways to combat these pressures.

No. 1: Sure, I agree, but maybe we should fight harder.

Hypothesis VI: *Since the expression of feelings is not sanctioned by the executive system, and since the subordinates will not tend to express their frustrations with their superiors, the superiors will tend to be unaware of the impact of their use of power.*

Evidence for Hypothesis VI

1. The meeting described to illustrate Hypothesis I and II also provide data for Hypothesis VI. As was pointed out, the meetings were planned by the executives to reduce centralization, dependence, and conformity. However, the executives evolved a plan for each meeting which rationally "sold" decentralization, relative independence, and nonconformity; while at the same time, the subordinates *experienced* the dependence, conformity, and centralization.

The observations of several segments of the planning sessions indicated not *one* clue that suggested the planners had any conscious awareness of the dichotomy between what they were saying and the conditions that they were actually creating. During the planning sessions, there were several enthusiastic moments when a "new pitch" with new data was uncovered to be available for presentation. Not one moment of discussion was given to the interpersonal impact. Moreover, although the "subordinates" in the meeting experienced the incongruency in all cases they reported that "this was natural" and "what the hell, that's how a business is run" because, "if you started worrying how people felt, hell, you'd never get anywheres."

2. Two executives from Department X met with a divisional executive to discuss a report which eventually was to be sent to the division. Manifestly, their problem was to differentiate between policy and practice because they had only a few pages, and they were asked to focus in this report on policy. On the latent level, according to the *divisional* executive, Department X felt slighted in last year's divisional report and this year deserved a more prominent position.

The discussion went round and round with the representatives of Department X trying to increase the scope of their report through the attempt to define policy and practice while the divisional executive attempted the opposite. Finally, one representative attempted to strengthen his case by citing the report of a rival department.

No. 1: We'll take another one. Let's take a look at Department Y. They've gone in to much more detail than we have.

No. 2 (to Leader in this situation): You say they're plans, but I say they're objectives. Maybe we should begin with a definition.

(No. 2 reads Department Y manual to support his view.)

LEADER: Well, obviously we have no clear-cut definition here. Maybe we can do it this way. Let's think of a possible definition of a plan.

(Discussion continues with little success.)

LEADER: Maybe the way to solve the problem is to table it. Let's say put anything you want into the report. After all, the important thing is not which are the objectives and which are the plans, for those are minor questions.

No. 1: Well, I think we could do this, but—

LEADER: Well, a lot of this is detail, and it's really only of interest to your departments.

(The representatives objected to the notion that what they intended to include was detail primarily of interest to their department.)

LEADER (begins to become impatient): Well, look, can we pass up this problem and simply decide what we want to say? When we are typing it up, then we can decide.

(It is important to keep in mind that the final report would be typed by the division executive's secretary and consequently such a suggestion could lead to the division man doing whatever he wished.)

The men continued the discussion by pushing for differences between plan and objectives. Finally the division man said, "I don't think we can define it. Let's not worry about that."

In the interview after the meeting, the division man said he did not believe the discussion was very fruitful, and that is why "*We* agreed to table it." When I pointed out that according to my notes he tabled the discussion, the division man became a bit flushed, smiled, and said, "You may be right. Come to think of it, I did stop it." He continued to say that he had to stop it because their real agenda was to emphasize how important their department was in the organization. I asked if he felt it might have been fruitful to discuss his view of their "hidden agenda"? The division man responded that such an attempt would be insulting to the two representatives. Such a diagnosis is probably correct because the subordinates were also influenced by, and behaved according to, the norms and values of the rationally oriented system. However, one might wonder the degree of time and human effort that may be spent in politicking and setting the stage for another attempt to influence the divisional manager. In the rational system the continual use and misuse of human effort is not insulting as long as the activity remains rational. Thus, we find that the social system can develop expectations in people to be used and misused. Once these expectations are internalized, the system has another strong source for maintenance as it is presently constituted.

Hypothesis VII: *In the rationally dominated system when feelings and attitudes hinder operations, then the tendency will be to modify the organization rather than deal with them directly.*

Evidence for Hypothesis VII

Because of management by crises, dependence, and conformity, pressures are placed to meet commitments to satisfy the executives, thereby reducing the crisis even though such commitments may not be realistic. Moreover, when it becomes obvious that the commitments are unreal, the tendency of the subordinates will be to "push the product through" even at the potential sacrifice of quality. The company objective of producing the highest quality possible is sacrificed (of course, only within safe limits) to meet an obligation. Thus, we find men committing "organizational sins" out of a sense of personal commitment. Another possibility is to ship parts of the product incorrectly, thereby gaining a few extra precious days.

Because of the extremely high level of aspiration toward excellence in product and customer service, the headquarters decided to "crack down." No attempt was made to ask responsible department heads to explain the reasons for the undesirable events. Such an exploration would tend to lead to the subordinates' feelings of dependence, conformity, and reactions to management by crisis, which incidentally was frequent enough to establish a famous phrase: "the crisis de jour."

The solution decided upon was to create an organizational quality control department independent of the other departments. Such action, thus, led to an increase in the quality of the new product arriving at the customer's door. However, it also increased the number of delays of new products, the rivalry and hostility, and protection activity among all departments because each wanted to make certain that if trouble did occur it would not be found responsible.

THE INTERPERSONAL COMPETENCE WITHIN THE EXECUTIVE SYSTEM

We have given data to illustrate the predictions made by our model. It might be helpful if we could use these data to somehow quantify the degree of interpersonal competence. Several methods were attempted, all of them ending in failure. The difficulty of developing systematic observations to define units was insurmountable, given the time limitations related to the action research emphasis of the project. We can understand more clearly Barker and Wright's conclusion that one of the most important requirements is the development of systematic raw data that describe with a reasonable degree of accuracy[6] the events that occurred. The traditional anthropological observational methods that I used were inadequate.

In spite of the difficulties, a rather simple and gross method was developed, which may give us some idea of the degree of interpersonal competence as well as of the difficulty in measuring it.

1. According to our model, interpersonal competence is a function of the degree to which an individual is aware of his impact upon others and they upon him, as well as the ability to solve problems in such a way that they remain solved.

If interpersonal competence is low, then we should find:

An increase in frequency where the executive's . . .	*A decrease in frequency where the executive's . . .*
a) Expectations of his impact are not consonant with the reported impact.	*a*) Expectation of his impact are consonant with the reported impact.
b) Awareness of where the consequences are not the intended ones is low.	*b*) Awareness of where the consequences are not the intended ones is high.
c) The solutions to the problems will tend to activate similar or other undesired problems.	*c*) The solutions to the problems will tend to activate similar or other undesired problems.

Our analysis would be more effective if we could differentiate the influence attempts into smaller units and in terms of their potency. Another important dimension that we were unable to study is the impact of the influence attempts upon the subordinates of the executives at the meeting. For example, if the leader influenced five subordinates to take certain action, the probability is quite high that this influence would be felt by many throughout the organization and with differential impact. These and other considerations could not be considered during this project because there was not enough

---

[6] Roger Barker and Herbert F. Wright, *Midwest and Its Children.*

time. As mentioned previously, this is another instance where the action's orientation of the research took precedence over known research procedures.

To test the hypothesis related to interpersonal competence, a simple quantitative analysis was made of the protocols. Every meeting observed had a formal leader. The leader was interviewed whenever necessary to ascertain his intended consequences or objectives for the meeting. Then all the others present at the meeting, whom the leader intended to influence, were interviewed after the meeting. They were asked to report the actual impact of the leader's influence attempts upon them. Each of the leader's influence attempts were scored for each individual he attempted to influence regardless of the length or intensity. For example, if the leader attempted to influence five individuals in one meeting, the total possible number of influence attempts was five. This would be the case whether the meeting lasted 10 minutes or three hours. If the leader attempted two unique and different influence attempts for each of the five men, the number of influence attempts would be 10. The word "Leader" is used to mean anyone who is attempting to influence (that is, was observed to be attempting to influence) anyone else. Thus, in a meeting, the leadership can vary. Each would be treated as a separate individual to be analyzed.

A sample from our records may help. This specimen is taken from the meeting used to illustrate Hypothesis I and II, Chapter 4.

The Leader's Reported Objectives and Results

1. *Primary objectives*
   a) To influence the plant managers to accept more authority and responsibility for their plants.
   b) To influence the plant managers to learn to diagnose their organization's structure.
2. *Secondary objectives*
   a) To communicate to the plant managers the divisional program in their area.
   b) To permit adequate discussion of the program so (1) appropriate changes can be made and (2) the program is internalized by the plant managers.

3. Results

Number of plant managers who:

a) Felt they were being given more authority and responsibility. 0

b) Felt they were being asked to learn to diagnose their organization's structure. 1

c) Felt they had adequate time to discuss and incorporate the program as their own. 0

d) Learned the division's program. 5

This means that out of a possible of 20 influence attempts, the Leader succeeded in six and failed in terms of his intended consequences in 14.

Another hypothesis is that the Leader would not be aware of the impact above. The evidence confirms the hypothesis. The Leader was interviewed after the meeting. He reported that in his opinion "most of the men" realized and accepted his attempts to push decentralization further, to help them learn how to diagnose their organization, to help them incorporate divisional objectives as truly their own, and simply to communicate the objectives.

According to our analysis there are 14 units of discrepancy between what the Leader perceived to be his impact and how the subordinates reported his impact to the researcher. In this case the leader was unable to predict accurately any of the 14 units.

Finally, we note that out of 20 influence attempts where the leader did *not* want to communicate or in any way reinforce centralization (that is, the subordinates' dependence upon him), he actually reinforced the very problems that he was intending to alleviate.

He said nothing in the interview to suggest that he was aware of the unintended consequences. As the interview was being terminated, the researcher asked for a few more minutes. He then made his own analysis, in which he showed how it would be possible to conclude that the meetings may have had these unintended consequences. The Leader smiled and said, "My God, that's interesting. I never thought of that. Complicated life, isn't it!"

In Table 13 the results are summarized for 10 meetings selected from the files.

We may conclude that our hypotheses were supported in terms of the over-all as well as the individual scores. The executives as a group were less aware of their impact and unintentionally solved fewer problems than they created. If we examine each situation individually we find that the executives actual score was less than the potential in all cases except five.

TABLE 13

INTERPERSONAL COMPETENCE SCORES

Meeting	No. of Influence Attempts	No. Succeeded	No. Failed
1	54	6	48
2	30	12*	18
3	10	0	10
4	30	12*	18
5	36	18*	18
6	21	12*	9
7	5	1	4
8	3	0	3
9	5	2	3
10	5	2	3
Total	199	65	134

* In all but five cases the successes represent time when the leader wanted to "needle" subordinates, and he succeeded in his objective.

In the five cases their score was as high in the success as in the failure column because they intended to needle the individuals and succeeded.

CONCLUSIONS

The observational data all illustrate hypotheses related to the model. The data also clarify some questions, such as the discrepancy between the reported (in Chapter 3) relatively high interpersonal competence and the predicted low interpersonal competence. The observational data suggest that the interpersonal competence is lower than the executives report and that they are apparently unaware of the discrepancy.

Again it should be emphasized that this organization is not atypical. Indeed, if our model is valid, these problems exist in all formal organizations in varying degree.

5

The Feedback of the Results

       The data have been collected and analyzed and organized into a pattern which the researcher believes is a valid reproduction of some of the interpersonal and organizational problems that executives face plus their causes.

I. THE OBJECTIVES AND VALUES OF FEEDBACK

The next step is to present the results to the executives. The primary objectives of such a presentation would be:

1. To help them explore the meaning of the results. How do they view the results? Are they valid, invalid? In which way are they incomplete? What implications for action do they see?
2. To explore with them the researcher's opinions on the same questions.

It was hoped that the feedback session would have at least two values to the executives. First, to help them to take the first step toward effective action; namely, to make an accurate diagnosis of their problems. Second, to explore further with one another the impact of their values, feelings, problems, as well as the needs of the organization, its problems, growth, and development. Such explorations, if effective, could lead the executives to new depths of understanding as well as to enlarge their scope of understanding. Thus, even if the executives were to reject the results and the training, hopefully they would have

99

had an important experience in self- and organizational understanding.

The feedback session also offers something to the researcher. First, the session could provide a validity check for his data and conclusions. For example, the executives have been diagnosed as holding certain values that tend to lead to a decreasing interpersonal competence, increasing interpersonal mistrust, conformity, dependency, and external commitment as well as to specific difficulties in decision making, management by crisis, and organizational rigidity.

A second value to the researcher would be that it would provide him an opportunity to make another (admittedly crude) assessment concerning the degree to which the laboratory method of education would help or frustrate the executives. Some degree of frustration would probably increase learning. However, too much frustration would probably lead to regression,[1] and in turn to resistance and minimal learning. The evaluation could be made by observing the executives' reactions to the data and to one another as they explore their meaning. The researcher could use the model of authentic relations as a guide to his assessment. He could, for example, observe during the meeting the extent to which the group is open to new ideas and the degree to which the members give and receive nonevaluative feedback, the degree to which the members own their feelings and permit others to do the same, and finally the degree of fight, flight, or work (in the Bion sense).[2]

If the executives' diagnoses are consonant with the researcher's, then they should see a discrepancy between what they say they value and how they actually behave. For example, most report they dislike conformity, dependence, mistrust, and so on. The research suggests, however, that they help cause these problems. The awareness of a gap between their behavior and their aspirations for the organizations could

---

[1] Roger Barker, Kurt Lewin, and Tamara Dembo, "Frustration and Regression," *University of Iowa Studies, Child Welfare*, Vol. XVIII, No. 1 (1941), pp. xv and 314.

[2] W. R. Bion, "Experiences in Groups," *Human Relations*, Vol. I (1948), pp. 314–20 and 487–96.

create within the executives a certain degree of disequilibrium or dissonance.[3] They may feel a strong need to close the gap. Such tension could provide a motivational basis for self-generated and controlled learning.

II. THE STRATEGY OF THE RESEARCHER AS A CONSULTANT

Once the data are gathered, analyzed, and formed into a coherent model that provides a valid diagnosis of the problem, the researcher is ready to feed them back. If the basic objective of feedback is simply to offer a clear presentation of results, then the researcher need only develop a well-written, well-bound, easily understood report; come to the feedback meeting armed with interesting charts and other instructional materials that will make the communication of the results easy; and select a capable lecturer who will tend to prevent difficulties from developing between the client and the researcher. Such a presentation may elicit warm praise from the management, partially because the report is enlightening. However, equally important is the probability that the praise may be covering up (1) their anxiety about what the researcher uncovered and (2) their belief that the presentation was nonthreatening. Such actions may win friends; however, they will not tend to help the executives.

THE RESEARCHER AS A CONSULTANT

It is at this point that the researcher is able to take on an additional set of values. He now becomes more actively interested in helping the client and less in adding to basic knowledge. He realizes that the information which he is about to communicate to the subjects can have a strong impact upon the organization. It may arouse anxieties, new problems, and so on. He feels responsible to be available to help the executives "work through" their problems and to grow in the direction they desire. He is going to be as intensely interested in

---

[3] Leon Festinger, *A Theory of Cognitive Dissonance* (Evanston, Ill.: Row, Peterson & Co., 1957).

and concerned about them as participants trying to help themselves, as he was interested in them as subjects.

The researcher, therefore, in my opinion does not choose between being a researcher or consultant. He must learn to be both. The choice is primarily one of diagnosing which role is appropriate at a given moment or in a given situation.

Taking on the role of consultant is going to require that the researcher develop new sets of values. How much help will he give? Under what conditions? What are the limits of his help? In a recent study, the findings suggested that employee alienation was positively related to high production. One top executive, upon hearing this, pushed the others to give me funds so that I could increase the employees' alienation, thereby increasing production. The president "got me off the hook" by saying that he would have "none of that damn alienation in my plant." I promptly agreed.

But how would I have replied if I were pushed? If I were to hesitate, the management would question whether I should continue my studies in their organization. They would tend to infer their confidence in me from how they observed me in dealing with such difficult decisions "under fire," which after all is the way they evaluate each other.

It is possible to structure feedback so the executive will tend to experience it not as an opportunity to place blame on various members of the organization but as an opportunity for them to solve real and meaningful issues, thereby beginning to increase their sense of competence as an effective problem-solving team. He will find that one of the factors that inhibits the achievement of this objective is that to the extent the diagnosis helps to understand a problem, until then not understood by members of management, they will tend to experience a sense of inadequacy. This sense of inadequacy can raise anxieties and guilt feelings within top-flight executives not accustomed to such experiences. To the extent the data fed back are new and upsetting, the researcher now turned consultant should, therefore, not be surprised if he finds himself on the receiving end of covert or overt hostility. This could take the form of questioning the validity of the research methods and the sample used as well as the conclusions. It could also take the form of raising minor questions about grammatical accuracy, typing errors, clarity of presentation, adequacy of reports. It could also take the form of rejecting the analysis by insisting that times have changed, that the results are not new, that more time is needed to study the results, and that they find the report excellent but wish to give it more careful thought. (We will call you, do not call us!)

Whatever the negative feelings about the diagnosis, it is important for the researcher-consultant to create a climate where they can be brought out. The researcher-consultant can use management's defensiveness to help them obtain the first set of "gut" experiences that are usually necessary if research efforts are to be used effectively. One of the most effective ways a client system has to "seduce" a researcher-consultant to prevent their own growth is to compliment him on the diagnosis and then to ask for his recommendations. It is at this point that the researcher-consultant might suggest that if the management is not able to suggest recommendations, then the diagnosis (assuming it is valid) has not been understood. If a valid diagnosis is thoroughly understood, one should be able to derive from it the prognosis. What can he do to help the executives fully understand the diagnosis so they can derive their own recommendations? For the executives' sakes he will do his best to refrain from behaving as if he were in a line relationship. However, he will work hard to act as a resource person if they desire him to help them work through their prognosis.

Usually two reactions tend to occur. One is the expression by the executives of sorrow and dismay, if not disappointment. After all, the researcher-consultant is supposedly a competent leader in this profession. He should have some positive suggestions. It is the responsibility of the one who makes the diagnosis to have some recommendations. This reaction is understandable. The diagnosis just fed back does not belong to the executives. They did not conduct it. Since the diagnosis is truly not theirs, it is easy to understand why it is difficult for them to develop prognoses.

As the researcher-consultant examines these feelings, he can find a rich set of learning experiences for the clients to consider. Could not their reaction provide rich, living data to show them how "irresponsibly" they feel toward something which they do not create? Perhaps this is a problem of their subordinates in the organization. Perhaps others, much lower in the ladder, feel the same way about policies announced by these executives in which they (subordinates) have little participation. Perhaps this will begin to help the executive to understand why their clearly written policies do not seem to create the same high enthusiasm in the subordinates as they do in themselves. If so, then if we can discover a process by which this feedback can become part of them, they will have learned a process which they can use to make their own policies more "living" documents throughout the organization.

Moreover, if their expectation of the researcher is that he should give some answers, because in the feedback situation he is the leader, what does this expectation imply concerning what they probably do to their subordinates? Perhaps this indicates that when they (as leaders) make a diagnosis, they feel they must make a prognosis. But if the above analysis is valid, what positive value is a unilateral prognosis? At best it gives their subordinates something to shoot at (just as they are behaving toward the researcher). But as they just experienced, if the leader (in this case the researcher) is skilled enough to answer all their objections, he succeeds in making the diagnosis *his* and not theirs. Perhaps, this also occurs when they succeed in answering all the questions of their subordinates when they, as superiors, are "selling" a new policy or practice.

If the researcher is not going to provide recommendations, how are they to be developed? The first tendency is for the management group to develop them. But usually if they go through experiences similar to those discussed above, it is not uncommon for someone from management to point out that if they develop them, they will have the same problem in making the recommendations *their subordinates'* as they are having in making the research-consultant's diagnosis their own.

Finally, the researcher-consultant can raise the question: To what extent does their strong desire for recommendations prevent them from exploring a previous problem (that is, their own group effectiveness)? For example, in a feedback session to a bank, events indicated that the officers' insistence that the researcher-consultant focus on recommendations helped to prevent the group from examining the extent to which they influenced, sanctioned, and created some of the problems discovered and discussed. One of the findings, for example, indicated a strong norm within the organization to have what the officers called "the right type." The right type may be characterized as an individual who manifests strong desires for security and predictability in his life, a strong desire to conform to the present organizational norms, and a dislike of hostility in himself or in others. After the results were presented, many of the bank officers agreed on their validity. One finally said, "Gentlemen, I recommend that we ask the researcher to develop a program to bring in more 'nonright types.'" There was quick agreement, and the chairman asked the researcher if he had any suggestions. The researcher replied that, given the present culture within the bank, a nonright type would probably not remain with the bank very long. This thought triggered off another one; namely, that if the officers are to develop an effective prognosis, they need to ask themselves to what extent they are of the right-type vintage and to explore further to what extent they (and the bank culture) would knowingly make the nonright type feel uncomfortable and frustrated.

In another situation the top management group accepted the researcher-consultant's diagnosis and focused quickly on asking him for his recommendations. The researcher responded in such a way that the group began to become aware of issues such as those discussed above. Especially painful was the conclusion at which they arrived; namely, that in forcing the researcher and themselves to arrive at specific recommendations, they never faced the implications of the fact that the data should be fed down to employees. When asked why they preferred no feedback to the lower levels, the conclusion was that they did not think such feedback would have a positive effect. In fact, some worried that such feedback might jell and make overt the present covert discontent. "It's best to let sleeping dogs lie." The researcher-consultant helped the executives to explore the impact of such a policy on the lower levels. Even with some careful discussion of the danger of not feeding back data to people who participated in the creation of and who are probably expecting to learn the results, the executives concluded that the safest course of action would be not to have feedback. Some researcher-consultants would continue to push for feedback to the lower level. A few would even require it. However, if a management group is that insecure in its relationships with subordinates, then it would probably only do more harm to all concerned to "sell" the management to accept feedback. If one can infer that executives who do not have trusting relationships with their own subordinates probably do not create trusting relationships among one another, then the case for not pushing for the feedback becomes even stronger.

Fortunately this was not a problem for this particular executive group. They were willing to feed back to the organization as much data as it could cope with. More important, they felt a strong need to spend adequate time to explore the implications. Again, we note the "core strength" of this particular executive group.

III. THE ACTUAL RESULTS

A six-hour meeting was held at a nearby country club. All executives were present. Each was given a report of the results. The researcher summarized the findings and encouraged discussion. He did not have any difficulty in starting a discussion. As we shall see, the session was extremely lively and open. Indeed, the problem was to find an opportunity to say something. As mentioned above, the major tasks during the meeting were to act as a clarifier, summarizer, confronter, and once in a while a protector, and to resist answering questions such as "Well, what can we do about this? What is the alternative that you offer?" The first reason for this resistance was the belief that many human relation problems are solved ineffectively because their complexity is not adequately explored. All too often, there tends to be a rush to make a decision. Such a tendency would probably be operating in this group of highly action-oriented executives. The second reason is that an early focus on solutions would probably lead the researcher to be the one who must provide them, and this would tend to create an undesirable dependence of the executives upon the researcher. Finally, an early focus on solutions also would tend to help the executives to deny the fact that the problems to be dealt with are rooted in their basic assumptions about man and their philosophy of management. The deeper the diagnosis, the less the problems are viewed as solved through techniques and more as requiring systematic diagnosis of one's values and development of a philosophy of management.

The two observers and the researcher independently concluded that the group showed less defensiveness than what might have been expected and much more willingness to explore, experiment, and modify. Unfortunately, because of lack of time we were unable to develop instruments with which to assess systematically these conclusions. This is another example where the commitment to action took precedence over the commitment to research. The importance of such instruments is recognized, and it is hoped to develop them in other laboratories or at other action-research programs. However, the problem was not neglected completely. There were some rather crude ways to evaluate our influences.

To present some relatively systematic indices of what occurred during the sessions, the feedback session was tape-recorded. The tapes were analyzed in simple and rather gross terms. We attempted to discover the major themes developed during the six-hour meeting. The procedure was as follows: The analyst (the author) listened to a tape recording of the session. As he listened, he would note the theme, who began it, the theme that preceded it, and those who participated in the discussion plus what they had to say about the subject. The content was obtained by recording onto a second recorder relevant samples of the original tape recording of the meeting. As a new theme arose, a new sheet of paper was used. If, at some point, the group returned to a previous theme, the analyst would simply return to the work sheet containing that information and continue his reporting.

IV. THE MAJOR THEMES
DURING THE FIRST FEEDBACK SESSION

Eleven major themes were isolated from the analysis of the tape recording. They are presented below in the order in which they arose.

Theme	Content
A...............	The difficulty of establishing the facts.
B...............	The proper role of the leader.
C...............	The scarcity of time to make effective decisions.
D...............	The difficulties and unpopularity of being a dissenter or deviate.
E...............	The mistrust of, and incompetence in coping with, our own and others' feelings.
F...............	The dilemma between centralized interpersonal relations and decentralized organizational policies.
G...............	Management by crisis.
H...............	The meaning of loyalty.
I...............	The meaning of openness and trust in human relationships.
J...............	The increasing department centeredness versus the decreasing identity to the organization as a whole.
K...............	The impact of the executive system above them upon their own system and upon their organization.

A content analysis of these categories shows that all the reactions and discussions of these men fit under the six "outputs" shown in our model in Chapter 2. No information was brought forth directly or indirectly that was not consonant with, or went beyond, the categories of "outputs" in the model. Below, we itemize all the topics that evolved during the feedback session. The reader is reminded that each topic represents a theme, a topic about which there was, *as a minimum,* majority agreement.

Categories of Topics at Feedback Session	Outputs of Model
A, B, C, D, E, H, and I.........	Interpersonal conformity.
A, C, E, G, and I..............	Interpersonal mistrust.
A, B, C, D, E, G, and H........	Dependence upon the superior and external commitment.
H, I.........................	Decrease in effective decision making.
E, G, H......................	Management by crisis.
A, F, H, and J..	Departmental centeredness and organizational rigidity.

All of the topics that were discussed illustrated one or more of the "outputs" in our model. Category K, the only one not included in the analysis above, actually dealt with the impact upon the executives of the system above them. In effect they talked about their conformity, external commitment, and interpersonal mistrust in relation to the officers above them. They stated that these phenomena caused (1) their decision making to be less effective, (2) management by crisis, and (3) increasing departmental centeredness and organizational rigidity. In terms of our model, the outputs of the executive system above them become inputs for their system. If this is so, it raises the important question of the validity of a strategy to ask these executives to change their values and behavior without the same occurring at least in the executive systems above. More of this later.

Let us turn to a more detailed description of each topic discussed during the feedback session plus some excerpts taken from the tape that illustrate the quality and nature of the discussion.

A. THE DIFFICULTY IN ESTABLISHING THE FACTS

The first topic discussed by the executives arose from their belief that the way to resolve emotional issues during a meeting was for the leader to "get the facts." One executive raised the question, "What are facts?" A discussion followed from which the group concluded that the way one saw the facts depended at least upon (1) the objectives that he was trying to reach, (2) the values that he held, and (3) the group that he represented. These insightful considerations made at the outset came back to haunt the executives at various times during the day when one of them pointed out that they were assuming that their view of the facts was a correct one.

B. THE PROPER ROLE OF THE LEADER

As a result of considering the questions "What are facts?" and "Who has them?" the executives explored the role a leader should take to determine the facts. The task of the subordinate, they concluded, was to take a selfish departmentally centered point of view. He should fight hard for his department's interests. It is the leader's responsibility to adjudicate and make a decision concerning which facts are the correct ones.

After evolving the role, the group began to question its validity. One individual pointed out that this led to inter-departmental rivalries. Another pointed out that departments were inherently interdependent, and this would lead to difficulties among the departments. The consultant added to the questioning by raising the possibility that if the leader became the judge, it would create highly centralized interpersonal relations and activities during meetings and in the rest of the organization. He pointed out that this would be contrary to the announced policy of the company to decentralize as much as possible. (More of this in category F.)

C. The Scarcity of Time to Make Effective Decisions

Another executive pointed out that time was an important factor. There never was enough time. Time seemed to work against the desire to make adequate decisions. If time was lacking, added the consultant, then the incompetent subordinate may use it to protect himself. As long as he knew that the leader saw himself as being responsible for establishing the facts, then all the subordinate needed to do was procrastinate long enough and time would coerce the leader to take action. An executive added that when this occurred the subordinate would probably no longer need to feel responsible for making decisions. Another pointed out the opposite; namely, that the *effective* subordinate was harmed by centralization in interpersonal relationships because presumably he wanted to be responsible for making decisions.

D. The Difficulties and Unpopularity of Being a Dissenter or Deviate

This comment lead someone to point out the dangers of being a dissenter. "How much freedom do we *really* have to disagree?" asked another executive. The executives concluded, "Not as much as they would like!" One more put it as follows: "Best advice is to be a 'yes man' but don't talk or act like one."

Below are some excerpts taken from the tape recording that illustrate many of the points made in A, B, C, and D.

No. 11:[4] The real reason for disagreement is the different ob-jectives and points of view of the participants in the meeting. They may have totally different objectives which they are unwilling to talk about. They may have selfish objectives; I may say, for example, "Don't worry about No. 2, let No. 2 worry about himself."

No. 7: If we use the word selfish or department incentive, it is not necessarily personal. That's the way we are because we must be, in respect to self-interest. Because if you're in charge of an ac-tivity like that of manufacturing, you have got to take a selfish interest to protect it. If you or anyone else should take the broad philosophical outlook, then manufacturing might lose a little bit.

No. 9: But there isn't any function that isn't interdependent. There's where trouble begins.

No. 7: This is the price of being in an organization. It is each one of our jobs to worry about our area. You should say to yourself, "I want to be sure that I have a number of people at the right time," or the right material or whatever it is. Let me give you an example of what I would call good selfish interest. In solving a manufacturing problem, if I would stand up and be strong enough, I would say, "My golly, I want to set schedules and won't even accept changes of any kind except once every six months." If the business was strong and manufacturing-oriented, it might happen. This is what I meant by real strong selfish interests.

No. 8: What happens? You know what happens. You listen to the facts on the other side. You're fighting for what you think is most desirable, and someone else is fighting for what he thinks.

RESEARCHER: No. 7, let me ask him this question. What No. 11 says makes sense, that each one has his own point of view. I think this makes sense. Then isn't it true that they, the top men, that they have this point of view? Well then, who has the facts? If there are three different points of view and who now is going to judge as to who has the facts?

SOMEONE: The top men.

SOMEONE ELSE: Right.

No. 7: All these facts have been presented, three or four or five different points of view, and perhaps the leader makes a deci-sion on the way he balances it. The proportion is more important of significant facts. I mean, everyone has the facts, but the significance of the facts is different for different people, and I think the best way this is done is by whoever is in charge of production. It's a matter of

---

[4] The numbers are a code for the actual names. The code is changed in each chapter.

values for the company, and I will cite a simple example. If I have the job of making those decisions on this little schedule, their difference of interests, for example, marketing interests, would sometimes put our manufacturing operations in a horrible position if we looked at those alone. Yet, facts would show to some extent that this would be a nice way to run the marketing organization. On balance it would save the manufacturing from spending tremendous amounts of money needlessly. Now there's a point. Somebody has to make a judgment decision after they think they have all the facts. This is the job of the leader.

No. 3: It seems to me you've got an overriding fact of the time interval in which you're allowed to make decisions. Time may not allow that course of action to be taken. That itself becomes a fact that bears on how people view the facts and how the boss will act.

RESEARCHER: It may be possible, then, to think of you now as bosses. Under those conditions subordinates really control the boss because all he has to do is procrastinate long enough and they know that the boss will come up with a decision.

E. THE MISTRUST OF, AND INCOMPETENCE IN COPING WITH, OUR OWN AND OTHERS' FEELINGS

The next major theme of the session was the difficulty that the executives found in coping with the feelings in their executive system. Some suggested that they did not trust feelings. Others reported that they believed the expression of emotions was a sign of immaturity.

The consultant pointed out that under these conditions, it probably would not be long before the subordinates learned to suppress their feelings, especially the negative ones. However, as was pointed out by others, it was the bottled-up negative feelings that required so much of a man's energy. Would this not harm the subordinates' productivity and creativity? Some illustrative comments were:

RESEARCHER (referring to the results): Not one of you reports that he really knows how to deal with emotions. If emotions must be dealt with, you state that they should be handled by whoever is responsible for that meeting. That's the leader's job. Feelings in this system are looked upon as immature. It's not cricket to get emotional. One man gave an example where two people got quite emotional and the leader, in effect, said, "Now cut it out, you're not kids." In a sense, what the third man may be saying in effect is, "Look, I don't know how to cope with these feelings except to damn both of you by calling you kids."

No. 11: Isn't that the product of training, if that's the right word?

RESEARCHER: I think so.

No. 8: Definite in upbringing.

No. 11: Yes, I think this is us. But isn't it something that one sort of develops in a culture?

No. 4: It may also be related to our satisfaction of the job as an intellectual experience. We value the intellectual rather than the emotional one, and, therefore, we shy away from feelings.

No. 1: I think we visualize our job as being one where rational judgment predominates, and in an emotional discussion we're not really performing our job.

No. 10: I think that we distrust the emotion or display of emotion by others.

No. 5: I think that if you've had some experience with short temper, as I have, you usually find out that when you blow your stack you also lose the base. You're seen as destructive. When you see someone else blowing his stack, you figure, "See, this guy's going to lose."

No. 2: It seems to me, however, that this pressure can lead someone to water down his convictions. This would be a little bit dangerous.

F. THE DILEMMA BETWEEN CENTRALIZED INTER-PERSONAL RELATIONS AND DECENTRALIZED ORGANIZATIONAL POLICIES

The next major theme was introduced by the consultant. He suggested that if, as was pointed out, feelings were not expressed, if they were the responsibility of the superior, and if they were associated with immaturity, then this might tend to strengthen or sanction subordinate dependence upon the superior.

The lead to a discussion of the difficulty in keeping everyone informed. A suggestion was made by one of the executives that one way to resolve the issues might be to create a file where a copy of every important letter would be kept for the executives to examine any time that they wished. Someone commented that this would help to increase their feeling of "being in the know." However, another executive raised questions about the value of the approach because some people might not write everything of value if they knew that the letter would be read by all. Still another executive added the possibility that others may use the practice to get people in trouble. They could send a letter to the file and later tell the executive, "You should have known—it's in the file!"

"Why must we all be 'in' on everything that goes on?" asked another executive. "Don't we trust one another?"

"Perhaps not," suggested the consultant, and he cited a number of instances where a meeting was held to convey information which, according to their own estimates, could have taken 15 minutes, and actually took nearly two hours. Many of the executives agreed that they did "go by the way of devious and careful routes" when the subjects were "touchy." But they insisted it was for their as well as for others' protection.

Some illustrative comments were:

No. 7: In the meantime, the main thing we have to do is get the product out, get the job done, no matter how unhappy we are. I don't believe that most of us, if we see that there's going to be an open clash, I don't think we seek it out. We tend to sneak around through back doors some place and line up as many people on our side as we can before we have to come to the ultimate crisis.

RESEARCHER: As I see it, the group meets head on anything that has to do with the job that requires intellectual professional competence. They don't fear that at all. They meet professional issues, and they try to discuss them. However, it is also clear that you see the leader's job to make sure that if the group gets off the track, he must get them back on the track of it; if they, the members, become emotional, the leader must somehow stop the situation. In a sense, what this does is to say to the members, "I, the leader, am responsible for resolving these decisions. If I'm the leader, although I may talk decentralization when I'm at a meeting, it's going to be highly centralized. I am going to be in charge."

No. 2: I'm a little concerned on this point; I mean, where a meeting can be centralized or not. I mean, if you have a situation, then what you're really saying is that the decision need not be made by the leader. Then there's no point in the meeting. So generally the only purpose of a meeting is to bring together some points of view, facts, you name it, in order to get some kind of a decision made. Or maybe to inform, but I'm talking about decision making. But I don't understand your comment about whether this is centralization or not.

No. 9: If it, leadership, operates properly when you call this meeting; if you're properly decentralized, each one of them will make their decision. The leader doesn't really have to make it.

No. 2: Well, he doesn't have to be there then. No point in the meeting. The leader has to put it together; somebody has to pull it together.

No. 9: Why? Actually, if subordinates learn at these meetings that it is the job of the leader to pull things together, they may let him do just that. They seek the boss to decide for them. If so, then this policy that it is the leader's responsibility to pull things together could protect the weak ones. How do you feel about this?

No. 5: I think that the meetings that we're directing ourselves are too often meetings where we choose decisions that should have been made by our subordinates. We invite to meetings those subordinates that fail on their own to come to an agreement.

But isn't this correct on not agreeing with their convictions? So then the purpose of the meeting is to bring it together at a focal point for the leader to arbitrate. He listens to both sides and says, "This is the way it has to be."

RESEARCHER: But the other side of this is interesting. If I am in finance or budget or manufacturing, then I know that all I have to do is hang on and eventually the leader will decide. Also, knowing that a leader will eventually make a decision could increase my feelings to dig my feet in and say "No" to take my departments point of view and say "No, no."

No. 11: I'd say another factor is working here, and that is when you have a meeting among more or less equals in different areas and there's a disagreement, everybody realizes that it's better to give in a little then go in front of the boss to volley the ball.

No. 7: Yes, which I think is healthy, perhaps.

No. 11: I think it's in our culture that whenever we're asked for a decision, we feel that if we don't make a decision we're not doing our job.

No. 10: I've seen a boss, in one case, throw it back to the job or guy and say, "Look, you make the decision; I think you should make a decision." Not very many of us do this very often. We think that because they come to us for a decision we should record a decision.

G. MANAGEMENT BY CRISIS

The next theme was the tendency or practice of "the man above" to create crisis to motivate action. "Why are crises necessary?" asked one individual. "They are," answered another, and continued, "Without them the organization would not be alarmed, and without alarm there is not the highest motivation."

The consultant asked if a crisis created at the top would not flood the organization below, keeping many people busy. Several agreed, and one made the further point that for every one crisis started "on top" two were developed throughout the organization.

Can a company *really* be operated effectively without pressure and crisis? The question was never answered, but the discussion showed that there was a wide range of opinions. Many saw the absence of crisis as a dream world. Those who believed in management by crisis tended to believe that the alternative of absence of crisis would result in a "fat and happy," "sloppy," "sluggish" organization that would soon lose its vitality. One of the executives commented that these were serious assumptions, and they tended to have far-reaching implications for how they as superiors lead and how the subordinates learned to follow.

Still others pointed out that management by crisis led to a situation that forced many of them to set goals they knew would not be achieved at the scheduled time. Another impact pointed out by one executive was that decisions usually made under crisis tended to be poorly thought through and even less effectively executed. Many nodded their heads in agreement.

The next question that came up was the definition of crisis. Although none was arrived at, it was concluded that the higher up the person upset, the greater the probability that his worries and questions would be magnified into a crisis—if he did not do so himself.

No. 7: And that's another thing. Now, the reason for this type of meeting is to make sure that we are aware of the hot, top, sensitive problems affecting not only our decision but others' decisions and the *reputation* of our company. The reason for it is to make sure that manufacturing and engineering, product control are sensitive and are fully informed of the so-called "danger signals," and every segment of the business is *alarmed* and *alerted*. Let's make sure that the top people in the company are aware of how critical problems might be.

No. 2: I think that the researcher has a point on this one, and to explore the question of why in that particular instance and similar ones we need three-hour meetings to report a fact, an event that has happened. In one sentence you can say what the event is and then stop. The researcher caught me up short on this one because I thought he made some points, and he asks why do we go into detail? Well, some of it is, I guess, rationalization, you know. Some of it is probably because you [his boss] might be asked all sorts of questions, and I feel as if I better brief you. The problem is when you call your boss and tell them that the x product is in trouble, they jump. "Why what happened?" you see, and we all create a crisis. I'm not saying it's necessarily wrong.

No. 9: Yeah, but this interest in detail—as it goes down every level, new questions get raised which weren't quite answered, and they explode new crises.

No. 7: Yeah, but, No. 2, this is true only on some. Only those that have created nationalistic interest, so to speak. Like Problem Y or something like that. The majority of these situations are internal divisional actions.

No. 2: Well, I don't know; it seems to me, bluntly, that sometimes we attempt to dodge the facts or dodge the actual situation by demanding more information.

No. 7: Although crises are distasteful things, their sole purpose —in my estimation, their primary purpose—is, as I said before, to make sure that all energies of the division are being focused on the critical problem in the right way and in the right balance.

No. 2: One of the problems is that generally—I think No. 10 would agree—that the schedules on all of the projects are pretty taut. I would guess that we miss in the region of 90 per cent of our schedules on anything dealing with projects or products testing.

No. 10: I would agree with this. We built this in. I think we should recognize it.

No. 11: None the less, there's enough taut built in that generally we miss. This being the case, if we could somehow talk about the important ones that we missed badly, openly. What do I do? I'll inadvertently say, "Hey, you know?" and, "I don't think that so and so is going to come in on time." You [boss] immediately look at No. 2 with big searching eyes and say, "No. 2, if you're not going to come in on time . . . ," and he's upset, and boom! [Laughter.]

No. 10: The thing that's really serious about this is, if you follow this down through the organization, the thing that's really serious about this is that if you create one crisis, as it goes down it creates three more. Although you have determined that this is now the most important thing to the company, when this becomes a crisis you create other crises, and these tend to smother the organization.

No. 11: Look, we're all crying about this trouble of having

these crises come and the way we get a thousand people all generating to give eight facts so that we can defend ourselves! Why don't we stop this?

No. 10: No. You don't stop it. At least in my experience all I do is run down the line and be sure that this crisis didn't create three more. In fact, I spent all my time doing that for about three years.

RESEARCHER: If the culture is one of crises, the lower you go the bigger the god the boss becomes, and then you're in worse trouble trying to stop it. No. 2 said, "I'm sorry I said it, but we missed 90 per cent." It's no secret. You know everybody knows right down the line, and the irony is that they do know it. One must just imagine what must be going on down at the lower level. As some said, "He comes to the office every morning and asks what's the crisis of the day."

No. 9: The thing that I have to do, is to train Mr. X in such a way that when a crisis happens he accepts it. Then he runs the interference and pulls a man off—one man, not hundreds—and he runs interference all the way down the line to be damned sure that this one crisis doesn't generate another.

No. 7: Wait a minute. Every week something is supposed to be accomplished. No. 4 still has tremendous schedules. Well, it seems to me the converse of this is that we sit here and we just let things go along, and the first thing you know one schedule is dropping behind another schedule or something else. Should we just go along saying, "Okay, fine, that's good, just keep the thing tapping along; it's getting slower and slower"? I know there's dangers. It would be much more pleasant for everybody. But when we make commitments, as many of them as we have, which all deal with products, we can't afford too many delays in them. But I don't hear any other way of dealing with the problem. I agree that a crisis puts things out of balance. Then turn it around to a positive basis and get people motivated without having them mad. You can't. I don't think we should.

I think the reason that our company really has succeeded is that there's been a central commitment, *a sense of urgency in all segments of the business, I think there's a greater sense of urgency in, perhaps, this corporation than in any of them I've ever been exposed to.*

No. 5: Well, No. 7, well, are you saying that the only way you can get urgency is contrive it?

No. 7: No, I'm not.

RESEARCHER: That's what I hear you saying. I see as an outsider that the chief motivation for commitment is crisis. And I believe that these people around this table and others may be capable of being committed with less crisis.

No. 7: No, let me put it another way. I think they are capable of being motivated to operate without crisis. But now we would like to avoid crises; we would like to operate from here without having any major crises.

RESEARCHER: I don't believe that.

OTHERS: No, no.

RESEARCHER: As an outsider I do not believe it. I think you would go mad without a crisis.

No. 5: People enjoy crises.

No. 2: Yes.

No. 3: Yes—that's true.

No. 11: That's our business.

RESEARCHER: In the interviews everyone was very clear in saying to me that you dislike crises, and yet when I observed them you actually created them.

SOMEONE: We hate them, but we love them.

A LOT OF PEOPLE: Yes, yes, this is true. This is us.

No. 5: We dig the hole for the guy to fall into. I think we honestly attempt to meet our schedule without strife, but we didn't really say if we thought we could make them when we started. I think many times we really, we're going to really try, and there's no question about that, but if we're missing 90 per cent, and that's probably true, the facts of the matter are we've got the crisis built in when we set the schedule.

No. 10: Yes, we're using the schedule, too, as a carrot for the donkey.

H. THE MEANING OF LOYALTY

Discussing the impact of management by crisis led to the examination of requirements placed by the organization upon loyalty. Most people agreed that they should go along with a decision once it is made even if they did not agree with it. However, they strongly rejected the requirement that they must act as if they agreed with the decision. They felt that this was the height of debasing a man's sense of dignity and of attempting to brainwash him. Furthermore, it was a sign of mistrust. If a superior truly trusted a subordinate, then the former should know that no matter how much the latter disagreed, once a decision was made, the subordinate would always strive to carry it out to the best of his ability.

Some illustrative comments were:

No. 10: Yes, we're using the schedules as a carrot for the donkey.

RESEARCHER: And a switch behind the donkey.

No. 10: Well, one or the other. The idea is to make him sprint all the way to the end of the course.

RESEARCHER: And pretty soon the donkey may get so brainwashed that either the carrot or the switch will have to be increased to motivate the people.

No. 2: The damaging thing is not so much that people follow the party line; it's obvious you have to, if you've chosen a course of action. The thing is to me in some cases it's almost degrading when it happens, too, when you say, "Believe him or else."

My point is that you've got a situation where there's two ways of doing it, and a decision has to be made because a decision can't be made two ways, so Mr. A, the boss, says, "Okay, we're going to do it this way." Now I think that anyone can accept that it's obvious that it had to be done one way. But what really has bothered me is when not only do you say you're going to do it this way but then the next two hours are spent trying to brainwash you into saying, "Well, if you were in my position, wouldn't you do it this way?" In fact, by damn it, I wouldn't; I'll do it this way and try to make it successful.

OTHERS: Right. Right.

No. 7: This is one of the great evils of business. So far, and this thing boils along for some time. You get up to the point where, by golly, someone gets tired of hearing and listening to all the stories and finally you say this is a decision. I expect it to be carried out, and I expect you to carry it on down through your organization and let go and make it work. This is one of the greatest evils that exists.

No. 2: You mean the fact that we do that, or the fact that we do not do it? Well, that we don't accept some of these decisions? No, I don't agree with that.

No. 5: No. 2 was saying we'd accept the decision, but you're supposed to say, "Oh, yes, I not only accept it, in fact I'm right behind it." I wouldn't sell it that way myself.

No. 2: After he's said that he will do it, he has to say, "I agree with you Mr. X," and Mr. X doesn't let him go until he says it, and I'm not referring to anyone in this room especially.

No. 10: Are you saying then that there's a contest of loyalty between you? It's not only that you follow the decision; you must eventually sit in front of me and tell me, "That's the way I would have done it." That's our problem.

No. 7: In our company, decisions are made and then people are brainwashed to agree with the boss rather than "Okay, it's your position, it's your prerogative to make a decision. My viewpoint was something else, but because I am part of the team, I will carry out the decision." They stop there. I think this is a hell of a good point.

No. 4: It again implies a real sense of mistrust of the human being, if you require him.

No. 10: It's forcing you to knuckle down to a position that you're not really proud of yourself. You walk out of this situation thinking, "Gee, I wish I hadn't done that."

No. 2: And, I think this has a worse effect. I think you can go even deeper, because you can say one thing that happens when you make a decision is that you accept your responsibility for it. Now let's trace this through. You made a decision; at that point you have the responsibility. And then you browbeat people into agreeing with that decision emotionally and intellectually and every other way. I mean you just force them to. What have you done? You've just gotten out of the responsibility, because if it ever comes up again, we, you, agreed with it. And how many times have you heard that?

I. THE MEANING OF OPENNESS AND TRUST IN HUMAN RELATIONSHIPS

"If," asked one of the executives, "management by crisis and our concept of loyalty implied mistrust, then perhaps it was dangerous to be open in one's feelings. Perhaps, there could be a problem of too much openness and too many feelings coming out." "Would not," asked another, "our subordinates become terribly hurt if everyone said exactly how he felt?" "How about ourselves," responded one executive, "could anyone get anything done under these conditions?" Perhaps not, but the other side of the coin was that at times we feel that we are not getting the full story from one another or from our subordinates.

No. 7: I also have the feeling that—I am very serious— that in most of the areas of business that, many times, I'm only getting part of the story. I always think it's me that there is something wrong with and I haven't got to the point where people will talk to me freely. I feel that people are holding back.

No. 9: Well, I get that feeling once in a while with you, but I feel that I'm wasting your time if I go on. I mean I feel that some meetings that I have, that people feel that way about me; but sometimes with you, sometimes I feel that if I fill you in completely it would probably take 30 minutes, and I don't think it's worth it for your time or mine.

No. 7: And I have many times the feeling in your case that I am not getting all the facts or not understanding them all; we're really not communicating at all. You have the feeling that you don't want to waste my time by comparing a lot of things. I have the feeling that I'm not getting enough of the facts.

RESEARCHER: Why isn't it possible for you?

No. 7: The reason I'm bringing it up is that I think there is room for improvement. I think that as I listen to some fellow on this side, I watch out of the corner of my eye; I can tell there are a lot of small discussions going on, and this bothers me more than anything else.

No. 2: There is one thing where No. 9 said there isn't enough time. It's a question of going into more detail, but I don't think that's what you're worried about. I think that what you're worried about is the fact that you're talking about a subject and you hear a couple of things right and a couple of things wrong, and what you're worried about is that there are a couple of things wrong that you're not being told about, and why aren't you being told? One fear— a second reason, I would guess—is: "well, I know this is a problem, and I'm going to get it under control, you know, and I don't need help to get it under control, so I'm not going to bring it up, because if I do bring it up, I'll get hell."

No. 10: So you know what's wrong in my problem, and if I say what's wrong, this is what happened up at that meeting at Y on the announcement of the product. I was terribly embarrassed, but those two teams had gotten together and Mr.———— kept saying that something isn't coming out right in this meeting. Boy, were you right. Everybody knew about what a sloppy operation this was.

No. 9: I can't remember one incident where you thought I didn't turn you in where it became important later that I should have.

RESEARCHER: As I hear it, No. 7 is saying that he feels he made a decision that he didn't think it was important or not a waste of time.

No. 7: And I suspect that this is related to me. I suspect that, perhaps, I am defeating myself somewhat from being properly informed.

No. 10: And then many of us say I better be careful. I won't tell him because I think I can fix these up; and if I tell him, he'll make a crisis out of it.

No. 7: So I should really approach this the other way. If you would say, "These are the ones that I think are important, and I really don't know exactly, but I'm working on them," there are two other problems that exist: "I will handle them, but don't worry about it; I just want you to know about it," and I should, as any of you should say, "Okay, fine, go right ahead."

J. INCREASING DEPARTMENTAL CENTEREDNESS

The consultant summarized and raised the question if the above would not tend to cause the subordinates to become further entrenched in the narrow view of their own department and that interdepartmental rivalries and conflicts would increase.

The executives agreed that this was occurring. However, many of them asked if this was not inevitable with "strong" leadership. At this point, one of the executives reminded the others that according to the interview results, the overwhelming majority of the superiors reported that the biggest weakness of their subordinates was that they were too parochial and narrow-minded in their view (Chapter 3). "Can we have our cake and eat it too?" he asked.

K. THE IMPACT OF THE EXECUTIVE SYSTEM ABOVE THEM UPON THEIR OWN SYSTEM

The meeting closed with a discussion of where the training should begin. Some of the men stated that the training program should first be offered to the corporate executives. They were concerned that the president would be placed in a difficult position if he had to lead the division with two different value systems. For example:

No. 2: If we trust ourselves more, we will decrease the amount of detail that we will require from each other and that the President will require from us. But then we will be incompetent to give the corporate president detailed information that the people at headquarters will still require.

(Researcher points out that there is an area in the division in which change can occur, that is relatively free from corporate influence.)

(President again emphasizes that this laboratory is voluntary; also emphasizes that once at the laboratory, they can really work out a diagnosis and then invite the corporate staff.)

No. 2: The thing that bothers me is that I can see that there are two different approaches to managing and gathering data. There is one the way we are operating now and one that is implied in what the laboratory stands for. The nature of the communication, the degree of depth, the values, are different.

Now when the President asks questions, some of it is internally generated. Some of it generated from above at corporate. The one from above requires a different set of values. I don't see how I can act on both sets of values.

PRESIDENT: I would react that you should react to these inquiries according to the values we in the division accept. It shouldn't worry you as to where it originates.

No. 2: This leaves you naked with respect to them above.

No. 9: Not as long as you are aware of the President's plight.

PRESIDENT: My objective most of the time is to shield you from the blasts that come from headquarters. This way I can decrease the crisis aspect.

No. 2: Okay. Let's say with laboratory values I communicate the truth—and I'm trusted—but you call headquarters and tell them the same. Then comes the penetration, detail, the "who's at fault?" "How do you really know it's going to be fixed?" and so on. My point is that you are in an untenable position.

No. 10: Let me amplify: This group is new to this method of operation. The information our President has to have for effective operation within and without is different.

No. 2: The only way I can solve this is to continue operating the way we are now operating.

No. 3: Unless the President tells you that this is a point he'll have to discuss upstairs or not.

No. 6: I think No. 2 is saying if we are operating our organization with trust, then the amount of information necessary is small. But, by past experience, we know that we can't get by with it, because they will not accept a frank statement based on trust. We come back and say, "My God, what's wrong, what's the story, and so on?" But I think we can cope with this. Also, things are changing. Inquiries in the past have been very penetrating, very detailed. And we've all been taught to be extremely detailed in answering.

Now you're generating here a philosophy of competence and trust, and you're saying if the someone says it will be on the road in three weeks, they [above] should believe him. This hasn't been the case.

No. 8: I am glad to say that this is beginning to change at headquarters. More and more they're saying, "Okay I trust you— go ahead." Maybe it's not happening as much as it should below me.

No. 5: I might say—without trying in any way to sell you— sure, I feel frustrated as to exactly what we'll get out of this—I have confidences that we'll learn something, just as we have today simply by discussing these problems.

V. SOME THOUGHTS ON THE VALIDITY OF THE EXECUTIVES' COMMENTS

Since we used the themes evolved at the feedback session as a check upon the validity of our research, the question arises: "To what extent did the agenda and the researcher influence the executives to make remarks that were consonant with the results? How do we know that the executives were not simply going along with the researcher?"[5]

First, there is no doubt that the agenda and the researcher influenced to some degree the behavior of the executives. Both provided stimuli with which to trigger off and maintain diagnostic discussions. The agenda was based upon the material in Chapter 3. Prior to the meeting each executive received a report where the replies to each question were described. No other information was given to the executives. The theoretical framework and model used by the researcher was not mentioned explicitly. However, even with these precautions the data the executives were given were certainly influenced by the researcher's view. The very questions upon which the replies were based were drawn from the researcher's theoretical framework. Moreover, although the researcher did not present his model formally, an analysis of the tapes would show that he tended to ask questions that helped him to make the points he felt were important. These points were obviously influenced by his theoretical biases.

The question, therefore, is not: "Were the executives influenced?" The question is: "Given the influence of the researcher and his agenda, did it coerce the executives to think and behave in ways that did not accurately represent their views?" I doubt it for the following reasons:

1. As one can infer from the protocols included, the executives did not seem threatened, hesitant, or passive. They questioned, modified, agreed, disagreed in a most spontaneous manner with the material that they read and with the views of the researcher.

Perhaps, one might counter, the men really did not agree, but they just talked to cover up their feelings. After all, the analysis does show that the executives do not tend to express negative feelings. In the writer's experience, when top executives disagree with the feedback of research results and

---

[5] This question is probably not very relevant for the reader who is deeply acquainted with extremely bright, intellectually competent, aggressive, challenge-seeking, top executives, who in this case happened to be highly successful in an extremely successful company. He would know that the probability of such men sitting in a room and going along with a researcher on basic issues with which they disagree is quite low.

when these same executives do not tend to express such feelings openly, then they politely read through the data, ask few, if any, questions, and bring the meeting to a quick close. After the meeting, they may hold one of their own and find a "polite" way to neutralize or get rid of the researcher.

In this case the executives not only participated enthusiastically, they also added to, and modified constructively, the diagnosis. Moreover, they created their own topics and spent much time discussing relevant human problems that were not in the report. More important, as a sign of self-generated interest, the executives prolonged the meeting two hours past the time it was supposed to stop and continued a formal discussion during lunch.

2. A second consideration is that if the group did not agree with the researcher, there is a strong probability that they could unite as a group against him. The analysis of the tapes showed no such movement even by one individual. Nor did the two observers report any such activity. Moreover, the present and future of these men is related to how *they* evaluate one another and not how well they get along with the researcher. If several were agreeing with the researcher and they knew the group felt that the data were invalid, then they would tend to incur the (suppressed) wrath of the others.

3. A third consideration is that after the meeting the executives were canvassed (by one of their own people, and away from the researcher) to see if they were to have a laboratory. The vote was unanimous for the laboratory. Also, the executive acting as liaison reported that at least 60 per cent of the men spontaneously told him that they felt they already "got a lot out of the session because we have heard the views of the others on important human problems which we rarely have time to discuss."

4. Although the session began by discussing interpersonal problems, it was not long before the executives brought into the discussion the organizational aspects of these problems. One reason for this may be their greater comfort in talking on the task-oriented level. This hypothesis is supported by the fact that when the men did return to talking about feelings, they talked about them in a detached, intellective manner. For ex-

ample, they might say, "Let's take manufacturing or finance," when it was evident that they were talking about the head of each of these departments who were seated around the table. Once in a while someone would slip and say "Now, Bill,[6] let's take you for a moment," then a pause and "I don't mean you as a person . . ." and so on.

The researcher did not attempt to induce the executives in their discussion to a more "here and now" personal level for several reasons. First, this was a feedback meeting, designed to help the executive diagnose the situation from their view-point. The intellective (cognitive) view is their strength, and that is where they tend to feel most competent. Being permitted to diagnose the situation with the tools with which they feel most competent, we hypothesize, would free them to explore as fully as possible the depth and people of the problems involved. They did this, in the writer's view, in a highly competent manner.

The second reason for not focusing on the interpersonal level was that it might have opened up emotionally laden problems that could not have been worked through by the end of the day. Another consideration was that the executives would probably attend a laboratory session which would provide them much more time to discuss the emotionally laden issues.

All this leads to the conclusion that the executives operated primarily on the task level. This is their forte. They are extremely competent on this level.

---

[6] The name is fictitious.

PART THREE

THE
LABORATORY
PROGRAM

6

The Nature of Laboratory Education

Our diagnosis suggests that if the executives' social system continues to maintain itself in its present state, the interpersonal competence will tend to decrease or be continually reinforced at a low level. The degree of dependence, external commitment, and conformity will also increase or be further entrenched. These, in turn, will tend to lead to less effective decision making, further organizational defenses, and deeper organizational rigidity. As a result, the organization will tend to require increasing inputs of human energy to achieve its objective, maintain itself internally, and adapt to its external environment.

The executives agreed that the diagnosis was accurate and asked for a program that might help increase their degree of interpersonal competence and the effectiveness of the organization. The next question that arises is: "What kind of an educational experience would help them achieve their goal?"

WHAT THE LEARNING EXPERIENCE SHOULD NOT BE

Typically, learning experiences are organized so the teacher is largely in control of, and responsible for, the information to be given, the rewards and penalties to be used, the degree of involvement of the participants, and, indeed, the entire organization of the course. The strategy behind such a learning experience is the same as that used to organize in-

131

dustrial organizations. Under these conditions such learning experiences will tend to:

1. Increase the participants' feeling of dependence upon and and submissiveness toward the teacher, because the latter has power over the former (through control of authority, reward, penalties, information, and so on).
2. Increase the participants' centeredness and conformity toward the teacher and his values.
3. Increase the participants' interpersonal and interdepartmental rivalries and conflicts.[1]

As factors (1), (2), and (3) above increase, the individual's internal commitment to learning tends to *decrease* and his *external* commitment tends to increase. External commitment exists when the individual is induced to learn through someone else's influence[2] (the teacher's). The source of the participant's motivation to learn is outside the self. It is usually stimulated by rewards and penalties on the part of his superior. Under conditions of external commitment, individuals will tend to learn according to the teacher's desires and as a function of the teacher's rewards or penalties. Since the learning goals are not defined by the individual, he does not feel responsible for them, and they will not tend to enhance his esteem as he achieves these external goals. Moreover, the individual will tend to expect more rewards from his teacher. If such rewards are given, the individual's external commitment is increased.

Such a learning experience is consonant with, and tends to reinforce, the basic assumptions inherent in the pyramidal structure about the quality of effective relationships. They are (1) the relevant human relationships are the rational, technical, logical ones; (2) that personal feelings and attitudes are not relevant; and (3) that learning is most effective as it is directed and controlled by a trainer.

We may conclude that if we create a typical learning situation, the executives are provided with an experience that

---

[1] See for example Chris Argyris, *Personality and Organization,* and *Executive Leadership* (New York: Harper & Bros., 1952 and 1957).

[2] External commitment is similar to Kurt Lewin's concept of "Induced Forces." See D. Cartwright (ed.), *Field Theory in Social Science* (New York: Harper & Bros.).

reinforces the very organizational and interpersonal factors and basic assumptions that are the causes of the problems the executives wish to resolve.

In reaching this conclusion we are not implying that the learning experience should be at the opposite extreme. We are not suggesting a completely nondirective, laissez-faire learning situation where the participants are in control and the trainer simply looks on. Nothing could be farther from our desires.

The educator will be in control of the learning situation. The executives at the outset will tend to be dependent upon him. The difference is, however, that he will strive to create an experience where the executives' dependence will tend to decrease, and their sense of self-responsibility and internal commitment will tend to increase. As Lewin and his associates pointed out long ago, there is a fundamental difference between a laissez-faire situation and one in which human beings develop a deep sense of commitment and responsibility. These two situations are on different continua.[3]

Recently, Harvey, Hunt, and Schroder have written an illuminating analysis of training which has direct relevance for understanding laboratory education.[4] They define a continuum of training conditions ranging from unilateral to interdependent. Briefly they are:

1. *Reliable Unilateral:* Arbitrary, but consistent, imposition of source-defined standards or absolute criterion. Person is valued extrinsically. Emphasis upon ends.
2. *Unreliable Unilateral:* Inconsistent control. Excessively high goals. Indifference and neglect.
3. *Protective Interdependent:* Encourages subjects to explore environment but guides exploration. Source anticipates failure.
4. *Informational Interdependent:* Encourages subject to explore environment. Reflects informational consequences to subject. Subject reacts to consequences of own behavior. Person is valued for intrinsic worth. Emphasis is upon process (means).

---

[3] Gardner Murphy, *Human Nature and Enduring Peace* (New York: Houghton Mifflin Co., 1945), pp. 295–312.

[4] O. J. Harvey, David E. Hunt, and Harold M. Schroder, *Conceptual Systems and Personality Organization* (New York: John Wiley & Sons, Inc., 1961), p. 132.

In terms of our model, the reliable unilateral represents traditional training. Laboratory education attempts to approximate informational interdependent learning.

THE BASIC ASSUMPTIONS
OF THE LEARNING EXPERIENCE

The learning experience we are suggesting requires a highly active role on the part of the educator. He actively seeks to behave *in the service of human growth*. He consciously and openly manipulates the learning situation so it mirrors as much as possible the following assumptions:[5]

1. The training program ought to emphasize the participant's responsibility for his own self-development. It recognizes that the teacher-learner situation is a deeply human one, and, thus, it should be structured so it mirrors the philosophy of self-development and self-responsibility. It makes a little sense to "teach" interpersonal competence in a situation where the educator-executive relationships are not authentic or do not nurture interpersonal competence.

2. The second assumption is that education in human relations is a matter of re-education. The problem is, therefore, to help the learner become aware of his attitudes and behavior and then to help him unfreeze them before he makes the decision as to whether or not he will change them.

3. The third assumption is that the process of re-education is basically the same as the one by which the individual received his "original" education. Thus, learning takes place in interpersonal, small-group, and intergroup relationships. The learning experience attempts to make maximum use of all three relationships to create conditions where human beings will learn anew from one another.

4. Human re-education is not only a matter of intellectual understanding. Re-education requires that emotional learning also take place. One of the crucial problems in human relations is that even after people "know" what effective human re-

---

[5] The manipulation is "open" in the sense that the activities are consciously and continuously made available to the "students" for their examination, rejection, or acceptance.

lationships are, few are able to behave accordingly. Even more tragically, fewer yet are aware of this discrepancy in themselves.

5. The most effective development in an individual (or an organization) tends to occur as he becomes more aware of himself *and* more accepting of himself. One can best change himself if he first develops a deep understanding and acceptance of himself. True self-acceptance will not tend to lead to stagnation or complacency. A complacent individual does not esteem or accept himself. An individual who esteems himself realizes that complacency is akin to psychological stagnation if not eventual deterioration.[6]

6. As the participant's sense of self-responsibility, self-esteem, and self-acceptance increases, he will tend to be more understanding of others and show a greater esteem for them. This increased acceptance of others will tend to decrease his and others' defensiveness. This in turn will tend to increase the probability of greater openness and freer use of new ideas and more tolerance toward new ideas. As these conditions increase, the probability of more effective individual and group activities will tend to increase.

7. Re-education in human relations should focus more on a change in basic values then on acquiring skills. The development of valid values will tend to lead automatically to the development of proper skills. On the other hand, the development of skills without appropriate changes in values becomes, at best, an alteration whose lack of depth and manipulative character will become easily evident to others. Skills follow values; values rarely follow skills. Skills can be used to illustrate values. But they ought not to be the basis upon which to develop human relationships.

In terms of our model the task of the learning experience is to help executives develop a new set of values or "inputs" about effective human relationships that will lead to increasing authentic relationships and interpersonal competence. (See Figure 2.)

---

[6] See, for example, the chapters by Maslow, Allport, and Goldstein, in A. Maslow (ed.), *New Knowledge in Human Values* (New York: Harper & Bros., 1960).

FIGURE 2

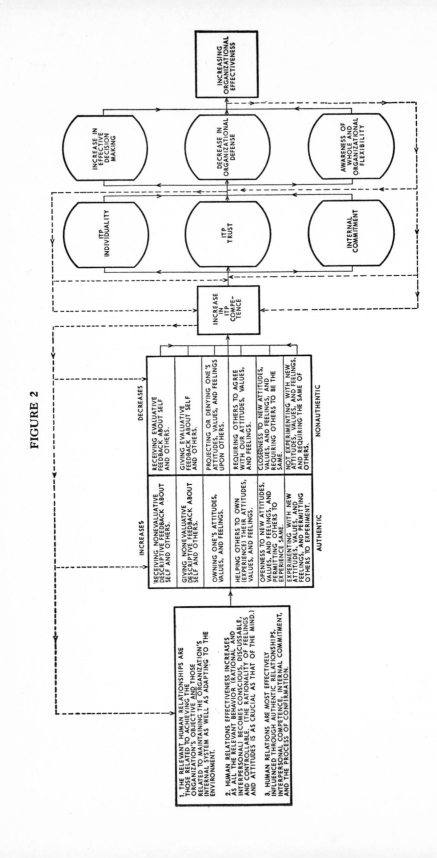

1. The relevant human relationships are those related to achieving the organization's objective *and* those related to maintaining the organization's internal system as well as adapting to the environment.

2. Human relations' effectiveness increase as all the relevant behavior (rational and interpersonal) becomes conscious, discussable, and controllable. (The rationality of feelings and attitudes is as crucial as that of the mind.)

3. Human relations are most effectively influenced through authentic relationships, interpersonal competence, internal commitment, and the process of confirmation.

LEARNING EXPERIENCE LABORATORY TRAINING: DILEMMA-INVENTION-FEEDBACK-GENERALIZATION CYCLE

Mouton and Blake provide an excellent description of the basic foundations of a laboratory.[7] Laboratory training, they write, stems from the procedure a scientist uses when he seeks new information or relationships. An experiment involves orderly comparisons between a standard situation and other conditions which are varied in certain significant respects from the basic situation. Changes in outlook and action follow from the discovery of new relationships through the examination of comparative conditions and their consequences.

DILEMMA

The strategy of experimentation begins with a dilemma. A dilemma occurs when, for a given situation, there is no sound basis for selecting among alternatives or there is no satisfactory alternative to select or habitual actions are no longer effective. In other words, a person doesn't know what to do.

What do people do when confronted with a dilemma? Do they begin to experiment or to invent? The answer usually is, "No." The *immediate* reaction is to try out *older* methods of

---

[7] I draw heavily in the next several paragraphs from Jane S. Mouton and Robert R. Blake, "University Training in Human Relations Skills," The University of Texas.

behaving with which one already is secure or else to get guidance from an "expert." In this way, the anxiety so invariably
associated with not knowing what to do can be avoided. In the
laboratory then, the anticipated first reactions by participants
to a dilemma are to try traditional ways of responding. These
"frozen behaviors" are ones based on more or less automatic
assumptions so deeply rooted that most individuals are unaware
of making them.

INVENTION

Only when conventional or traditional ways of dealing
with a dilemma have been tried—*unsuccessfully*—are conditions ripe for inventive action. Now people are ready to think,
to shed old notions because they haven't worked, to experiment, and to explore new ways of reacting to see if they will
work.

The period, when old behavior is being abandoned and
when new behavior has yet to be invented to replace it, is an
"unfrozen" period, at times having some of the aspects of a
crisis. It is surrounded by uncertainty and confusion.

One way of dealing with a dilemma is to look backward to
trace the steps that lead to the present impasse. By doing so, it
may be possible to spot points at which the present dilemma
could have been avoided and also to develop a clear perception
of what is required if the situation is to be solved.

FEEDBACK

Fullest learning from the dilemma-invention situation occurs when two additional types of actions are taken. One is
feedback, the process by which members acquaint one another
with their own characteristic ways of feeling and reacting in a
dilemma-invention situation. Feedback aids in evaluating the
consequences of actions that have been taken as a result of the
dilemma situation. By "effective" feedback we mean that feedback which minimizes the probability for the receiver or sender
to become defensive, and maximizes the opportunity for the
receiver or sender to own, to *be*, his value, feelings, and attitudes.

GENERALIZATION

The final step in the dilemma-invention cycle is *generalizing* about the total sequence to get a comprehensive picture of the "common case." When this is done, people are searching to see to what extent behavior observed under laboratory conditions fits outside situations. If generalization isn't attempted, the richness of dilemma-invention learning is "lost."

To summarize, the laboratory should provide as many opportunities as possible for the executives to:

1. *Expose their behavior* as well as their thinking. To reveal the way they perceive the world, the values they hold, and the behavior that is genuinely their own.

2. *Receive feedback* about their behavior and to give feedback about the behavior of others. Learning occurs when they can become more aware of their impact upon others and others' impact upon them. Awareness is fundamental to learning the relevance and effectiveness of their behavior. Finally, they can modify, correct, or confirm their and others' ideas and behavior through effective feedback.

3. *Create an atmosphere* where human beings are willing to expose their values, attitudes, and feelings, and where they are able to give or receive effective feedback.

4. *Intellectualize the learning* into a rational, consistent, cognitive framework. This would enable the executives to understand, organize, and integrate the new learning so it can form the basis for effective action.

This requirement points up the importance of providing as much research and theory as is possible and relevant to the learning achieved.

5. *Experiment with new ideas, values, and behavior.* To make the new learning a part of the self, one needs the opportunity to experiment with it, modify it, so that it becomes an organic, genuine part of the self, and finally to develop from it new ideas, values, and behavior.

THE NATURE
OF LABORATORY EDUCATION

How can a laboratory be created whose organizational structure is consonant with the assumptions and characteristics listed above? Before we attempt to answer this question, we need to remind ourselves that organizational structures are fundamentally strategies to co-ordinate, control, and influence human activities designed to achieve some goals. The influence, co-ordination, and control is usually accomplished through the definition of policies and the use of leadership, rewards, penalties, and the distribution of and control over information.

We may now ask, "How would the laboratory cope with the leadership, rewards, and penalties, and control of information?" Experience suggests that if the values implicit in authentic relationships are to be maintained, the following would tend to occur:

1. Wherever possible, *leadership* will tend to be controlled by the members. They will tend to assign leadership to that individual who at a given moment they perceive as most capable of helping them achieve their objective and who needs to be of help. This is what Knickerbocker and McGregor and others have called "shared" or "distributed" leadership.[8]

2. *Rewards and penalties* would also be controlled by the individual members. Each participant will tend to feel a sense of responsibility to use them in such a way that the objective of the laboratory is achieved, internal commitment to work and authenticity are increased.

For rewards to enhance self-commitment, self-responsibility, and interpersonal authenticity, they must be distributed in a particular manner. For example, the individual will be rewarded who is furthering the progress of the laboratory and who is aware that he is doing so. Similarly, penalties will tend to enhance self-commitment, self-responsibility, and authenticity when the individual knows that what he is doing is not furthering progress of the laboratory or it is violating the group culture.

In other words, rewards and penalties would *not* tend to be used primarily to reward or penalize others in the traditional

---

[8] Douglas McGregor, Irving Knickerbocker, Mason Haire, and Alex Bavelas, "The Consultant Role and Organizational Leadership: Improving Human Relations in Industry," *Journal of Social Issues*, Vol. IV, No. 3, (Summer, 1948). See especially pp. 5–40.

sense of these words. Rewards and penalties would be given to *confirm*[9] to the individual that others feel as he does. Under these conditions the reward does not motivate gratitude toward others as much as deep feelings of emotional satisfaction that others see him to be as successful as he sees himself. Such feelings not only enhance one's own self-confidence and internal commitment, they would also tend to increase his feelings of respect and confidence in his fellow man. Similarly, if penalties are necessary, they will be given to a man who realizes that he has not done well. Under this condition the penalty confirms to him that others also see him as being as unsuccessful as he sees himself. Penalties under these conditions could, if given appropriately, imply a real trust in the individual's capacity to receive "negative" confirmation without "cracking." To put this another way, the source for motivation to increase learning and work on a laboratory will tend to stem from one's competition with his own previously established goals. Under conditions of internal commitment and psychological success the motivation for realistic increases in productivity and achievement is almost limitless.[10]

Finally, rewards would not tend to be given by others to an individual who feels he has not done well, even though others believe he has done quite well. Such behavior could be perceived on the part of the rewardee as "playing favorites" or "flattery" or simply incompetence on the part of the rewarder.

If the rewarder desires to give some rewards in the situation above, to be consistent he would first attempt to clarify the different views with the individual involved. If his view develops correctly, he would have helped the one to be rewarded to see for himself how well he has really done. Then a reward can be given, because it becomes an act of conformation.

Similarly, penalties would not tend to be given when the individual to be penalized feels he has done well. Again, the first step is to help the one to be penalized to see for himself how

---

[9] In the sense that Buber uses the concept of confirmation.

[10] Kurt Lewin, Tamara Dembo, Leon Festinger, and Pauline Sears, "Level of Aspiration" in J. M. V. Hunt (ed.), *Personality and the Behavior Disorders* (New York: The Ronald Press Co., 1944), pp. 333–78.

poorly he has done. Then a penalty can be given, because it becomes an act of confirmation. The emphasis, in giving rewards and penalties, is to diagnose first in order to confirm.

We may depict the position that we have taken on rewards and penalties and the act of confirmation as follows: In column labeled "Mr. A" we depict his view of his behavior. In cases (1) and (4), A believes he has done well and in cases (2) and (3) poorly. In the column labeled "Mr. B" we note that he believes A has done well in (1) and (3) and poorly in (2) and (4).

	Mr. A	Mr. B	Confirmation
1.	+	+	yes
2.	−	−	yes
3.	−	+	no
4.	+	−	no

The process of confirmation occurs in cases (1) and (2). Under these conditions Mr. B's reward (+) or penalty (−) confirms A's view of the situation. Such rewards and penalties enhance self-actualization. Mr. B will not tend to reward or penalize A in cases (3) and (4). He will first diagnose the situation so he or Mr. A changes his view. Once this is done the signs will change to either two pluses or two minuses. We then revert to the first two cases. We are *not* implying that rewards or penalities should never be given under conditions (3), where A feels he has done poorly and B feels that A has done well, or (4), which is the reverse. We simply maintain that under these conditions, rewards and penalties will not tend to reinforce self-responsibility and self-actualization.

There are other conditions which influence the impact that confirmation has upon self-responsibility and self-actualization in human relationships.[11] For example, one may hypothesize that the impact of the process of confirmation will vary as a function:

a) Whether or not what individual A did was in the direction that he intended. The impact of confirmation will differ if A's acts that are being confirmed are (1) motivated from within or induced by others, (2) if they are related to central or pe-

---

[11] Just prior to publication, a new book appeared which presents an important contribution to understanding the process of confirmation: O. J. Harvey, David E. Hunt, and Harold M. Schroder, *Conceptual Systems and Personality Organization* (New York: John Wiley & Sons, Inc., 1961), chap. iii.

ripheral needs, and (3) if they are related to one or several needs.

b) Whether or not A expected to fail or to succeed. Clearly, the impact of the act of confirmation will differ if the individual expected to fair or to succeed. The expectation of success or failure, in turn, is a function of the individual's perception of (1) his competence, (2) his freedom to use his competence, and (3) his previous experience of failure and success under similar conditions.[12]

3. *Information* in a laboratory will tend to be collected and used in such a way that it tends to increase the feelings of self-responsibility, self-commitment, and authenticity. Such information should be, as much as possible, nonvaluative and descriptive; and gathering of data should be under the control of, and for the use of, the participants. Under these conditions each message is "owned" by the sender and sent in such a way that it does not imply that the receiver must accept it or that the sender is correct. Also, information would not tend to be collected to control human behavior. Information collected would tend to be returned immediately to the relevant individuals to help them control or modify their behavior if they wished to do so.

Although a laboratory attempts to organize as many of its learning experiences as possible according to the suggestions above, it is by no means limited to them. For example, lectures, discussions about concepts, theory, and research findings are usually held under conditions more representative of the pyramidal strategy. Thus, a laboratory contains experiences that represent both points of view as well as experiences that represent a combination of the viewpoints. However, the majority of the learning experiences tend to emphasize the values of the laboratory as outlined above. This is the case because a laboratory is designed to help human beings develop, as quickly and effectively as possible, interpersonal competence and effective group functioning.

We are not implying that industrial organizations—or any

---

[12] The work of McClelland and his co-workers is relevant in this connection. D. C. McClelland, J. W. Atkinson, R. A. Clark, and E. L. Lowell, *The Achievement Motive* (New York: Appleton-Century-Crofts, Inc., 1953).

other type—ought to reorganize themselves completely according to the laboratory structure. A laboratory structure effective for educational purposes may not be effective for producing goods and services. For example, it may be that the organization of the future will be composed of several structures, one of which approximates the laboratory strategy, another pyramidal strategy, and so on. Decision rules will be developed to guide the participants in their selection of the proper strategy for their decision making.[13]

EXAMPLES OF LEARNING EXPERIENCES IN A LABORATORY

The proper number, nature, and combination of learning experiences provided in a laboratory is not known. Much research needs to be conducted before systematic suggestions can be made. At this time each laboratory is usually designed according to the implicit or explicit theory, set of values, and previous experiences of the trainers.

In our case, we find the following learning experiences to be consonant with our point of view:

1. DIAGNOSTIC EXPERIENCES

For individuals to develop effectively, they must first feel deeply that there is a need for doing so. Unless each participant feels a genuine need for development, there will tend to be little self-controlled learning.

The diagnostic procedure can be of two kinds. The first is educator-controlled, where most of the insights come from him. An example would be the diagnostic session we planned where the researcher's diagnosis of the executive system was presented to the executives. The objective was to show them that in the researcher's opinion there was a discrepancy between how the executives' think they behaved and how they actually behaved. Also, the researcher attempted to show that the executive system was creating some of the very behavior that they said they wished to avoid (for example, conformity, external commitment, interpersonal incompetence, and so on).

---

[13] Chris Argyris, "The Integration of the Individual and the Organization" (mimeographed, 50 pages), Yale University, May, 1950.

The second type of diagnostic procedure is where the executives observe their own behavior and then diagnose it. For example, it is possible to ask some of the executives to role-play a particular decision in group discussion. The behavior could be taped and observed by the remaining executives. After the data are collected, the executives can diagnose for themselves the degree to which they create conformity, external commitment, and so on. Each type has advantages and disadvantages that will be discussed in a subsequent section.

2. THE TRAINING OR T-GROUP

The core of most laboratories is the T-group. It is most difficult to describe in a few words. Basically it is a group experience designed to provide maximum possible opportunity for the individuals to expose their behavior, give and receive feedback, experiment with new behavior, and develop everlasting awareness and acceptance of self and others. The T-group also provides such possibilities to learn the nature of effective group functioning. Individuals are able to learn how to develop a group that achieves specific goals with minimum possible human cost.

The T-group becomes a learning experience that most closely approximates the values of the laboratory regarding the use of leadership, rewards, penalties, and information in the development of effective groups. It is in the T-group that one finds the emphasis on the participants' creating and diagnosing their own behavior, developing distributive leadership and concensus decision-making norms to protect the deviants, and, finally, sharing as much as possible all the information that is created within, and as a result of, the T-group experience. Again, we are not suggesting that organizations be administered like T-groups. However, we are hypothesizing that they should include structures like T-groups for certain selected decisions.

There are several publications available that one might find of value in understanding a T-group.[14] We may simply

---

[14] Leland P. Bradford (ed.), *Theory of T-Group Training* (in press); Robert Blake and Jane S. Mouton, *Training for Decision-Making in Groups* (Austin, Texas; Department of Psychology, University of Texas, 1958); Irving Weschler and Jerome Reisel, *Inside a Sensitivity Training Group*, Industrial Relations Monograph No. 4 (Los Angeles: Institute of Industrial Relations, University of California).

summarize a few of the major characteristics by following McGregor.[15] The learning is of special importance because it differs sharply from that which occurs normally in group situations. Some of the learning comes from the educator, but most of it is provided by the members to each other. The "ground rules" the group establishes for feedback are important. With the help of the educator, the group usually comes to see the difference between providing help and attempting to control or punish a member, between analyzing and interpreting a member's adjustment (which is taboo) and informing him of the impact it has on others. Typically, certain features of everyday group activity are blurred or removed. The educator, for example, does not provide the leadership which a group of "students" would normally expect. This produces a kind of "power vacuum" and a great deal of behavior which, in time, becomes the basis for learning. There is no agenda, except as the group provides it. There are no norms of group operation (such as *Robert's Rules of Order*) except as the group decides to adopt them. The (experience) is for some time a confusing, tension-laden, frustrating experience for most participants. But these conditions have been found to be conducive to learning in this field. Naturally, some individuals learn a great deal, while others resist the whole process. It is rare, however, for an individual to end a two-week experience feeling that he has learned nothing.

Mouton and Blake describe the T-group which they call a *development group* as follows:

The fundamental-dilemma-producing feature of a human relations laboratory is the development group. The development group is composed of 8 to 12 members, whose explicit goal is to study their own interactions as a group. No leader or power structure is provided. No rules or procedures are given to structure interaction. No task, topic or agenda for discussion is inserted to serve as a guide for action. Thus, the group is faced with critical dilemmas in several fundamental areas of relationships in a group situation. What shall we do or talk about? How shall we relate to one another? What are our rules for interactions? What can we accomplish? How do we make a decision on any of these things?

---

[15] Douglas McGregor, *The Human Side of Enterprise* (New York: McGraw-Hill Book Co., Inc., 1960), pp. 220–21.

All of these issues and many more are dilemmas initially present in the development group. Thus, the stage is set for the first step of the learning cycle.

In addition to group level phenomena, much attention is centered on individuals trying out new and different ways of relating to each other. For example, an overbearing, long talking person may try being silent for an extended period of time; a person who withdraws when under attack may experiment with more aggressive forms of reactions; feelings may be openly expressed. The dilemmas posed by the development group impel inventive, seeking, searching behavior on both the group and the individual level.[16]

3. Consultation Groups

Another frequently used learning experience is to break down the participants into groups of four. Sessions are held where each individual has the opportunity to act as a consultant giving help and as an individual receiving help; the nature of help is usually related to increasing self-awareness, self-acceptance with the view of enhancing interpersonal competence.[17]

4. Lectures

As is pointed out above, research information and theories designed to help organize learning are presented. Typically the material is presented at a time when it is most clearly related to the learnings that the participants are experiencing in a laboratory.

As learning develops, it needs to be tested and enlarged. T-groups, consultation groups, and so on, are highly protected experiences. For example, time pressures, crises, the necessity for rational behavior are kept to a minimum. There comes a time when the individual must begin to try out his new learning in situations that more nearly approximate real life. There are three kinds of experiences that help along these lines.

5. Role-Playing of "Real" Situations

As a result of the original research program, much data were collected illustrating situations in which poor communi-

---

[16] Jane Mouton and Robert R. Blake, *op. cit.*, p. 8.

[17] In a later section we will discuss the difference between help provided at a laboratory and that provided in therapy.

cations existed, objectives were not being achieved as intended, and so on. It is possible in a laboratory to role-play many of these situations to diagnose them, to obtain new insights regarding the difficulties, as well as to develop more effective action possibilities. These can be role-played by asking the executives to play their back-home role. However, for other problems, important learnings are gained by asking the superiors to take the subordinates' roles.

6. DEVELOPING AND TESTING RECOMMENDATIONS

The research study also identified a number of problems that the executives felt would be extremely important in the future. These are the long-range problems that plague an organization; typically its members do not have time to analyze them thoroughly in the back-home situation (for example, effectiveness of decentralization).

In a laboratory, however, time is available for them to discuss these problems thoroughly. More important, as a result of their laboratory learnings and with the assistance of the educators, they could develop new action recommendations as well as diagnose their effectiveness as a group in developing these recommendations. Have they really changed? Have they really enhanced their effectiveness?

It was also possible that the executives might wish to invite to the laboratory their superiors, peers, or subordinates who they feel are intimately related with the problems. Time could be profitably spent examining the new recommendations. Also, the session could be so designed that they could provide the executives an opportunity to "test" their new behavior.

7. INTERGROUP

One of the central problems of organizations is the intergroup rivalries and hostilities that exist among departments.[18] If there is time in a laboratory, this topic should be dealt with. Again, it is best introduced by creating the situation where the executives compete against one another in groups under "win-

---

[18] Chris Argyris, *Personality and Organization* (New York: Harper & Bros.); *Executive Leadership* (New York: Harper & Bros.); and "Human Problems with budgets," *Harvard Business Review.*

lose" conditions. As Blake[19] and Shephard[20] have shown, it is possible to provide to executives such learning experiences for regarding the causes and resolutions of intergroup conflicts.

THE LABORATORY VALUES VERSUS THE VALUES OF THE EXECUTIVES' SOCIAL SYSTEM

Neither the executive system nor the laboratory is a unitary system with completely consonant values. We have shown that the executives tend to value nonemotional behavior rationally. However, there are times when the executives deal with emotions and interpersonal relationships. Similarly, the laboratory focuses primarily upon the emotional and interpersonal, but it, too, must deal with the rational. It is a fundamental working hypothesis that effectiveness of the laboratory or the executive system is related to some, as yet unspecified, combination of the interpersonal and the rational.

However, there are some differences between the laboratory and the rational executive systems. Under stress and tension these differences may be overemphasized by the executives in order to provide themselves with emotional support. Thus, there will tend to be a temporary polarization in the executives' perception of the laboratory values versus the values of their own system. The executives will tend to see their system as emphasizing rational behavior, the suppression of the emotional, and interpersonal (in the name of common courtesy) and the use of power correctly through the unilateral control over rewards, penalties, and information (in the name of efficiency and practicality).

On the other hand, during the initial stages, the values of the laboratory will probably be seen by the executives as emphasizing the expression of the interpersonal, especially such difficult-to-express feelings as hostility, agression, love, caring,

---

[19] Robert Blake, "Psychology and the Crisis of Statesmanship," *American Psychology*, Vol. IV (1959), pp. 87–94; and Robert Blake and Jane Mouton, *Clinical Treatment Versus Laboratory Training Techniques as Approaches to the Induction of Change*, April 21–23, 1960.

[20] Herbert Shephard, "As Action Research Approach to Organization Development," *Management Record*, NICB, June, 1960, pp. 4–7.

and so on, and the use of power through mutually shared and distributed control over rewards, penalties, and information. These requirements, at first blush, especially to a highly emotionally involved executive will tend to be seen as requiring people to be discourteous, to blow their tops any time they wish, to tell someone to go to hell if that's how you feel, and so on.

To make matters more difficult, because the laboratory will tend to be a new situation for the executive, his behavior will not tend to be efficient (that is, follow the shortest path to the goal). There will be much exploratory, trial-and-error behavior. Errors and false steps will be made at the very time that each is being most cautious. Frustration and conflict will occur as well as feelings of ambivalence. These, in turn, will tend to lead the executive to vacillate, to shift his ground. He may be easily influenced and easily led, especially by his fellow executives. His resistance to suggestion will tend to be low.

To the amazement of the executive, in spite of these obvious difficulties, the staff does not seem to do anything that he can see to help him, but seems to work hard at creating difficult situations. Once they have placed the executive in the situation, they seem to retreat and watch him struggle. It is not difficult to see why the executive may feel quite hostile toward the staff. A somewhat more difficult hostility for the executive to see is the hostility that he probably has built up internally against himself. For years he has been operating quite "effectively." He has been getting the job done—and doing it fast. Now he finds himself up against a new situation in which his competence does not tend to measure up to his own level of aspiration.

If the laboratory staff tends to respond to the executive's difficulties by providing lectures that give, or experimental situations that provide, logical reasons to "prove" that the staff is correct, the staff will tend to deal with the problem by using the rational unilateral approach. Taking the rational approach is an easy step because the staff leaders presumably have more information on effective human relations than do the executives. However, the strategy has two serious disadvantages. First, it may drive the executives to counter the staff arguments with logical evidence that their views are not valid. Such a situation could lead to the executives' "uniting" against the staff in a win-lose intergroup battle. The second difficulty is that it "teaches' the executives that when the staff is "under attack" they tend to revert to the very behavior that they are asking the participants to modify.

There are two other alternatives which seem to skirt the difficulties above, although they do create other ones. However, these other difficulties can be used by the staff as the basis for new learning for both groups.

First, following the concept of authentic relationships, the staff should hide nothing, including the rationale behind the nature of the laboratory and their own behavior. Although this is presently being done in some laboratories, in my opinion, one should go further. For example, a rationale for the laboratory is usually based on the fundamental assumption held by the staff that the executives' interpersonal competence tends to be low relative to their rational competence. The staff believes that if the executive group is left to behave "naturally," it will tend to create dependence, conformity, interpersonal mistrust, and so on. If this is the case, the staff should communicate these beliefs to the executives in as caring, warm, and rational a manner as they have at their command. For it to "reach" the rationally oriented executives, the communication needs to be bolstered with rational evidence. As the reader has seen, we obtained evidence (from the research) and presented it to the executives.[21]

The attitudes and feelings with which the staff communicates these views are crucial. If the executives feel the data are used to "clobber" them, they will quite understandably become doubly hostile. However, diagnostic data can be communicated so it conveys the impression that the staff "cares" for the executives so much it has gone to great pains to check and recheck its findings before it asks them to consider a laboratory experience. For example, a medical doctor learns how to communicate various laboratory and clinical diagnostic findings in order to communicate to the patient the importance of certain therapy.

However, a result of this approach is to create a feeling on the part of the executives of dependency upon the staff. Historically, laboratory staffs have attempted to skirt this dependency

---

[21] In a laboratory composed of executives from different companies, the evidence needed could be obtained by conducting some very simple research interviews at the outset of the laboratory.

relationship by not communicating openly their assumptions about the interpersonal competence of the participants. In not doing so, they have created, in my opinion, a deeper dependency plus an equally deep mistrust based upon the participants' feelings that the staff is "holding back."

Instead of skirting this particular dependency relationship, we planned to face up to it as a "natural" one. The staff would not be establishing authentic relationships if it did otherwise. How could we expect the executives (in the social system of the kind described in the previous chapter) to develop a diagnosis which suggests that they are influenced by the values of their social system which will not tend to enhance their effectiveness?

Moreover, if at this point they do become dependent upon the staff, the staff can reflect this back to the participants, pointing out its naturalness as well as its potential trap. If the staff and the executives can develop methods by which this dependence becomes interdependence, then the executives would have developed insight and skills they can use "back home" when they are in the position of being the "expert."

The second strategy, therefore, is to utilize the dependency situations as a learning experience. This means that the staff will tend to reward and encourage the expression of the negative and hostile feelings that the executives probably have as a result of their dependency, frustrations, and so on. For example, the staff should be able to respond to the defensive reactions by descriptive nonevaluative feedback; by permitting the executives to own their feelings, and by suggesting ways in which they can enlarge their openness to new values and set the stage for experimentation. If this behavior is successful, the executives have experienced not only an effective way to resolve difficult emotional issues; but they have had an opportunity to experience emotionally the defensiveness, frustration, and so on, that their subordinates tend to experience "back home."

Hopefully, this is enough by way of introduction. Describing a laboratory is indeed a difficult task, as the reader has seen by now. One more step might be helpful. Let us become much more concrete about the strategy of a T-group, the core activity of a laboratory.

7

Interpersonal Authenticity
and the T-Group

       □ In the previous chapter, the T-group experience has been described from various points of view. I should like to present in some detail a preliminary statement of a framework developed for viewing a T-group experience. This is done for two reasons. First, to show how the same model used to diagnose the executive system in planning the laboratory can also be used to guide the "educators'" behavior in a T-group.[1] As far as I know it is the first time that the same model has been used to guide all three activities.

The second reason is to help differentiate the laboratory and T-group sessions held in this program from others. It is important to do so, lest the reader infer that all T-groups and laboratories are alike. There are important differences among them. At this stage of development, it is important to preserve the differences. For example, I feel more distant from some of my colleagues working in laboratory education than I do with some individuals who have serious questions about the entire process. It would be sad indeed if attempts were made to create a conformity to one or a few points of view. As it is, the differences encourage disagreement and discussion, which in turn could lead to further empirical research.

---

[1] I use the term "educator" fully realizing the potential confusion with its traditional meanings. I use it to emphasize that in my opinion an educator is interested in the total individual, that is, the emotional as well as the intellective. Historically, the term "educator" has been limited to the intellective dimension.

153

A Frame of Reference for Understanding T-Groups

If one examines the model that purports to describe how interpersonal competence decreases (Chapter 2), one will note that the inputs are the basic values people hold about effective human relations. According to the model it is these values that need to be influenced if interpersonal competence is to increase and if the "negative" outputs (conformity, dependence, management by crises) are to be decreased. The modification of the values is a major objective of the T-group.

Changing values is difficult for two reasons. First, changing the values of individuals effectively requires that the educational processes used should not violate the very values that the executives (in this case) are being asked to consider. Most lecture and discussion teaching is typically based upon values similar to those that the executives presently hold (for example, the teacher is in control; he directs; he focuses on the objectives; and he emphasizes rationality). Consequently, there is a need for a significantly different *process of education*. The second reason is that values are not on the same order as skills to influence people in order "to keep them happy." Values are the emotionally rooted, intellectually expressed "personal directives" that individuals hold that serve to compel their behavior in a particular direction. They cannot be "taught," "issued," "sold" or "plugged into" people (who have an opportunity to choose freely) regardless of the oratorical, persuasive and pedagogical skill of the teacher.

Lewin[2] pointed out years ago the first step is to unfreeze the old values. The group members need to be placed into a situation where they can see, experience, and evaluate firsthand the impact that their present values (about effective human relations) have upon each other and the group. In our case, this means the T-group experience should first help the executives to experience for themselves the relatively high degree to which they (1) give evaluative, defensive-producing feedback (2) do not own, indeed, are not aware of their feelings (3) do not help others to own their feelings, (4) are not, or

---

[2] Kurt Lewin (Gertrud Weiss Lewin, ed.), *Resolving Social Conflicts* (New York: Harper & Bros., 1948).

permit others to be open, and (5) to experiment and take risks.

If such a training experience can be created, then they will experience the impact of their clobbering as well as the resulting mistrust and nonauthenticity in their relationships. Also, as they generate their own frustration for "not being able to get started," for not making quick decisions *and* as they see that all these are *their* responsibility and not the educator's, there may be aroused within them an emotional as well as intellectual awareness, of the (unintended) consequences of their present behavior upon each other and upon the organization.

If so, the members should then tend to begin to experience a sense of internal disequilibrium or "dissonance." On the one hand, they have typically viewed themselves as helping others to develop themselves as well as to develop an effective organization. Now they "see"—through their own experience—that the behavior they felt was effective actually may be a major cause of the problems that they dislike (for example, conformity, dependency, management by crises, and so on).

The initial reaction of the members will probably be one of struggle to project the responsibility upon others (for example, the educator) and everything (the T-group or the laboratory) but themselves. However, if the educator does not become defensive (and this tends to be most easily accomplished if he has literally said very little during the initial sessions) then the members have little choice but to face their own behavior, each other, and the human culture which they have begun to create. It is usually an unsettling experience for individuals to realize that when left to their own resources and competence, the result tends to be a culture that clobbers, suppresses human individuality and growth. Indeed, many groups discover that if left to their own resources, they have the capacity to create a situation similar to the groups created by the Chinese brainwashers.[3] Typically, the reaction to this uncomfortable revelation is to attempt to "jam the blame for this down the educator's throat." However, as the group develops adequate intellectual and emotional strength, the members begin to face the issue squarely. They begin to admit that they have just experienced a rela-

---

[3] E. Schein, *Coercive Persuasion* (New York: W. W. Norton & Co., Inc., 1961).

tively inhuman situation created largely by their own hands.[4]

They now have a choice of beginning the long, painful, confusing process of altering their values or the choice of entrenching themselves deeper into their old values. If they select the latter course (which, empirically speaking, is rarely chosen), then the educator can push for consideration of the choice for growth. However, he can not push very far because if he is not careful, he could easily create a situation that results in the members feeling that they are being coerced to change in spite of their decision not to do so. Under these conditions the individuals would be placed in the educational system that is similar, in terms of values, to the present executive system.

If the members choose to experiment with growth, then they are ready to move forward. The decision to move on is not easily made. It tends to involve "proving" to one's self that it *is* one's self who is responsible for some of the problems that one is facing. The degree of willingness to consider change varies with groups and within the same group at different times. Some members are ready to move forward earlier than others. This differential readiness for change could be an asset, because if all individuals were equally ready for change at the same time, there would be an overloading of the communication channels. Also, it is useful to have some people resisting, because they will tend to provide the testing that the new ideas require if they are to be internalized.

The Expectations of the Members

The T-group experience begins with the educator making explicit that it is designed to help human beings (1) to explore their values and their impact upon others, (2) to determine if they wish to modify the old values and develop new ones, and (3) to develop awareness of how groups can inhibit as well as facilitate human growth and decision making. Thus, a T-group does not begin objectiveless as far as the educator is concerned.

---

[4] In the language of Harvey, Hunt, and Schroder, the members came expecting a reliable unilateral type of training. They are actually exposed to an informational interdependent training experience which they interpret as being primarily unreliable unilateral training experience. Hence, the frustration and aggression.

It has a purpose, and this purpose, for the educator, is emotionally and intellectually clear.

However, the educator realizes that the purpose is, at best, only intellectually clear to the members. He believes that one of the initial activities of the T-group should be to create the conditions where the members can "project" their behavior, diagnose its consequences, and "own up to them." Only after these conditions are fulfilled will the members have "seen" the purpose emotionally as well as intellectually.

To begin to establish these conditions, the educator states that he has no specific goals in mind for them. Moreover, he offers no specific agenda, no regulations, rules, and norms by which they should act. This "vacuum" of leadership, goals, and so on, is created so the members can fill it with their own leadership, goals, rules.

There is very little that is nondirective about a T-group educator's role. He is highly concerned with growth, and he acts in ways that he hopes to enhance it. He is nondirective, however, in the sense that he does not require others to accept these conditions. As one member of the T-group, he will strive sincerely and openly to help establish a culture that can lead to increased authentic relationships and interpersonal competence. However, he realizes that he can push just so far. If he goes too far, he will fall into the trap of masterminding the education. This is a trap in which the members would be glad to see him fall, since it would decrease their uncomfortableness and place him in a social system similar (in values) to their own. In other words, his silence, the lack of predefined objectives, leadership, agenda, rules, and so on, are not designed to be a malicious or sadistic activity to hurt people. True, these experiences may hurt, but the hypothesis is that the pain is "in the service of growth."

Anyone who has taken the responsibility to create such learning conditions knows the tremendous responsibility that the educator accepts. The conditions could hurt beyond the expectation of the educator. He must be ever alert to sense the impact and to protect individuals who may need it. Thus, the educator does not intend to retreat from the group or shirk his responsibilities.

THE MEMBERS' INITIAL EXPECTATIONS OF THE EDUCATOR'S ROLE

At the outset, the group members typically expect that the educator will lead them. This expectation is understandable for several reasons. First, an educator in our culture tends to do precisely this. Second, because of the newness of the situation, the members may also fear that they are not competent to deal with it effectively. They naturally turn to the educator for assistance. It is common in our culture that if one member of a group has more information than the others as to how to cope with the new and difficult situation, he is expected by the others, *if he cares for them,* to help them cope with the new situation. For example, if I am in a cave with 10 others who are lost and I know how to get out, it would be from their viewpoint the height of noncaring not to help them get out. Finally, the members may turn to the educator because they have not as yet developed much trust for each other.

The problem for the educator is not how he should withhold his resources. The problem is how he can use his information, wisdom, and skills in the service of individual and group growth.

One way that I have found to be helpful during the early stages of a T-group is to tell the group that I understand how they could feel dependent upon me. But I believe that learning can take place more effectively if they first develop an increasing sense of trust of one another and a feeling that they can learn from one another. I freely admit that silence is not typical of me and that I need to talk, to be active, to participate. In fact, I may even feel a mild hostility that I am in a situation in which I cannot participate in the way that I desire. Thus, anything they (members) can do to help me "unfreeze" by decreasing their dependence upon me would be deeply appreciated. I add that I realize that this is not easy, and that I will do my share to help decrease the dependence upon me.

One way the educator can help the members to decrease their dependency upon him is to support those individuals who show early signs of attempting to learn. This would be especially true for those who show signs of being open, experimentally minded, and willing to take risks by exposing their behavior. How can an educator accomplish this?

There are several cues that may be helpful. First, he can look for individuals who are not so highly upset by the initial ambiguity of the situation that they are ready to begin to learn. One sign of such an individual is one who can be open about the confusion that he is experiencing. He is able to own his feelings of being confused, without becoming hostile toward the educator or to the others. Such an individual is willing to look at his and others' behavior under stress, diagnose it, and attempt to learn from it. Some of these individuals even raise questions about other members' insistence that the educator should get them out of the ambiguous situation.

Another opening that the educator can look for is insistence by one of the individuals that the educator has created the ambiguity just to be hostile. The educator can provide such an individual with feedback to help him see the impact that his behavior (that is, hostility) is having upon him. There are two reasons for this intervention. One is to reinforce (with feelings) that the educator does deeply care for them and that he is not consciously attempting to be hostile. Secondly, the intervention may help to unfreeze others to explore their hostility toward the educator or toward each other. Such explorations can provide rich data for the group to diagnose and from which to learn.

Some educators believe that they should not make their strategy explicit. They prefer to interpret the members' negative reaction to the confusing T-group situation and to the educator's silence, as a sign of a deep dependency upon him. They believe that the group will not tend to progress unless they "work through" their authority problems with the educator. In my experience, a strategy of this type infuriates the members because they can see (and they are correct) that *he is* partially responsible for their predicament. They are also infuriated because his interpretation is on such a deep clinical level that they do not understand it. The result is that they experience an even deeper dependence upon the educator at the very time that he insists they decrease their dependence upon him.

To resolve the resulting hostilities, the educator is required to delve into deeper levels of behavior. But, in doing so, the educator has created a self-fulfilling prophecy. It may be true that any dependence that human beings experience can be ultimately related to a deeper tendency for dependence upon authority. It is *also* true, however, that many human beings have worked through or have suppressed this basic dependence so they can operate relatively effectively in reality. If they have not, then I question if they belong in a T-group (more of this later). The educator through his pushing the members to deeper clinical levels can create an emotional situation where, indeed, these deep feelings do become operative. At this point, he is correct that the group will not move forward unless the members resolve their basic dependency problems.

Another approach commonly used, which seems to me to be equally dysfunctional for learning (but may be valid for therapy), is for the educator to remain absolutely silent as the group struggles through their initial confusions and frustrations. Under these conditions the educator in the eyes of the members is "teaching" them by his behavior a very strange lesson. Growth occurs when the leader psychologically separates himself from the members. The members' anxiety that the educator does not really care for them is, in their eyes, confirmed by the silence. The anxiety is also confirmed if the educator behaves differently inside the T-group than he does outside. If, for example, he tends to talk and participate freely outside the group, this apparent lack of genuineness may understandably be interpreted by the members that under the difficult T-group conditions, the educator is not able to establish authentic relationships.

Jerome Frank suggests that there is nothing more anxiety-producing than uncertainty. It is understandable that the members immediately feel dependent upon the educator because he is viewed as having information that will help or that will harm.[5] If an educator through his silence comes to be perceived by the members as desiring to harm them, they may adapt, Frank suggests by outward conformity to escape reprisal and/or by becoming resentful and hostile.

On the other hand, Frank continues, if one (and this is

---

[5] Jerome D. Frank, *Persuasion and Healing* (Baltimore, Md.: Johns Hopkins Press, 1961), p. 34.

consonant with our position) engenders hope, exhibits a sense of caring, one may directly improve the members sense of well-being, heighten their self-confidence, and increase their openness and willingness to learn.[6] At the same time this would also strengthen the sense of dependency. However, it is suggested that dependency "in a climate of caring" can be used to develop growth and autonomy.

To summarize the objective of the educator, therefore, is to develop an effective membership role in the group. But this is the objective of everyone else in the T-group. All members have the same challenge. Now, the idea that the role of the educator is different from the member roles vanishes. Any difference in role is now seen as being valid primarily during the early stages of the T-group. According to our theory, he can accomplish this by helping himself and others to establish authentic relationships. Another way to say the same thing is to state that the T-group has at the outset one member (the educator) who is presumably more capable of establishing authentic relationships than are the remaining members. The members, therefore, have a resource who can help them increase the degree of authenticity in their relationships within the group. They could, however, utilize him in such a way that no one develops.

THE EDUCATOR AS A MODEL AND THE PROBLEM OF MIMICKING

The educator's behavior now may serve for what it is, as valid a model as he can manifest of how he would attempt to help create an effective group and integrate himself into that group so he becomes as fully functioning a member as possible and others have a similar opportunity if they wish.[7] The model is his; he admits owning it, but he is *not* attempting to "sell" it to others or in any way to coerce them to own it.

Viewing the educator as a source of "model behavior" leads to the question of the members' simply learning to mimic

---

[6] *Ibid.*

[7] This view is similar to the existential view that the commonality between the therapist and patients is their quest for "satisfaction through lessening self-deception." Hugh Mullan and Iris Sanguiliano, "The Subjective Phenomenon in Existential Psychotherapy," *Journal of Existential Psychiatry,* Vol. V (Summer, 1961), pp. 17–34.

him. Most educators tend to believe that mimicking is a sign of "regression," "overdependence," "poor growth," and so on. Although this may be the case, there is an alternative view that may be worth considering.

After one has begun to "unfreeze" his previous values and behavior, he finds himself in the situation of throwing away the old and having nothing new that is concrete and workable. This tends to create states of vacillation, confusion, anxiety, ambivalence, and so on.[8] These states in turn may induce the individual to "hang on" to the old with even greater tenacity. To begin to substitute the new behavior for the old behavior, he must see (1) that he can carry out the new behavior effectively and (2) that the new behavior leads to the desired results.[9]

One may predict that under these conditions individuals are going to try out any bit of behavior that represents the "new." This is one important purpose of the T-group. Experimentation is not only sanctioned, it is rewarded. If one is experimenting with new behavior, then one may predict that he will tend to defend himself from experiencing failure. One relatively safe defense is to "try out the educator's behavior." It is at this point that the individual is mimicking. Instead of condemning this behavior, I find it perfectly natural. It does help to reduce the probability of psychological failure, and it does give the individual some behavior with which to experiment. The educator should behave so the individual can feel free to mimic and *to talk about the mimicking and explore it openly, because* it would be helpful if he could become aware and accept the fact that he does *not* own the behavior. The behavior with *which he is experimenting is the educator's.* If the educator is not anxious about the mimicking, the member may begin to safely explore the limits of the new behavior. He also may begin to see whether or not the educator's behavior is, for him, realistic.

For example, in one session the members of a T-group attacked one member for "acting too much like the educator."

---

[8] Roger Barker, Beatrice A. Wright, and Millie R. Gonick, *Adjustment to Physical Handicap and Illness,* Social Science Research Council Bulletin 55, 1946, pp. 19–54.

[9] Ronald Lippitt, Jeanne Watson, and Bruce Westley, *The Dynamics of Planned Change* (New York: Harcourt, Brace & World, Inc., 1958).

"What are you trying to do, pull an Argyris?" someone asked. The individual responded that this was a crucial question in his mind. The more that he listened to himself, he continued, the more he heard himself, "saying things that the educator had said or would probably say." He asked the group for any help that they could give him to test to see if the new behavior is really him or if he is mimicking. A deep and open discussion ensued in which the members evolved the following learnings:

1. Initially, the behavior was not really the individual's but the educator's.

2. As the individual experimented with aspects of the educator's behavior, he began to experience some success. The success was enough to lead him to the conclusion that he wanted to incorporate the new approach.

3. Because of the experience in the T-group, he was intellectually and emotionally aware of the dangers of dependence and mimicking and of the value of accepting oneself. It followed for him that trying out the educator's approach was only a first step. The next series of steps turned out to be, for him, much more significant and difficult. After testing and tentatively accepting a new bit of behavior, he then had to modify, and internalize it until it was integrated and consonant with his self. He also had to experience as many of the value implications of the new behavior as he could. Next, he had to develop a value which he could make explicit to himself and to others that became a personal command and acted as an influencer of his behavior in relevant situations. In addition, the individual eventually found that he was capable of creating new behavior which went beyond the educator's repertoire, the T-group members, and indeed the entire experience.

4. The members' pointed out that it was possible for them to see behavior in the member that was genuine to that member. Thus, as the member began to increase his psychological success in developing the "new" approach, he began to feel the new approach to be a part of him, and the members began to confirm these feelings.

5. The process of incorporating new attitudes and developing consonant behavior is, therefore, one of progressively "observing," "testing," "modifying and molding," and "expand-

ing," "creating" new behaviors, and *simultaneously* organizing
these experiences with the use of a value which then provide
the "personal command" to behave in a particular way under
specific conditions. The process is a complex one which does not
evolve in the simple sequence described above. One can be creating new behavior, testing other, modifying still other, or re-
testing some of the "original" from which one had thought he
had evolved an approach that was his own. In this connection
Luchins and Luchins[10] have suggested that we differentiate
between *cognitive imitation* and *rote imitations*. The former is
repetition when one understands the principles underlying the
behavior, or understands why it leads to success. The latter is
repetition devoid of such understanding. Cognitive imitation
can lead to growth and may be facilitated in a T-group.

6. Finally, the members concluded that in spite of their
initial fear of one of the members, mimicking was partially
valid. However, the exploration also helped them see that they
were projecting upon him some of their own concerns as well
as desires.

The analysis suggests mimicking can lead to establishing
authentic relationships. Once this possibility is admitted, we
can see several reasons why increased authenticity in relationships will *not* tend to lead to *continued* conscious or unconscious mimicking. First, since the individual who mimics does
not own this behavior (it is the educator's), he will not tend to
be responsible for it, and indeed the behavior will not be truly
his. To the extent that he is not accepting of it, he will tend to be
defensive toward himself and toward others who provide him
feedback about what they tend to perceive as his nonauthentic
behavior. This would be especially true under stressful conditions. To the extent that this occurs, the others (and he) will
not experience authenticity in their relationships. The mimicking behavior will therefore fail.

Another reason why mimicking tends to fail is that no one
educator can provide "models" of "proper behavior" for the full
complexity of situations in which the individual is immersed

---

[10] Abraham S. Luchins and Edith H. Luchins, "Imitation by Rote and by
Understanding," *Journal of Social Psychology*, Vol. LIV (June, 1961), pp. 175–
97.

during the laboratory and especially away from it. The person who attempts to learn through mimicking is therefore dependent upon and limited by his relationships with the educator. Ultimately, he will have to find himself in a situation with no appropriate model of behavior to use and will tend to regress to the old, or he will tend to be highly confused and ambivalent and tend to behave in a way that is clearly not himself.

We may conclude therefore that mimicking can be a first step toward growth. If, however, it becomes the only step, it will not lead to self-development. Realizing that all mimicking is not necessarily harmful may also help the educator to be more open and articulate about the values he believes can lead to increased authentic relationships and interpersonal competence. For example, I find it quite comfortable to admit and encourage mimicking in such activities as giving and receiving nonevaluative feedback, owning and helping others to own their feelings, openness, and risk taking. Anyone who learns these basic human skills (which for me includes developing the appropriate values) will not tend to become dependent, submissive, conforming, or require others to do the same. Depending upon the educator to help formulate a model which one can consider can lead to growth if the model itself is composed of these activities that lead to growth. Such dependence will tend to be temporary and in the service of growth.

The discussion of mimicking raises another question that plagues educators in T-groups. It deals with the relative value of education that focuses on skills versus that which focuses on basic philosophy. I am persuaded that effective change occurs when one's philosophy (or pattern of values) changes. However, I am equally persuaded that one cannot change one's personal philosophy by being only "philosophical." It is improbable for individuals to learn the philosophy without at times concentrating on the techniques. Individuals are understandably loathe to accept a somewhat new philosophy and apprehensive about their achieving competence in using it. It is at this point that the exposure to skills becomes valuable. The individuals can try out the behavioral implications of the philosophy. Moreover, they might test the relevance and worth of this philosophy to them by seeing if they are able to modify the skills and create new ones. It is through the process of actively modifying and creating new behavior and skills that the individuals can gain some feeling for the flexibility, applicability, and effectiveness of the philosophy.

Philosophy and its concomitant behavioral skills need not be separated from one another. The experience with skills can, if it is seen only as a means to an end, lead to the development and acceptance of a personal philosophy. The development of a philosophy, in turn, can lead the individual to increase his competence in modifying and creating new skills so the behavior he manifests is consonant with his self. Skills are to personal philosophy what empirical research is to basic theory in the sciences.

Educator Dominance and Member Dependence

Many T-group educators are anxious lest they do too much talking within the group. One of the commonly held hypotheses is that much talking on the part of the educator is a sign of group dependence upon him. But is this necessarily the case? An educator who typically says little could dominate the group with one sentence while a leader who talks much could bore the group for hours. In terms of our framework, the sheer amount of talking by the educator does not necessarily signify dependence. The question translates itself to: "Does what the educator say tend to enhance the degree of authenticity in the human relationships?" Thus it is conceivable that under certain conditions the leader would not say anything for two hours, while under other conditions, he could be the major contributor. Both could help to enhance authentic relationships.

Let us take an example.

It is quite common for the members to arrive at a point where they ask each other to vote on a "there and then" topic (that is, a topic which deals with situations outside the members' T-group experience). If I, as an educator, were asked to vote, I would respond that I could see that this was an important topic for them to discuss, but I would have to vote negatively because such discussions have not helped me to become more aware and accepting of self and others. I would not, as some do, tend to ask them, "I wonder why we are doing this" with the objective of throwing the discussion back to them, because this would be dishonest. I am really *not* wondering. I believe I know why they are doing it. And perhaps more important, I believe they feel that I know. Dishonesty does not lead to authentic relationships. If I am going to be questioned and coerced to talk, then I should prefer to do so rather than knowingly not be genuine.

Several questions may be asked at this point. Some would ask if such behavior does not rob the group of the opportunity to experience the futility of the "there and then" subjects. The answer is: "Not necessarily." If a group really wants to discuss a "there and then" topic, in my experience, it does so. Moreover, at times, I have found it possible to vote, "No," explain why, and then encourage them to try it if they wish.

The other possibility is that if it is important for them to learn to feel the futility of the experience, then I ought to say so. But do I really know it is necessary? Moreover, if I vote for a futile experience and later one of the members learn that I (the educator) knew it would be futile, it gives them the impression that I am at best, a manipulator, and at worst, a nonauthentic "clobberer" of group members. Can learning occur when the educator is perceived as a noncaring, nonauthentic individual?

The position above leads to some new difficulties in my experience. If the vote for a "there and then" topic is early in the history of the group, the members tend to see the "there and then" topic as relevant. Moreover, they are probably feeling quite frustrated for not being able to decide on a topic to discuss. If the educator votes in the negative that is usually in the minority, his vote is viewed as an unpopular if not hostile act, and he may be attacked. The educator is urged to "join up" and "go along with the overwhelming majority." In my own experience, if I maintain my position the group may override me and go on to have a futile experience in problem solving. This is their perogative. After the episode is over, it is then analyzed, and much learning usually takes place. The group may also see my view, and the tide may turn in my direction. If so, I tend to ask the group to help me explore and express the feelings that I had while I was a deviate. This usually brings us to the topic of establishing group norms and the sanctions necessary to protect the deviant.

During these discussions, I may be accused of blocking the

group, a feeling which each member may have had about other members but as yet has not said so openly. If I am told by someone that I am blocking the group, I usually feel thankful for the feedback and say so. Then I ask others how they feel about this particular behavior of mine. I attempt to accept their hostility as well as their praise if such should arise. The members soon learn that I will do my best to be open, to create conditions for others to be open where each one of us can own his feelings. In my experience, the probability for dependence upon me decreases, because the members experience the "safeness" of being hostile toward or praising me. Praise tends to be a problem because it is given so frequently, in our culture, to placate others, and to cover up interpersonal problems as well as to control human relationships. Under these conditions people have difficulty in dealing with praise because they do not know how to trust it.

In another instance—again early in the group's history—I told someone that I could not trust his feedback to me. He replied that this was not a gentlemanly answer. If I didn't trust him, I should say this to him outside the group. Again, the hostility on his part is understandable, and I said so. I probably had violated his (and others') standards of gentlemanly behavior. I then asked for feedback from others to check this hypothesis. It was largely confirmed. This request raised the issues of "How open do we want to be?" "How trusting are we of one another?" "Is it possible that if we are open, we would hurt one another?" All these questions are central ones for a T-group if it is to develop.

INDIVIDUAL VERSUS GROUP INTERVENTIONS

Some T-group educators tend to make most of their interventions on the individual personality level, some on the interpersonal level, and still others on the group level. The criteria for selection of the level of intervention are, for the most part, implicit and related to the personal biases as well as to the model each educator has developed of his role.

Authenticity theory provides some clear-cut suggestions regarding the strategy of interventions. First, an educator following authenticity theory would not tend to make interventions that in essence are clinical interpretations, especially genotypic or latent, that are beyond the members' comprehension. As is pointed out below, the members of the T-group are presumably selected on the basis that they are able to learn from others and help others to do the same. Individuals whose defenses are so great that they are unable to learn from the non-evaluative descriptive feedback should not participate. If they continually cause such defensiveness in themselves or others that a skilled therapist is needed with clinical concepts to make sense of the interchange, then they ought not participate in a T-group. Clinical interpretations, however, might be necessary if an individual is unexpectedly threatened by the T-group experience and requires emotional support. If possible, such interpretations might be made outside the T-group. If the individual is not able to continue without further clinical support, it might be best for all concerned that he leave the T-group.

On the other hand, interventions on the interpersonal level are central to authenticity theory. The educator *at the outset* would tend to focus on those interpersonal interventions that tend to help the members (1) to become aware of their present (usually) low potential for establishing authentic relationships (2) to become more skillful in providing and receiving non-evaluative descriptive feedback (3) to minimize their own and others' defensiveness, and (4) to become increasingly able to experience and own their feelings.

Although interpersonal interventions are usually made at the outset, it is important that the T-group *not* be limited to such interventions. After the members receive adequate feedback from one another as to their inability to create authentic relationships, they will tend to want to become more effective in their interpersonal relationships. It is at this point that they will need to learn that group structure and dynamics deeply influence the probability of increasing the authenticity of interpersonal relations. For example, as soon as the members realize that they must become more open with those feelings that typically they have learned to hide, they will need to establish group norms to sanction the expression of these feelings. Also, if members find it difficult in the group to express their important feelings, this difficulty will tend to be compounded if they feel they must "rush" their contribution and "say something quick" lest someone else takes over the communication channels. Ways must be developed by which members are able to use their share of the communication channels. Also, group norms are required that sanction silence and thought so that members do not feel coerced before they have thought it through to say something, out of fear they will not have an opportunity to say anything later.

An example of the interrelationship between interpersonal and group factors may be seen in the problems of developing leadership in a group. One of the recurring problems in the early stages of a T-group is the apparent need on the part of members to appoint a leader or a chairman. Typically, this need is rationalized as a group need because "without an appointed leader a group cannot be effective." For example, one member said, "Look, I think the first thing we need is to elect a leader. Without a leader we are going to get nowhere fast." Another added, "Brother, you are right. Without leadership there is chaos. People hate to take responsibility and without a leader, they will goof off."

There are several ways to cope with this problem, each of which provides important but different levels of learning. One approach is to see this as a group problem. How does leadership arise and remain helpful in a group? This level of learning is important and needs to be achieved.

Another possibility is first to help the group members explore the underlying assumptions expressed by those individuals who wanted to appoint leaders. For example, in the case illustrated above, both men began to realize that they were assuming that people "need" appointed leadership because, if left alone, they will not tend to accept responsibility. This implies a lack of confidence in and trust of people. It also implies mistrust of the people around the table. These men are suggesting that without an appointed leader the group will flounder and become chaotic.

In an attempt to use the incident above to help develop trust, the educator may raise the issue and ask the group to explore the assumptions implicit in the above statements about the importance of leadership. In this case, however, someone took the initiative and suggested that the comments above implied a lack of trust of the people around the table. Another individual suggested that another dimension of mistrust might also be operating. He was concerned how he would decide if he could trust the man who might be appointed as the leader. The discussion that followed illustrated to the group the double direction of the problem of trust. Not only do superiors have feelings of mistrust of subordinates but the latter may also mistrust the former.

One of the defendants of the need for leadership then said, "Look here, there is Mr. B over there who has been trying to say something for half an hour and hasn't succeeded. If we had a leader or if he was appointed as the leader temporarily, then he might get his point of view across." Several agreed with the observation. However, two added some further insightful comments. One said, "If we give Mr. B authority, he will never have to develop his internal strength so that he can get his point across without power behind him." "Moreover," added the other, "if he does get appointed as a leader, the group will never have to face the problem of how it can help to create the conditions for Mr. B to express his point of view." Thus, we see that attempting to cope with the basic problems of trust in a group can lead to an exploration of problems of group membership as well as requirements of effectively functioning groups.

Trust, therefore, is a central problem in a T-group. If this can be resolved, then the group has taken an important step in developing authentic relationships. As the degree of trust increases, "functional leadership" will then tend to arise spontaneously because individuals in a climate of mutual trust will tend to delegate leadership to those who are most competent for the given subject being discussed. In doing so, they also learn an important lesson about effective leadership.

Moreover, as was pointed out previously, the group will have to learn how to make decisions, to share power, rewards, and penalties in such a way that authenticity in human relationships is enhanced. This will require learning to become proficient in group census, consensus, distributed leadership, as well as establishing norms that sanction deviant behavior and the expression of the uniqueness of each member. In short, interpersonal authenticity and group effectiveness are intimately related.

Another reason why the group members ought not limit their interventions and learnings to the interpersonal level is that a group will not tend to become an effective task-oriented unit without having established effective means to diagnose problems, make decisions, and so on. It is as the group becomes a decision-making unit that the members can "test" the strength and depth of their learning. The pressure and stress of decision making can help to show the degree to which authenticity is apparent rather than real. It can also provide opportunity for further learning, because the member will tend to experience new aspects of themselves as they attempt to solve problems and make decisions. Similarly, as we have seen in our model, intergroup problems are central in organizations; therefore, intergroup training activities can also lead to further testing as well as enlarging of the learning that the members receive. However, according to this view, intergroup experiences ought not come until the members have learned enough on the interpersonal and group effectiveness level that they are able to achieve whatever goals they set and fulfill their aspirations regarding authentic relationships.

To summarize, a T-group educator guided by authenticity theory will at the outset tend to make most of his interventions on the interpersonal level. After the members evolve enough learning regarding their ineffectiveness in giving and receiving feedback and are ready to move on to acquiring and practicing the new behavior, it is important that they focus on creating an effective group. Thus, the idea uses both interpersonal and group interventions.

Some Differences between Therapy Groups and T-Groups

What is the difference between T-groups and therapy groups? Certainly both may be said to attempt to help the individual become more aware and accepting of himself and others. If so, how does a T-group differ from a therapy group? As research progresses, we will probably learn that T- and therapy groups differ only in degree. Perhaps, especially at these early stages, it may be more useful to accent the differences in order to add to the necessity of inquiry.

T-groups and therapy groups are the same in that change in human behavior, attitudes, and values do occur within them. But unless these changes are specified more concretely, we have not said much, since changes in behavior and attitudes can and do occur in everyday human relationships.

One way to differentiate T-groups from therapy groups is to say that a T-group should attempt to focus on that level of insight that all the members can provide one another. This will probably rule out—not completely, but as a rule—most of the deeper clinical insights that the educator is competent to offer.

There are at least two valid reasons for this suggestion. If the feedback to be received is going to be at that level which will tend to create an encounter primarily between the educator and any given member, then the remaining members will become observers while (if the insight is valid) becoming even more dependent upon the educator.

Second, therapy tends to go on in a particular culture or milieu. The therapeutic processes are primarily valid for the therapeutic setting and not to be used in an active sense in everyday life. Thus, a therapist in a social setting (for example, a meeting) may sense that one of the causes of a given individual's problems may be related to a fixation at an early childhood level. However, he will not tend to be able to communicate such insights to the individual because (1) the individual has not asked to be a patient and (2) a particular relationship would have had to be developed before such insights are communicated so they may be of help, and (3) awareness of the cause can be of minimal help to that individual while he is working in the meeting.

The point being suggested is that the clinical processes are powerful, and their power (in terms of helping the other) is largely limited (as perhaps it should be) to the therapeutic setting. A T-group should help individuals to develop those relationships and processes that can be used in everyday life.

Bettelheim's analysis, which I unfortunately read too late,

describes better than I do the point that I have been trying to make.[11] Bettelheim suggests three reasons why psychoanalysis (and perhaps a good deal of clinical psychological theory) does not tend to offer guidance toward what is the positive nature of man, his "goodness" and "greatness."[12] First, psychoanalysis has emphasized pathology and primarily its destructive influences. Second, it assumes that the goal for self-realization is achieved by ridding a man "of what ails him." Third, and this comes closest to the point I attempted to make above, it is a powerful but highly specialized, conditioning social situation. Consequently, it is unable to draw from the wealth of health in the environment. Thus, psychoanalysis is a philosophy which by ". . . being fascinated with pathology ends up (without really wishing to) by neglecting life."

A T-group, on the other hand emphasizes the constructive, healthy, positive aspects of life. It has to, if for no other reason than that the educator is not there to lend his skilled professional advice to analyze the pathological aspects of their behavior. The group, if it is to succeed, must rely primarily upon its *member* resources with minimum depth interpretation from the educator. Without conceptual tools to get at pathology or their deeper motives, the members must discover what Bettelheim calls the "good experiences" of life, those that are the heart of sane living. If they are unable to do so (even with the help of the educator) then the group will be left at the mercy of the destructive forces and eventually fail. Here is a crucial reason why T-groups need to have as their goals the increased effectiveness of all members and of the group as a whole. These goals act to coerce (responsible) members to behave constructively. Otherwise, since they lack the clinical concepts to cope with destructive pathology, they will tend to fail. This also illustrates why T-groups need to be composed of relatively healthy individuals, that is, individuals who have available to them and are able to help others express constructive, caring behavior that can overcome the destructive tendencies.

---

[11] Bruno Bettelheim, *Informed Heart: Autonomy in a Mass Age* (Glencoe, Ill.: The Free Press of Glencoe), pp. 21–28.

[12] This is not true for the works of men such as Rogers, Maslow, May, Fromm, Kubie, and Sullivan.

Thus, T-groups differ from therapy groups in terms of level of behavior considered for examination. In the T-group, the majority of feedback remains more or less on the immediately experienced and/or observable level. The deepest one may go would be to the preconscious. One may receive feedback about the impact of one's self upon others as well as to give feedback on the impact others are having upon that individual. To put this another way, the feedback should remain as much as possible on the level of *nonevaluative descriptive feedback* of how one is affecting the others, as reported by those others and not by an expert (or anyone else) in terms of inferences about why the individual is behaving as he does. One difference between a T-group and everyday relationships is that eventually everyone receives the feedback presumably in a climate of support and openness with minimal distortion or evaluation on the part of the sender.

Immediate experience of others does not tend to be in terms of motives, needs, and so on. These are concepts that may be legitimately used to explain the probable underlying personality dynamics of human behavior. However, such explanations are not, from this viewpoint, an objective of the T-group. The dynamics of human behavior are best understood in a clinical relationship where an expert is present to make such inferences. Nothing is as disruptive and nonauthentic in a group as 12 lay individuals attempting to provide "two-bit psychoanalyses" of each other. Also an excellent way for an educator to create strong dependence is to make clinical interpretations obviously beyond the capacity of the others. If an educator feels a clinical analysis is important for a given individual, he may offer such help to that individual and on a private basis.

Although it may not be relevant to ask the "why" questions regarding psychodynamics of individual personalities, it is possible to ask many "why" questions at the group level. For example, "Why is a group having decision-making difficulties?" or "Why is the group unable to support the deviant?" are questions that can be answered substantially by simply asking the members to examine their communication channels, consensus activities, and so on. Also, it is possible to ask an individual a "why" question about behavior related to the group's culture. Thus, an individual can feel uncomfortable in being "open" when the group's culture is restrictive and does not sanction openness. Finally, the "why" questions that explain an individual's strategy in a group are certainly open to questioning. For example, the question "Why are you supporting him?" is admissable if we are looking for a reply on the level of "I am supporting him because all of you are clobbering him, and I want to hear his view." However, a question that attempts to get at the deeper psychological needs—for example, "Why do you need to support the oppressed?"—would not be relevant.

To summarize, a T-group is successful if the individual can become more aware and accepting of himself and can help others to become more aware and accepting of themselves, through giving and receiving minimally distorted, nonevaluative, descriptive (of behavior) feedback. The requirement implies that self-awareness and acceptance that must come from other than such descriptive feedback is not relevant to the T-group.

The requirement also implies at least three attributes that are necessary for each individual to manifest. First, a relatively strong ego that is not overwhelmed by unconscious conflicts. Second, the individual's defenses should be so low that he can hear what others say to him accurately and with minimal threat to his self, without the aid of a professional scanning and filtering system (that is, the therapist). Third, the individual ought to communicate his thoughts and feelings with minimal distortion. In other words, the operational criterion of minimal threat is that the individual does not tend to distort greatly what he or others say, nor does he tend to condemn others or himself.

This criterion can be used in helping to select individuals for the T-group experience. *If the individual must distort or condemn himself or others to the point that he is unable to do anything but to continue to distort the feedback that he gives and receives, then he ought not to be admitted to a T-group.*[13]

---

[13] I believe the "compulsiveness" or "rigidity" of behavior is the same phenomenon that Dr. Lawrence S. Kubie suggests is the heart of neurotic problems. *Neurotic Distortion Of The Creative Process* (Lawrence, Kansas: University of Kansas Press, 1958), pp. 20–22.

To put this another way, T-groups, compared to therapy groups, assume a higher degree of health—not illness, that is, a higher degree of self-awareness and acceptance. This is an important point to make to those attending a laboratory so one may make it clear that individuals ought not to be sent to the laboratory if they are highly defensive. Rather, the relatively healthy individuals capable of learning from others to enhance their degree of effectiveness are the kinds of individuals to be selected to attend.

8

The T-Group: Examples
of Major Themes

□ To provide the reader with some idea
of the subjects discussed at the labo-
ratory as well as the "climate" developed, I will attempt to describe in highly summarized form some of the discussions that
took place in the T-groups and in the sessions on organizational
diagnoses. Selections are taken from these two types of sessions, because they represent nearly 80 per cent of the learning
situations. The remainder of the time was spent in lectures and
a few sessions on individual development.

Let us now turn to the T-groups.

Session I

As often happens, the first meeting began with an extremely loud, deafening, uncomfortable silence. Someone finally broke it by laughingly asking the man next to him where
he was born. After the whispered reply the group broke out
into hilarious laughter probably related more to the high degree
of uncomfortableness then to anything else. At a deeper level
the concern regarding "Can we get this group going?" could
have mirrored the fear of failure.

Interestingly enough, someone raised the question, as to
whether people worried about failing in the company; two
supported this as an important issue. The discussion was picked
up by a member who "carried it" outside the scope of the group
seated around the table by commenting that this fear was true
in all of industry. The discussion of failure continued with the

178

subject being referred to "some particular leader," a "hypothetical group," "those kinds of people who have fear." Someone brought the discussion closer to the group by saying, "Don't you [any of you] often feel discouraged—" Another almost brought it clearly to a particular individual around the table by asking, "Let me ask, don't you think that you push [pause]—I mean don't you think personally . . . don't you think *individuals* push—not anyone specific—push to stifle?"

No. 2 pointed out, "It is interesting that we have started by talking about one of the most negative aspects of our business." Educator A asked No. 2 if he wasn't implying that people around the table may have fears. No. 2 nodded his head affirmatively but said nothing, nor did anyone else.

No. 7 then suggested that fear of failure is not a good thing to have. It can make a team weak. Educator B remarked he felt No. 7's comment could make him feel that "fear of failure was bad." "Perhaps," he continued, "I need to feel free to say that I have fears of failure without fearing I'm going to be clobbered or seen as 'weak.'" The discussion continued with No. 7 concluding that perhaps "I'm really talking about my own makeup. Maybe, I don't like fear of failure." Others began to open up by providing examples of how "people" hide failure. No. 2, for example, described a hard-driving executive who gets "trapped" into a discussion and, "suddenly you discover that he is at war, inside." Interestingly, No. 2 discovered later on that *he* was such a leader.

The "positive" aspects of failure were explored with the suggestion by No. 4 that it may "keep people moving." Most people agreed that fear of failure can do this, but wondered if it was good for the company. They pointed out that it caused conformity, dependency, fear of risk taking, fear of thinking, and compulsive desire to "go, go, go—and keep going." The group also concluded that they tended to rationalize failure (*a*) by blaming the other departments, (*b*) by saying it's not important, and (*c*) by pushing to kill a point that is threatening.

The discussion expanded to the exploration of other motives. Some issues that were discussed were the need to be essential to essential decisions, the need to have one's abilities recognized, to obtain power, to identify with an important organization.

This led to an exploration of the meaning of loyalty. Some illustrative comments were:

No. 5: I feel badly inside when I disagree with my boss but don't say anything. In fact, I act as if I agree. Then I leave the meeting and act as if I never agreed. I ought to say to my boss, "I disagree."

No. 2 (nods affirmatively): I rationalize it by saying 51 per cent of any decision is what you do after you've made it.

No. 7: Let's assume we made a decision, and you didn't like it, and you defended it to others. This isn't dishonest. You're part of a team. You shouldn't feel you're a hypocrite. Your conscience shouldn't bother you.

No. 10: Maybe it depends upon the depth and scope of the decision.

No. 3: Does this mean that we can never stop a meeting until complete consensus?

No. 10: It's damn difficult to "sell" this position to high up by those below.

No. 2: Maybe we simply must defer to the leader. It's the boss' ultimate responsibility. I have learned to shut up and not defend something that I don't believe in. I then let the boss defend it.

B[1]: I wonder how the boss would feel. However, doesn't he want support from the subordinates?

No 7: This is one of the penalties against individualism in a large organization. We cannot have complete agreement. We don't believe in all things. Yet we *must* uphold policies.

No. 10: But is this operating most effectively.

B (to No. 7): I hear you're telling people around the table that they shouldn't have some of the feelings that they have.

No. 10: But I for one don't listen to him [No. 7]. The hell with him [laugh].

No. 7: Let me defend myself. I was trying to tell No. 10 that he shouldn't feel badly.

No. 11 (to No. 7): I shouldn't feel badly about defending that which I believe. These are *my* feelings!

No. 7: No—I—

No. 10: The point is not whether I should or should not feel badly. It is: Do you help me explore my feelings?

No. 7 (smiles): I can see that I may have been stifling.

---

[1] A and B represent the two educators.

No. 2: Why should anyone want to hold onto and explore his feelings? What good does it do?

B: Let's ask No. 10.

No. 10: I'm not sure I understand your question.

No. 2: What good does it do to have these feelings?

A: Is it a matter of good? He has them.

No. 2: Okay, but if you say to me that you have strong feelings and it hurts me, I'd say, "Okay, change them." You ought to rationalize yourself to the point of not having them. The feelings are purposeless.

No. 10: You're using me as an example, let me answer. That comment would really hurt me. Worse than telling me to jump overboard.

No. 4: Wait a minute. You brought your point up so that we can discuss it.

No. 10: Yes.

A: But, what encouragement do we give him if we tell him he is wrong for feeling this way?

No. 2: Wait a minute—that's unfair, darn it.

B: If we are going to make it unfair, let me add another aspect. I felt, No. 2, that you were saying to No. 10 that if he were as intellectually bright as you, he could intellectually rationalize his feelings just as you can.

No. 2: Maybe that's it. Let me say what I *really* thought. I've had the same problem—It hurt me, too, and I kick myself for it, then I have to say, "What good does all this do to me?" I was trying to convey this to No. 10.

No. 10: This is a great difference.

No. 2: Yes, I see—I really pushed.

B: And one of the values about this learning is that you became helpful to No. 10 when you told him the problems that you had in this area and how you have strived to resolve them.

No. 2: That's an interesting observation.

Obviously these short vignettes of the first meeting do not even begin to describe the richness, complexity, difficulty, confusion, and exploration that occurred. The most one can hope that they do is give the reader a feeling for the kind of themes (content) discussed and the processes of the discussion. The group began by talking about fear of failure in "other" organizations and "other" people. Soon they began to get closer to the people around the table. This led one of the men to point out that fear of failure was a problem in their company. The educator attempted to help the individuals to talk about their own feelings of failure. Perhaps the topic was too difficult to discuss, because a short silence ensued. Note the educator did not push for his topic. He suggested a direction, but he left the choice up to the group.

The direction was changed by a member, No. 7, who suggested that "fear of failure is bad." The group started to talk about their feelings openly but did so with these feelings that were "more acceptable" and "safer" to discuss.

Basic feeling needs were then explored. This led to the concept of loyalty, which was examined in terms of the concept of loyalty "back home." With the help of the educators, the concept was also explored in terms of the kind of loyalty the men were requiring of one another around the table. For example, when many people felt that feelings shouldn't be explored and No. 10 felt the opposite, they attempted to coerce No. 10 to agree with them. "Loyalty" to the group at this particular moment meant agreement with the majority. The members then became aware that they probably did the very same thing back home to the deviant. Finally some, especially No. 2, became aware that he was telling No. 10 not to own his feelings because he, No. 2, had tried to do this in the past and felt that he had failed.

This interchange indicated one of the major kinds of learning that can occur in a meeting. The members explored a human problem in terms of its individual, small-group, and organizational aspects, seeing how each level influenced the others.

Session II

The session began with several questions and comments, probably with the hope that one of these might lead to a fruitful discussion. Some of these were: (1) "Are we really at our top effectiveness?" (2) "Maybe we are more marginal" (3) "I'm wondering if we really understand our own feelings" (4) "You've got to capitalize on what you are."

No. 2 commented that the group seemed to be trying to get started. He added, "To me, we're warming up. I feel like an 18-year-old." Someone added, "Soon we'll *really* say what we're really thinking," and another said, "I've already come to realize that maybe we haven't been saying what's really on our mind." This statement verbalizes something that people may not have been fully aware of, namely, how much they tended to withhold feelings. This awareness led to an insightful discussion about how open one can be with feelings. In reading the discussion below, one might recall the diagnosis in the previous chapter that 100 per cent of the executives felt that feelings were not important in and should not be considered relevant to business.

No. 1: It isn't safe to be open.

No. 6: I dismiss problems that aren't in my shop.

No. 2: I am upset when someone forms an opinion of my motives. They're wrong—I think that he thinks I am a dog, and I dislike this.

B: And I did this to you in the previous meetings [explains]?

No. 2: Yes—exactly.

B: The fact that you didn't mention it made me more uncomfortable because I felt that I had upset you.

No. 7: If he had really learned, wouldn't he had been open and told you that he disagreed?

B: And also express his resentment.

No. 2: Yes, I felt resentful. It's true that I didn't say so.

No. 7: I suspect that if a person in our company said, "I resent it," it would cause a person to withdraw. I'm not saying it's bad.

No. 10: We all have hidden feelings. I'd rather have my hidden feelings communicated in a hidden manner.

No. 2: My problem is when my motive is misunderstood.

No. 7: It's a good point—happens to me, and I probably do it to others. I resent someone saying, "It's really this way; you don't understand?" I resent this. They aren't listening to me.

No. 2: This raises another concern. If my motives are misunderstood, imagine what happens down below.

A: Maybe when we speak of resentment, we dislike them because we fear that they will last forever. Maybe we resent only for that moment.

No. 7 and No. 6: Agreed.

B: We speak as if we can hide our resentment. I sensed No. 2's resentment even though he tried to hide it. I now feel our relationship is more open because I can say what I really feel.

No. 7: Maybe in our culture it's wrong to have our feelings so close to our sleeves.

No. 10: I really don't think it's humanly possible to have real open discussion.

No. 8: You can do it when you're drunk.

A: The trouble with the "drunk" strategy is that it assumes "I'm going to find out about him without him finding out about me."

B: I felt that some of you are really asking how far we can go—

A: We cannot tell you how far. It is up to you.

No. 1: Are you implying the greater openness, the more effective? Maybe we should hide feelings.

B: Can they be hidden—for example, were No. 2's feelings hidden?

No. 4: Even if we don't get a deep understanding of why we feel the way we do, it's important that we do not seem to be hiding things from one another.

B: You ask, "Should we communicate our feelings?" My view is don't kid yourself, you are—

No. 2: There is a long tradition in business of not expressing our feelings.

No. 7: All my life I have been taught that distance between subordinate and superior was good. I interpret our thinking now as that this works against us.

No. 4: I would like to feel that you're giving directions because you're competent—I should feel your respect—not because there is a distance.

No. 7: So the superior must gain the respect by really knowing his people.

B: Maybe this is related to the problem that we had at the outset. No. 7, you said we were being very coy—like 18-year-olds; maybe we see a manifestation of this practice in our group.

No. 1: I always thought a superior should keep his distance because the more mystery about him, the more respect people will find in him.

The less a subordinate knows about a superior's feelings the more respect the superior will receive.

No. 4: This is the military system.

B: I am not saying that we must share our innermost feelings. I have feelings that are private. I am suggesting that there are a whole host of feelings, especially about our relationships, that communicate whether we think we do or not.

No. 2: That's a good point.

A: Maybe we're working on our problems of membership in this group? How far do I have to go to be accepted?

No. 8: As I see it, we have a back-home rule that says that we hide feelings. This rule is now operating here. Maybe let this rule go for a moment and experiment. What would happen if we expressed our feelings and tried to deal with them?

No. 10: The reason we don't express feelings is that we have found if we do, we may get into trouble.

No. 1: This is what I mean. I'm worried. If we are implying that we should express our feelings, then I'm worried because my sense of values are that I respect a person for *not* saying what he feels.

No. 2: I think we're polarizing; maybe we're polarizing against what we think the educators want.

B: As No. 10 said, ultimately it's up to you to decide what feelings we shall express.

No. 6: We tend to cover up negative feelings. If you're going to be negative, cover up. Part of the rules.

No. 7: Maybe No. 6 is saying that majority of people in this room say that it is pleasant to avoid negative feelings.

No. 6: For example, in an evaluation session, I have no trouble in telling him positive things; but negatives—that's another matter.

No. 5: I can't understand No. 1's view that it's good to hide feelings. I think this is bad.

No. 10: Maybe one of our problems is that we don't trust one another; maybe the boss man is responsible.

No. 4: If I suspect you're closed, then I will resent you for not taking me into your confidence.

No. 7: Maybe you're not really saying all that you think— right now.

No. 4 (blew his ———): Maybe that's right.

No. 10: I am keeping things secret because the boys above keep things secret.

No. 2: This implies mistrust—do they trust us? We have that problem with setting targets. That's why the majority are unreal.

No. 7: Do you really think the targets are unrealistic?

No. 2: Yes—yes. [others nod heads]

No. 4: Why do we agree to these goals? Why don't we say the truth?

No. 7: You know, this is interesting. In this company it's a great problem to find out exactly the state of a project. I tend to feel that I'm not getting all the facts. Then I wonder; I get resentful.

(A discussion of how we do this to one another.)

No. 7: This is a key subject—really hurts. I get a stack of stuff to do, things that I resent. I feel it weakens my position if I say the Top Boss said this. Yet, we are saying it would be helpful for a subordinate to know the pressures on this superior.

No. 1: You might be interested. Since everyone covers up where something originates, the people below simply do not know where things originate.

No. 2: What really bothers me, I don't mind being called dull, stupid, incompetent—that's the objective side. But to be called directly or worse yet by implication, lazy, insincere, lying—that side *really* cuts me.

The problem is that when the challenge is made, it is never

clear which he means, and then one interprets its personal side and, boy, that really burns me.

A: If we know that we're hurting someone, then we can repair the relationship.

No. 5 and 9 and OTHERS: Yes.

No. 1: Why should we repair our relationship?

No. 2 (to No. 7): When you say, "I'm bothered that people are withholding the facts," are you saying that people don't know the facts or that, by god, they know the score, but they won't tell you—they're lying to me?

No. 7: I don't really think it's the other guy's fault. It may be me. Maybe I have mannerisms that cause people to hold back.

No. 1: I have a clue. I have a clue. When someone says we're in trouble, our first question is, "What have you done about it?" Now if you've had to have done something, then people aren't going to report trouble until they have tried something. So they hide information, sometimes until its too late.

No. 5: Also, we ask *who* made the mistake—who did it—fire the guy.

No. 3: You mean, who besides you.

No. 7: This is important for me. Good point. We're saying that we stifle facts because people won't report something they haven't figured how to lick. How can we create a climate so that he can tell us when the problem occurs?

No. 2: I see it differently—we have to be careful so a change won't mean that the subordinates will report too easily and let someone take the responsibility.

B suggests that No. 2 may now be expressing feelings about his subordinates that he dislikes his boss to feel about him; for example, subordinates will tend to slough off if they feel *free* to be responsible.

(Group decides that there must be a threshold to this so that not all problems are sent up. Group also concludes that they have been creating mistrust by table pounding, getting "who done it.")

No. 7: This is a philosophy of the company for years. If there is any trouble, always look for the guy who made the mistake and fire him. This is the first thought I have. But maybe we're working against ourselves.

No. 4: I've heard this: "Are you a weak manager? Why don't you run a tight shop. Gee whiz—move." So I get worked up and pick up the phone, and that's action. You're really playing for keeps. And people move. But now I wonder if it really happens down the line. Does this really happen at lower levels?

No. 1: We're really to be the same way.

No. 5: Very definitely. I've learned in this company—you bore, clobber, push.

This raised hell on the climate for men to make an honest creative mistake.

OTHERS: Yes. Yes. Yes.

The discussion above began with an educator helping No. 2 express openly his resentment toward the educator. This helped No. 2 and others to experience the lack of a "danger" as well as the value to express feelings openly when in a relationship where individuals are attempting to develop a higher sense of trust. This led the group to discuss some of the reasons why in their "back-home" world it was wrong to express feelings. This, in turn, led individuals to explore their sincere views that it would be dangerous—indeed, ineffective—to be open. Note that neither educator told them that they must express their feelings. One educator did say that he found people tended to have great difficulty in hiding feelings. Another suggested that they may want to use the sessions to experiment with varying degrees of openness, to see the consequences.

This discussion brought out how "hiding one's feelings" and "the proper distance" between superior and subordinate were highly related. The men began to see that a distance between individuals created from fear of expressing feelings may be a source of interpersonal mistrust. This led one individual to show how the mistrust led to organizational difficulties. Since they were uncomfortable with negative feelings, the superior tended to set targets and change them without the participation of the subordinate. Conversely, the subordinate hid difficulties with reaching targets for fear that the superior would blow up. Eventually, the difficulty did rise to the surface, and the superior did blow up, largely—as one member said—because he felt he wasn't kept informed. He wondered if the subordinates told him the truth. None of these feelings were expressed. Therefore the subordinate saw the blow-up as confirmation of his original view that he should not express his feelings to the superior. This, of course, set the stage for the next blow-up and developed increasing mistrust.

Another member pointed out since he does not tend to discuss the trust problem with his subordinates, he attempts to resolve it with tighter controls, such as budgets, increased pressure, and closer checking. These organizational techniques, the group now realized, actually helped to make the problem worse. This is an example of how increasing openness can have significant effects upon organizational factors. Again, however, no one is suggesting that to increase interpersonal trust and openness will tend to resolve all the problems. It does, however, help to bring the problems out into the open where they can be discussed, analyzed, and appropriate action taken.

Speaking of action, the reader will sense very little action taken during the laboratory in terms of making organizational changes. There are three reasons for this. First, the members increasingly realized that their big problem in the past has been that they have been taking action much too fast. They tended to oversimplify complex problems, thereby developing oversimplified solutions. Since the solutions did not tend to be effective, and since the subordinates (at all levels) tended to withhold their feelings regarding the ineffectiveness of the superiors' decisions, the superiors saw the cause of the failure of their decisions as being in the subordinates. The superiors, however, did not tend to express their negative evaluations. However, the subordinates sensed them. The result; both felt that the other mistrusted him.

The second reason was that as the laboratory progressed, the members valued increasingly the time available to work on such factors as trust, openness, and so on. Time and time again they would ask that the group not spend too much of the "precious laboratory milieu" to make decisions that could be made back at home. Finally, the participants also realized that if they made decisions at the laboratory, they would tend to be seen as unilateral ones by the subordinates who were not there. This would probably act to increase the mistrust.

Session III

It is not uncommon for a group that has gone through, for the first time, an emotional as well as intellectual diagnosis of itself to retreat at a subsequent next meeting. There is usually a realization at this time of how open the group is able to become. This confronts each individual with several questions.

The first is a choice situation. "Do I want to continue? I can see now what may happen. I find myself saying things that I have always felt but rarely explored." Second, "Who is doing this to me? Is it all my responsibility? Perhaps it's the educators. Maybe they are leading me without my realizing it." (Something the executives found out they do all the time to their subordinates.) Third, "If I go deeper, I had better check to see if (*a*) others want to dig deeper (*b*) if I can trust them with the information which leads naturally to (*c*) my wondering about the others' motives for being in the T-group."

All these are important questions, and to the extent they are explored (or exposed) openly, the individual will learn much more about himself and the others from his company as well as the educators.

The educators are a special problem to the group members. It would take an entire book to discuss their role adequately. Suffice it to say that they represent to the group authority figures, who, to make matters more difficult, do not seem to behave as most authority figures behave. This problem, as we shall see in the next few sessions, becomes one of the major levers by which the group helps to develop itself.

For example, the session began with, as is pointed out above, an expected "regression" to topics that were safer and less difficult to discuss. This continued for about a half hour when one of the educators asked, in effect, if the group wasn't taking flight from its task. He added that they certainly could do this if they wished. He wanted to test his perception and to see if others wanted to continue the discussion. This comment partially opened up some people's unexpressed confusions about the T-group, their pent-up feelings about the educators, and both of these led them to explore their own loyalty to, and motivation for, being in the group. This in turn led to a discussion about "back-home" loyalties and then to an organizational arrangement that corrodes loyalties. None of these topics were "worked through" during the meeting. However, as we shall see, they set the stage for a more complete discussion in the next several sessions.

B: Nostalgia and crutch—maybe we're using this discussion to prevent us from doing what a T-group is for.

No. 2: I was wondering how long it was going to take before you lowered the boom.

B: In effect you're counting on me to lead the group.

No. 11: Why not—you're the leader.

No. 7: I think they're teasing B.

No. 1: Oh, we're supposed to know what the T-group is for [laugh].

B: I don't know how to take it—as overt or covert hostility. Let's explore it further. Perhaps others have some feelings about me or the T-group experience.

No. 1: My point wasn't meant to be hostile, although I'm glad you told me you took it that way [loud laugh].

No. 4: It was an accident.

B: Honestly, I don't believe this. I think No. 1 is expressing some important feelings of his own and perhaps of others.

No. 1: I wasn't hazing you. Simply reminding you that I was confused. Since you indicated we're on the wrong channel, honestly, I'm interested in knowing how to get to it.

A: Why are you confused?

B: Maybe, you're looking at A and myself in the same way that you look at your leader back home.

No. 7: Okay, we're off the track, says B, but I don't know what to do to get on the track. Please help me.

No. 8: Maybe he says he doesn't know what the track is.

No. 1: Since I was enjoying the discussion, it was upsetting to learn I was enjoying the wrong discussion.

B: This discussion also raises a question as to how involved people are to make this T-group successful. Perhaps some of us do not want it to be a success. This is fine, but perhaps we ought to make it explicit.

No. 8: Maybe we don't understand what is successful.

No. 11: It wasn't centered around us.

No. 2: You [No. 11] just put No. 3 on the spot.

No. 11: Yes.

No. 2: And [laughs] I miss putting you on the spot.

No. 3: I think in working with people around the table, I can predict how you will predict, but I don't understand the motives behind decisions. It'll help me to predict more accurately.

No. 10: I don't consider this real. I would be very careful not to be open here but open back home.

No. 2: Interesting, because so far I have gotten a better understanding of you here than I ever got back home [to No. 10].

No. 7: I'll be frank—I have no inhibitions here. I'll say everything that comes in my mind.

A: Perhaps it's easier for you to say this.

No. 3: The gratification for me is that for the first time I'm learning about you as a person. Getting to know your motivations and to predict your behavior.

No. 2: Why would you want to be able to predict our behavior?

No. 3: It's easier for me to evaluate my relationships with you.

No. 7: I'm surprised, since we've known each other so long.

No. 10: Is this surprising? We're a team, each representing our own specialties, not identified with the division.

No. 7: I would have thought loyalties are to the division.

No. 10: Personal loyalties may be to an individual but not to the institution.

No. 9: We'd all like to be the best in our specialty.

No. 6: At the moment I, too, feel I'm a professional first and division man second.

No. 7: I disagree in theory because I'm not a professional and, therefore, have loyalty to the whole.

A: Does this mean we can't have a division group?

No. 2: Time will make a difference; I need to have the feeling that our division is the best.

No. 10: Our loyalties come high when an outsider attacks us.

No. 2: It seems to me we need to have high cohesiveness when we're not being attacked.

No. 4: Maybe we're not convinced that this kind of a meeting cannot really do much for us.

No. 2: It might be that we have varying identifications with the division. I believe that although our emotionality may be lower, our level of commitment may be deeper. In this group any commitment made is damn deep. The anticipation here is that we'll live with it for a long time.

No. 7: And as I see it, the value of this is to help us open up and say exactly what we think and feel to each other.

No. 2: Another personal motivation: I feel misunderstood; and now that I see this as an opportunity to get things on the table, maybe I won't be misunderstood as much. My motivation is to see this get pretty deep.

No. 11: I know I give you difficulties back home. I'd like to know what is my impact on you. I try to be understanding of you, but I wonder how I really am seen.

(The discussion turned to the product control functions.)

No. 2: Fundamentally, I disagree with Policy (x). My constant fear it that this feeling radiates out, even though I try to hide it. I hopefully want to do the best to make it work and to minimize the negative impact of the watch-dog function. The very fact that my people know there is a watch-dog department motivates them to do a less complete job.

No. 9: I agree with No. 2. I personally believe it should be somewheres else.

No. 2: On the other hand, we can't make this change overnight. Like morphine, we're accustomed to it.

No. 11: That isn't my problem. I'm trying to understand if you think I really trust you, or if I try to maneuver you into something.

(No. 2 implies he has difficulty with No. 11 because the latter is as professionally competent as No. 2.)

(No. 7 wonders if this isn't an example of barriers between the two.)

(No. 2 defends the use of a less competent guy in testing so that testing doesn't tell engineering what to do.)

(No. 6 points up that each department has its own narrow view and that no one is taking an over-all view.)

No. 2: You are attempting to move to co-operativeness, but when the chips get down in a tight situation, then I think you're much less co-operative. By the way, I do this to you. Under a hot one, we're at each other's throats. You're saying, "For heaven's sakes, this machine won't work," and I say, "For hell's sake, you are doing your job correctly."

No. 7: My impression is that you [No. 11] are overly sensitive, polite, and too cautious. Now this may not be wrong, but for my case I wish you'd be more directive. You're too nice, too courteous, too tactful; therefore, not getting over the urgency.

No. 2: Yeah, but the pleasantness is like fine crystal. You can see through it. I know exactly what he feels!

No. 10: Is there anything wrong with this? Doesn't it help if we're polite and diplomatic? Won't it make life easier?

No. 2: Well, I look at it this way. Mr. A comes up to me and shouts. Mr. B comes up, is quiet, and has a 45 pistol aimed at me. Now, frankly, the shouting doesn't bother me. It's that 45 I'm worried about. All the sweet talk in the world doesn't convince me that guy with a 45 is less threatening if he talked sweet.

Session IV

The previous session ended with a discussion of how several people saw each other, their degree of trust, and so on. Involving as it was for some, it apparently acted to exclude others. Those "excluded" felt that the four were talking about a problem not relevant to the entire group. Also, a fact that would not be evident by these data, this problem was discussed outside the T-group in another session. This frustrated No. 3 to the point that he openly stated that he had been holding back. No. 11 utilized the opportunity to open up even further and tell No. 2 that he feared that No. 2 was trying to take over.

No. 3: Damn it, I think we're still being protective. I know what I felt like saying during the last session: "Okay, I've had enough of the four of you." I'd like to get in on this. But I guess one of the problems is that we're going to be together when we get back home, and, therefore, I guess I'm being cautious.

No. 11: Are we really opening up all the way? Isn't this how we behave back home? If we can tackle the problem here, we'll go a long way to solving ours back home.

I feel we have personal "take-over" motivations; for example, I am afraid of yours [points to No. 2]. I'd be afraid to let you alone with my subordinates. You did it at the last meeting, and I was scared. Created a lump in my heart.

No. 9: I'm concerned about this.

No. 2: It is difficult for me not to be involved in the product when we've helped to plan it. Maybe if we can forget history of the product. . . .

No. 10 (to No. 2): Your insistence to respond on a work level to set the record straight. To me you were evidencing a great characteristic of yours: to say something.

No. 2: Well, that isn't the way I see it. I'm glad to know how you see it.

A: No. 2 shows a lot of ability to punch but to dodge when someone punches back. You dodge, and its hard to reach you.

No. 2: It's certainly interesting to see that I'm dodging. Let me explain my viewpoint.

B: But there you go again dealing with a viewpoint and the relationship.

No. 2: Well, I don't know what you want me to say. I'm a dog. . . . I'm no good?

No. 10: I don't think he or I want you to say anything. It's that this group will not succeed unless we deal with relationships.

No. 2: Okay, maybe let me try this way. What can I do about what appears to you and others as a dodge—or talking for the sake of talking?

No. 8: This is good, because this is what we do back there.

No. 11: Right, if we can learn to deal with the problems in this group, we can learn to deal with similar problems back home.

No. 10: You know, I also see now that although we work with one another, this is not a close group. We *really don't know* each other personally. You know, I've never stopped to think about this. I always felt I knew you fellows. But now I realize that this isn't the truth. So I suggest we really work on the here-and-now problems.

No. 1: I agree; it seems to me when we get thoroughly involved, then we learn. In my opinion No. 11 has made an excellent effort. I think we disregarded it because we don't really know how to handle it. There are problems that are dynamite that we're not talking about.

No. 4: I, too, feel that we are not facing the crucial interpersonal problems. We are always regressing back to where we can hide behind our professional specialties.

No. 2: I finally see what happened. No. 11's point that we do take over, and he used me as an example. I jumped at the illustration or back home—I did not fail the problem.

No. 11: What happens when someone takes over?

No. 3: My mental energy switches to how I can cut him off at the pockets. Get him in a box. This is one reason why if we stop this take-over, we'll save countless time and energy.

(Others agree.)

No. 11: I listen to the first few words; then I stop listening and decide how to block him.

No. 4: How can we differentiate between take-over and trying to be of help?

No. 10: The degree of interest a person shows in listening to others—help others to express themselves.

No. 5: I feel hostile toward take-overs. I'd like to shut them up.

No. 1: How do we find out if it is a take-over?

A: Why don't we find out by asking?

We see how the discussion began with one man accusing another of trying to take over his department. In an attempt to reply, No. 2 learned that he was seen as dealing with the problem primarily on the intellectual level, omitting the interpersonal level. At first No. 2 responded "and understandably so" defensively. However, he was able to eventually gain enough insight to ask others for help. This not only brought him some helpful feedback, it helped to unfreeze other members, to talk about their dislike of "take-over" and their "under the table" strategies to cope with it.

The records show that the group then related their learning about one another to their back-home situation. For example, they concluded that "taking over" in a meeting implies a lack of faith and trust in others to make effective decisions. They then explored the degree to which the company encouraged and sanctioned "take-over" by advancing those people who expressed this kind of aggressiveness. "This is how people are advanced. It is a fact of life." And another said, "Boy, I can now see more clearly why it was smart, at a meeting with the top, to have a point no matter whether it was important.

Talk—talk fast." The group explored how it could recognize take-over behavior in themselves and others more effectively. This, in turn, led to individuals' exploring how they might reduce "take-over" back home.

Session V

In session five the group began to deal with the people who had the greatest power, the educators and the President.

The discussion began with an exploration of the need "to fight." The President rejected the idea of "fight." "We don't *really* fight. These are normal ways of doing business."

No. 4: I'm not sure. Before I would have not described these as fights but as strong discussions. Now I am not sure.

President: I don't know. These strong discussions don't bother me.

No. 11: It might not have bothered you. It certainly bothered me!

(No. 4 and others nod and agree.)

No. 10: Do you enjoy a fight?

President: Yes.

No. 2: Why do you hate to have it called a fight?

President: I dislike a fight because people are getting personal, breaking up things.

B: I am comfortable in calling it a fight—for me—yours is a protective comment. Don't call this a fight. This a good group.

No. 8: Fight is not good or bad. It is an ineffective way to run the business.

No. 6: Pretty tough to listen and compromise when people get hostile.

No. 4: Do you get anything done if feelings are in the way?

No. 10: What struck me is that the President can't say anything in this group without someone jumping on him. I do it.

No. 3: He has relinquished his ability to punish us, and we're getting him!

No. 2: Maybe a greater motivation is to make sure he understands us.

A: It is not uncommon to have ambivalent feelings about a man with power.

No. 11: But you know the educators jump on him more than anyone.

Others: Yes. Yes.

No. 1: In fact, you have been jumping on everyone.

No. 8: Maybe we want to "beat" him [President] into line.

No. 5: Also maybe here we're going to prove to ourselves that we don't have to agree if we don't want to—without being vindictive. I think—just to prove it to ourselves—that we can do it.

PRESIDENT: Another reason I feel that I'm not as forceful here as I am back home is that I'm a little more cautious. Maybe that is a little incentive to some to open up and jump in.

B: You have helped to unfreeze me. I can tell you what I think. The other reason that you get feedback is that you tend to tell other people what to do and how to feel. This invites feedback that clobbers.

PRESIDENT: Maybe the manner is which I disagree tends to squelch others. I don't want to squelch others. But I do want to get my views across. Maybe one thing I can learn is to disagree without having the suppressing impact.

(B agrees but points out that interpersonal change isn't enough. The structure tends to create dependence problems.)

No. 2: This is sure disturbing. I find it happening in my area. I'd like to feel free to argue and disagree without implying to people that they must jump on my band wagon. Later on I call and ask why something is going on and they say, "Well, you said so!!"

No. 11: Sure, the President is pretty directive, but let me tell you its already much less disturbing to me when he says, "I really disagree with you." I say, "Okay, and I can feel free to tell you."

No. 6: The President shouldn't stop saying exactly what he feels with the clarity he wishes. This is a two-way street. Now I see he's not trying to cut us off.

B: What would happen if No. 2's subordinates could be helped to learn how you feel about creating conformity? It might unfreeze them more as it has here.

No. 2: Yes, I want to have an impact on my subordinates, but I don't want them to become identical with me.

No. 10: Regardless of who the person is, if this is a fraction of authority, we resist and resent authority.

B: We resent the dependency.

OTHERS: Yes. Yes.

No. 10: Even if we get patted on the back, rewarded, we can resent it.

A: Does it mean that the President can't do anything?

No. 4: He can learn what we're learning here.

B: Perhaps some day he can attempt to change parts of the organizational structure.

No. 10: If we accept that we cannot change the structure for the next five years, then what can we do to avoid doing to our subordinates what we have been doing here to one another and what is being done to us from above? We need an interim solution.

No. 2: One thing that I've learned: If the people within the structure learned your real intent, they would be influenced less negatively.

We see that the group began to explore openly some of their feelings about the President. He encouraged these expressions by asking for more feedback and exploring new possible ways to behave. This, in turn, helped others to explore their probable impact upon others. Finally, one of the educators cautioned not to see the interpersonal factors as complete solutions to the problems. Some day the organizational structure and controls will have to be examined. The group agreed but, with the help of the other educator, explored what a superior can do, at this time, to begin to resolve some of these problems. In this connection, the records show that the group led by B[2] also discussed the possibility that some subordinates need to be dependent. This led to a discussion of the subordinates' responsibilities to help alleviate these problems.

About a half hour later B received some strong feedback about his impact upon the group. The educator reported that he found the feedback very helpful. Other members in the group reported that in addition to the value of beginning to be less dependent upon the educator, this discussion had the value of their seeing how the educator attempts to cope with his problems of authority. Also, the discussion helped them to explore how they could develop group consensus so similar misunderstanding would not tend to occur.

No. 11: You [B] really screwed this thing up.

No. 2: Wait a minute. He may have screwed up the reading of the reports, but was that the only thing we wanted to accomplish?

No. 6: I am not convinced he did.

No. 11: Yes, he did. When someone tried, you said, "I am not sure others want to talk about this."

B: Yes. I said as a member, I'm not sure the group wants to talk about this. I assumed that we would test my views. If the group wants to read the reports, they would say, "Damn right we do," and we'd read the reports.

No. 11: You've got to remember one thing. You're like the President. Whether you want to be in the group or not, we see you as imbued with something we don't have. You're helping us. When you help something go "Plop," it stays "Plop."

---

[2] The reader is reminded that A and B represent the two educators.

B: This is very helpful.

No. 7: Why couldn't we say, "Pardon me?"

B: I do want to read the report. I think I asked that very question.

No. 7: No, you didn't.

B (becomes defensive): Let's listen to the tape. It is in these [tapes].

No. 10 and No. 7: Agree that it is not matter of how you said it, it came out negatively. I didn't have enough steam to come back.

No. 6: I think if the group was really strong, it would have gone on.

No. 2: I agree that we can get stronger, but I think if we asked the group it would have been 50–50.

B: This is the view I have.

No. 1: You are overlooking the fact that you are seen as the leader. What is frustrating is that the report seemed to some of us to be assigned, and some came prepared to complete our assignment.

B: The objective is to generate data. I can see, however, that you are telling me that at least you two feel that I have the same problem that I tell the President he has in this group; namely, not aware of his impact. This is very helpful. Knowing this, I can deal with it.

No. 7: Maybe if we had known how to get consensus, we could have moved. I don't know, and maybe this is something we have to learn. Maybe we have to develop these rules in our group.

A: This is the first time the question has been raised. How do you find out what a group thinks?

No. 9: Yes, how do you know when a group is with you?

No. 2: Yes, this is frustrating. When I tried to sense what's going on in this group, I found it difficult.

Session VI

The discussion about the influence of the educator partially reported above was continued during the beginning of the sixth session. One way to view the discussion was that 11 people were expressing their natural feelings about being in a subordinate, dependent position. Some believed that the educators knew exactly what was happening, but they were not saying so in order that they could control and "brainwash" the group. Others believed that the educators behaved the way they did to permit the group to develop its own internal strength.

In some sense, both of these hypotheses have some validity.

The educators were controlling and directing. However, they were attempting to guide the group so the group would become *less* dependent upon them. (Thus, control and power can be used in the service of growth and development. The reader may recall above how the educators encouraged feedback about their impact and attempted to modify their behavior accordingly.) As we will see in a moment, the educators continue the same strategy. They attempt to show that they deeply respect the questions that the members have. Also, they imply by their minimal defensiveness that they believe their (educator) behavior is also justified and valid. Note how this seemed to help the members explore some very deep feelings that they had about people with power. This discussion (1) helped to integrate the educators into the group so that (2) they and the members could more clearly express their individuality which (3) led to the possibility that the members might understand at a deeper level the feelings that they expect their subordinates to have of them plus the feelings that the subordinates probably hold. Thus, when some members object to the "aggression" against the leader, they may also see how they would probably feel if their subordinates gave them similar feedback. They may, as some did, reach the conclusion that their feelings about the sanctity of leadership probably "showed through" whether they wanted them to or not. Consequently, these feelings were probably operating to influence negatively the subordinates.

No. 3: Don't you think it is an encouraging sign not to accept the leadership of the educators? We can stand on our own two feet.

No. 8: Maybe we may create an in-out group.

No. 5: Are the leaders trying to mold us in a pattern?

No. 9: No.

No. 2: No.

No. 1: Yes, I have that feeling. I feel B is trying to mold us at times.

No. 10: We do have a "holier-than-thou" attitude in the company. Maybe we have been shaken. We've realized that we're not so all-perfect.

No. 5: Yes, and in a defensive way we're ganging up on the educators.

No. 2: I feel unhappy about discussion of the exclusion. It seems to me the educators are part of the group. I feel very uncomfortable because we're coalescing by excluding them. I think they have much to offer.

No. 6: I've been one of the vocal dissentors of their [T] activities. I think there is a built-in resistance because there is a spillover from the directorially oriented lectures.

No. 11: It bothered me. I told B that he screwed up the meeting. I guess that puts me back to day one. But my real reaction is I now realize that I may have to live with your position as one of the facts of life. You should be in the group.

No. 1: That's interesting. They've only been out of the conversation for five minutes, and everyone is remorseful [laughs].

No. 6: Is it possible to be an educator and a leader?

No. 10: Perhaps a way to bring them back in, if they ever left it, is to examine what No. 7 said. It is true that we feel back at home that we think we are superior. But maybe we need to examine ourselves.

No. 5: But we *are* superior—as a group.

No. 6: Yes.

No. 3: I think No. 10 has a point. We all enjoy this feeling of superiority, and we get a bit defensive when we see it threatened.

No. 6: I agree with this.

No. 1: I want to agree with No. 10. I was critical of the educators because they had something we didn't have, *not* because I was superior.

OTHERS: Yes. Yes. Yes. Yes. Yes.

No. 4: I have a lot of confidence in the group that we can punish anyone if we feel it's necessary. So I think we can afford to bring the educators in. They're not a problem.

No. 9: My feeling is we need the educators. They've got resources.

No. 2: This has been an extremely uncomfortable discussion.

No. 1: Why?

No. 2: I wonder; for example, yesterday we jumped on B for jumping in, but we have been doing this to all of us. Why should it be related to whether he is in the group or not?

No. 1: You shouldn't feel uncomfortable.

No. 2: But I *do* feel this.

No. 1: I think you don't like to discuss this because this is a topic you don't like.

No. 10: I have been using the educators as a tool to help us talk about the educators. I don't think we're really talking about the educator. I think these problems are ours.

No. 2: I was. Frankly, I got a hell of a lot of help from both the educators.

No. 7: Maybe we're not rebelling against the educators. Maybe we're saying, "Give us more freedom."

No. 9: I'd like for us to get the educators in.

No. 4: Maybe they don't want to come back.

No. 8: Why don't we ask them how they feel about the last 15 or so minutes?

No. 3: Now we're putting them on the spot.

No. 11: No, I don't think they have to say anything.

A: Well, I found this fascinating. Compare it with the first night, when you said you were a closed group. But now we may see that we weren't. I agree with No. 10. We're beginning to become a group.

No. 11: It's interesting that we've had to come here to develop a group. Now I see that you have to pay a price. One is time. It takes time to develop a group.

No. 6: It seems to me that we must be careful not to let this group become a clique.

No. 1: It never occurred to me, because if we're learning anything it is how to be more open and, therefore, not have cliques.

No. 5: I've been thinking how I could apply it at home.

No. 7: I have not thought of this group as becoming a special group.

No. 6: But we have had a special experience here.

No. 10: But this does not necessarily stratify us.

No. 2: It is interesting to note that we've been talking about the group.

B: Can I say how I feel?

No. 5: I'm relieved that you're talking.

B: My job is to become a member so my skill and knowledge are seen as resources rather than a threat.

The discussion indicated to me that for some I wasn't a threat and that for others I was. And for those who were a bit unhappy with me they felt free to say so. Both of these realizations helped me to feel closer to the group.

Then I also wondered if you don't have the same problems with your subordinates that you have with us.

No. 10: Makes sense to me.

Others: Yes.

B: The way I feel more accepted as a member so I can release my skill and knowledge without being fearful is when someone is free to say, "Hold it—you're dominating" or "Like hell he is."

No. 4: I have a very definite feeling that, by God, we've made a decision.

No. 1: I have a feeling that we've had a complete discussion.

No. 4: Last night I was disturbed that we had not formalized enough how we make decisions. Now I feel it's formalized enough. Maybe now we trust ourselves more and we don't need as many rules. Then, as I say it, I wonder if I'm kidding myself.

No. 7: I don't anticipate to see a pattern. It's our sensitivity that's getting better. I can feel the group has arrived.

The conclusion that the group members were becoming more open, sensitive, and aware of the emotional level eventually led the group to discuss another interesting topic. The group began to explore how high intellectual competence can be used to create personal disequilibrium, increase interpersonal mistrust, and cover up personal insecurities. This seems to me to be an important point to consider. There are many who suggest that if top executives are intellectually capable, they will tend to be effective. In this connection it is interesting to note that several members who perceived themselves as not having "verbal dexterity" began to feel much better.

No. 3: One thing that is true is that this group has a tremendous level of verbal dexterity which we can use to cover up our feelings. We know the words to deal with a point but we can also knife pretty deeply.

No. 11: I think I did this to No. 2 when I said I did this to hit him as hard as I could. I felt badly afterwards.

No. 5: I must say that I've had a great difficulty in dealing with your "verbal dancing." I feel it hides real feelings and ideas.

No. 7: Interesting.

No. 10: Yes.

No. 6: For example, I really felt this with No. 5 when he said it.

No. 8: Perhaps verbal dexterity hides the individual's insecurity.

No. 5: This is the way it affects me. Of course, I may be rationalizing.

No. 7: This puzzles me. I always felt that one of my weaknesses was that I didn't have the verbal dexterity, and you say that this isn't so good.

No. 4: It seems to me that we're now being more open, and the need for verbal dexterity might not be as great.

No. 6: Isn't this inbred in our company? You never say, "I don't know." If asked and you don't know, you just start talking.

No. 10: Why should we be afraid to say, "I don't know"?

No. 6: I feel this is the way the top feels. They want all sorts of details.

No. 10: Should it bother you? After all, if you're not supposed to know. . . .

No. 6: I don't think it should bother me, but it does.

No. 7: I had the same feeling for a long time. I had to know everything. Believe I had this changed. I have learned it's much better for me to say, "I don't know." I think this creates confidence.

B: Other side is that when you don't know because your ideas are not clear, "thinking out loud" does not tend to be sanctioned.

No. 9: This is the problem I have had with you. "If you don't know, by God, you're not there." "Run it."

If you can say, "I don't know," it might help to get the subordinates to reflect.

Session VII

The meeting began with several comments that individuals felt that the members' degree of leveling was increasing. Someone pointed out how this would help increase trust.

No. 3 asked if the group wanted to discuss the "penalties for not knowing." For example, he suggested that when a mistake is made back home, the top invariably attempts to pin it to one person, when in reality many were involved in the decision. The fear that one might not be prepared with an answer creates a tremendous pressure within the organization to brief the "higher ups" with details, lest they be asked a question from the very top. The members agree that "an awful lot of hours could be saved if people didn't demand so much detail at a moment's notice." The group explored the possibility that the need for detail suggested that top management may not really trust the divisional officers.

No. 3: And if the superior will be comfortable and accept the "I don't know," and if we support this, we will have helped the company and move decisions ahead faster and break up the tremendous report gathering done "just in case."

No. 10: There is a fear to say, "I don't know." What will the boss do?

No. 11: It seems to me we can't do much about corporate headquarters, but we can do it here.

No. 7: But even corporate recognizes. I always have the fear that someone will ask me an x-level question.

No. 2: They really ask for much too much detail. We get frightened, so up goes the paper work to be protected.

No. 8: This makes our system an advisory one. We go up to them to argue our case before a judge. And the worse thing we can do is not have all the details.

No. 7: Good point. I think we have little confidence and trust in our decision-making process, come to think of it.

(No. 3 gives example of an extremely minor question asked. He doesn't know, so he calls. It gets back, and the subordinates are wondering is that all he has to do is call on that?)

B: How do *we* show lack of trust of one another?

No. 2 (Gives an example): It was a lack of trust in, frankly, you [President]. I felt that if you had your way, you would have wanted —— fired, and I thought it through far enough to be convinced that this was wrong.

B: What would have happened if you could talk about your fears? [Gives an example.] This could get to the point that you and he [President] may not trust No. 2 in firing people.

No. 2: B has a good point.

PRESIDENT: Yes, in all honesty, No. 2, I do feel you're weaker in handling the people problems.

No. 2: And I've felt this.

PRESIDENT: And by the way, I get this from above. Not as much. I think they are trying to leave us alone. Every time some major problem hits, I get put on the spot. "What's going on there?" "Are you a weak manager?" "Do you have incompetent people?"

No. 2: I think I'm trying to move in the direction of recognizing the importance.

No. 7: This discussion is important for me. Is it for anyone else?

OTHERS: Yes. Yes.

No. 7 (Gives evidence of how he senses that he is not trusted and how he begins to mistrust): "I get irritated." "My position of authority is threatened." By God, they had not done what they agreed to do. I was really disturbed and mad. So this leads me to mistrust and to increase the checking.

(Others in the room bring in further data on the problem.)

No. 7: But shouldn't corrective action be taken? How can we run an efficient organization if people are not disciplined?

No. 10: I don't think they're saying that people should not be disciplined. They're saying that it's damn difficult to publicly discipline one more when many people had responsibility. He becomes the scapegoat.

No. 2: We are agreed that discipline must occur. And that we can't be completely fair. However, the crucial question is: How do we cope with the guy who is partially guilty?

No. 9: Trust can only be developed by a climate. Instead of top picking at the climate, they pick at the detail.

A: You're trustworthy as long as you don't make mistakes.

No. 11: Or, when is the time that they're going to find out that we're not keeping up to our responsibilities? Why can't we go to the top and tell them exactly what is going on?

No. 4: To make matters worse, under tension we also hear things differently. There was a difference in view.

No. 2: Yes, and let's dig deeper. When we at the top decided that Mr. so and so should be fired, and so on, then every iota of responsibility was determined right there. [Centralization.] The subordinates can feel no responsibility.

At the root of all this, and what is revolting to me, is that we are making a decision we should not be making. I guess my emotional reaction is so strong that I hide facts.

Session VIII and IX

The previous session ended with the members gaining insight into how they tend to make their subordinates more dependent upon them and less responsible for decision making. The next few sessions were concerned with much personal feedback. Each individual, whenever it was appropriate, gave the other feedback about his impact.

Intermixed with the personal feedback was a discussion about the importance of trust in decision making and the difficulty to hide feelings. It is interesting to see how each of the members struggled with the problem of leveling with an individual when he did not trust the individual. Several attempted to get the group to agree that such feelings should be hidden. However, many gave examples of how they could sense when some were really hiding feelings.

No. 7: One thing that I've learned time and time again is the importance of trust, especially in decision making.

No. 11: I agree. For example, take the new policy that came out which was a surprise to me. I began to wonder how many meetings were held and I wasn't invited. I began to mistrust a little, and I knew that this wasn't right. Yet I couldn't help it.

(Group explores ways which they show mistrust toward one another.)

No. 10: Let me ask this question: Can we hide our views about our peers and subordinates?

No. 8: I'm amazed how hard feelings are to hide. Every time I think I've covered them up, people have sensed them.

No. 11: It's clear if we chose to operate as a real cohesive group, the degree of trust and openness has to increase.

(Group agrees that under trust A can say to B, "There are things going on which I can't share with you at this time," and there are no difficulties.)

No. 6: Can we say that we don't trust that behavior?

No. 10: Should we do this openly? Isn't it too dangerous? After all, we can get this across without saying it directly.

No. 3: But this is mistrust if the guy senses that you don't trust him.

No. 7: I can sense if No. 10 doesn't trust me just by looking at his eyes.

No. 11: In our company each has found a diplomatic way to say, "I don't trust you."

(One gives example, "Have my fellows seen these figures yet? Now this is a polite way." He is cut off by several members.)

No. 5, 3, and 7: Boy, that really burns me up.

No. 7: I would be offended if someone said they didn't trust me.

No. 5: Maybe, we're saying that we can trust the person but not the facts.

No. 3: Some people say your [No. 7] face is hard to read. I don't think so. I think that I can tell when you've made up your mind. Then I watch you listen to the guy. But the curtain is really closed. It seems to me that if we have openness and trust you would bring it out.

No. 7: Very good point. But I worry about being premature or upsetting.

A: Instead of saying I don't trust you or me, let's focus on the particular relationship.

No. 7: Yes, my reaction would be to inspire me to do something.

No. 11: Leads to a need for communication as to what's going on.

No. 8: Yes, I agree. Sometimes I feel there is a mystery and I'm behind an iron curtain.

No. 1: I don't share No. 11's feeling that I need to be brought into the picture. Interesting to see the different reactions that we have.

Another important discussion was the one where the members explored how they tended to coerce others to develop into their image. This topic came up elsewhere and was a central one during the entire program.

No. 7: To me personally, one of the highlights of these sessions is to learn how people are really motivated. You don't say, "Grow damn you, grow and grow on my wagon." I now see that I violate principles of growth all the time. I see now that you fellows see me as trying to create you in my image.

No. 8: And was I relieved to hear you ask yesterday how you could change, because I wondered inwardly whether I would or could grow with you.

No. 7: What bothers me is how unaware I was and now how to accomplish this. I'm beginning to learn.

No. 8: The way I see that we've been doing this for years is telling the person: "I want you to grow." "Tell me how you want to grow." "No, that isn't the way I want you to grow."

No. 2: I am impressed how easy it is for the leader to force his characteristics on to others. [Explores in detail how he did it with people around the table.]

No. 3: No one is going to change me beyond my tolerance points. I consider this a threat to my personal integrity.

No. 2: But we ought to be open to changing our own tolerance points if it is necessary. I'm against image development, but the subordinate must be open.

No. 1: Sometimes I feel that I'm invited into a group meeting because my boss thinks I'm more like him than I think I am.

A: You feel then you're going in on false colors.

No. 7: I hear No. 1 saying I really don't want to let the group know me as I really am.

No. 1: I suspect that there is some truth.

Perhaps these comments are enough to provide the reader with some idea of the kind and levels of discussion that occurred during the T-groups. The final sessions were taken up mainly with personal feedback which helped the individuals understand one another at a level they reported they had not reached before.

9

Organizational Diagnostic Sessions

Although the T-groups constitute the core of the laboratory, there are other learning experiences offered in the program. One sequence of these was called "organizational diagnosis." As the name implied, the focus was upon diagnosing the organization's problems. The group began by holding (at the laboratory) several "natural" meetings on company problems that would have been held back at home. During the first meeting, three fourths of the group participated in the meeting. One fourth acted as observers. The observers noted the crucial moments of the meeting, the leadership styles, the nature of decision, and so on. These observations were discussed in detail, giving the group insights into what they were doing to one another as well as experience in using the new concepts they were learning.

At the next three meetings, the total group participated in diagnosing the problems that they created for one another and for the organization, as well as those that the organization created for them. These diagnostic sessions took relatively deep slices into problems, exploring as many of the facets as the group could develop. Although it was possible for the group to take action, they decided against too quick decision making. They were especially worried about making major policy decisions without involving members of the organization not present.

Before giving the reader a few examples of the topics discussed, it is important to add that along with analyzing specific issues, each member selected another member to observe him during the meeting and to give him feedback on his impact. These sessions became extremely absorbing. The members spent about twice the amount of time as was originally planned. In all instances the staff had to intervene to stop the program.

The group began with an analysis of the status of the personnel function. Some of the personnel people, especially those coming from line organizations, tended to see themselves as having a somewhat lower status because personnel problems are "not part of the go, go, go of the company." One man said, "I feel that personnel discussions are seen as 'sand in the wheels of progress.'" This led to the diagnosis that most staff functions are seen by the line as "second class," as "hurdles to be overcome."

The second major area to be diagnosed was the competition for "people, money, and space." The new budgets on people and money created many conflicts among groups, each bidding for the scarce supply of money and labor. Budgets and personnel freezes only tended to compound the problem.

"Why," asked someone, "haven't we sat down to really work through these problems?" "Perhaps," continued another, "we are in a fairly rigidly prescribed environment. Maybe since we never *had* to think seriously about resolving these problems, we don't do it." "It's so much easier," added a third, "to go to our bosses and let them make the decision." "They're so much smarter [smiles], and they like to make decisions," concludes a fourth.

The competition for and pressure from the lack of personnel, money, and space created many administrative headaches for each group that was attempting to keep up, if not increase, its own programs. "Since none of us have enough time, we get those things done that are regimented, scheduled, and required; consequently," concluded another, "we never have time to be imaginative, and this worries me more than anything else."

The superiors' attempt to knowingly and unknowingly dominate and control was the next topic of discussion. The subordinates concluded that one reason they had not done much about some of these problems was that they did not tend to feel highly responsible for such problems. "We love to complain and go around damning the boss but not take the responsibility."

This led to an insightful discussion on how superiors tend to control. Two of the members agreed with one's observations that there were bosses who kept the subordinates in conflict in order to keep them dependent upon the boss. "I'm not sure if we worked these things out that we would come in conflict as much as the boss might want us to." Their superior nodded and said, "That's a very honest statement."

The discussion of how easy it is to fall into the role of being submissive continued with a discussion of the directiveness and impatience of many bosses. Someone added, "After a while, under these conditions, it's easier to go to the boss and say we have a problem and watch him work hard at solving it." Another executive commented, "If we're sure a decision will wind up in the boss's office, then we lose any sense of responsibility. We don't really feel committed to it."

Speaking of commitment, several members agreed and none disagreed (overtly at least) with the comment, "I'd rather lose a decision by fighting it out with my peer than by losing it through edict. Then I think the boss is playing favorites."

The superiors added another dimension to the problem by exploring ways in which they perceived the subordinates coercing or enhancing their dependence. "Subordinates come to my office," said one superior, "poorly briefed and without facts." "These are times," suggested another, "when I feel, by God, I'm going to kick everyone out of my office who isn't really familiar with the problem."

The subordinates agreed this does happen. However, as one pointed out, many times they felt there was not much sense to being briefed ahead of time because one would only have to wait while the superior was also briefed.

They continued by pointing out that superiors tended to create administrative situations of a "someone will win" and "someone will lose" variety. Some superiors insisted that strong functional loyalties were a good thing. "Sure, get together and fight it out. Neither of you should feel you have to give in. Come to me." This, however, pointed out a subordinate, only tended to create feelings of increased dependence upon the leader and a feeling that one was going to court instead of to his boss. Perhaps, added another, the executives tell the subordinates to fight because if they did, they must eventually come to the boss for a decision. This automatically gave the superiors some control over the subordinates (four members agreed and nodded their head in agreement.)

"I wish," continued a subordinate, "that you would give me hell for *not* settling something with my peers. Then I'd be more motivated to work with them. Now, as it is, I feel confident that all I have to do is pick up the phone and you'll settle it."

A related outcome of the interdepartmental rivalries is the "energy spent in building up our own or knocking down some one else's status."

The final problem discussed in some detail was the tendency of finance to hold secret most of the important figures. "It is a sign of personal mistrust not to give out figures." This leads line individuals to mistrust finance and to always wonder, "What's he up to?" One executive described the informal ways he "smuggles" some secret finance information in order to resolve a particular problem, "I dislike the secrecy because in addition to the things the fellows have already said, you [to finance] imply that I don't have the brains to keep secret information to myself." All the line agreed. One added, "Moreover, since people do not know the real facts, they assume that finance is holding back 20 per cent, so they keep fighting, hoping that they'll get it." "It's real hard," continued another line executive, "to feel that you are a part of a team if in some plays you cannot get into the huddle."

In a different session the individuals explored the meaning of many of the past and present human relations policies and practices. Some typical comments were:

> Sensitivity isn't something you can command or issue. We cannot legislate sensitivity.
>
> I have a distrust of the gimmicks that we are trying to use to maintain high employee morale. We ought to get to basic

causes. For example, increasing use of standards, restriction of jobs rather than job enlargement.

How fixed are we in our present personnel and other programs? Aren't we operating on effects rather than causes?

We ought to have a belief that we would be more efficient, survive. If you accept this, then we must back our present policies if these are correct. If they are correct, then we must push them.

We ought to develop manager ability to diagnose the complexity of the situation.

We must re-examine the present methods we are using, because many of them aren't really solving the basic causes.

Now we realize the difficulties of developing innercommitment. My God, how do you do this? I just gave up on myself.

In addition to the personal feedback that each individual received, the following kinds of learnings were also noted:

How we clobbered one another trying to get the job done.

How we misunderstood each other.

How our anxieties influenced what we see "in" others, and how we ought to handle them and the problems.

Even though we were trying to be of help, many times we made things worse. As one man told the other, "You were trying to create the right atmosphere, but if you would have only kept out a bit, it would have been better."

How advice can become an order.

How safe it is to reject something from a powerful person when we are uncomfortable with power.

The values of being open. The inner satisfaction of facing reality, and the interest with which others tried to understand.

Finally, the men learned by experimenting that the leadership functions can be shared when the members feel a deep responsibility to achieve the goal and keep the group operating effectively. They also began to see how increased involvement through true participation actually increased commitment to the implementation of a decision.

It was also interesting to note how uncomfortable the leaders of the meeting felt in experimenting with what they felt was a somewhat more passive leadership with which they are accustomed. As one leader said, "I felt that the meeting was forced in the sense that you and I were holding back." Another leader added, "I was sure forced. Something would come up, and I would force myself to keep out." "I'm glad you did," added two others. "It was worth the effort," added another.

To summarize, some of the major problem areas discussed were (1) the relatively lower status of staff units and manufacturing personnel, (2) management by crisis, (3) control through detail, (4) interpersonal conflict, (5) fear of failure, (6) functional loyalties and interdepartmental fights, and (7) conformity to leadership pattern that may be characterized as directive, articulate, and controlling.

In closing, it should be emphasized that the T-groups and the organizational diagnostic sessions eventually fused so that one could not tell, at times, what kind of meeting was being held. This was the hope of the planners of the program. The problem of training in real life is to integrate the use of interpersonal competence with intellectual and professional competence. At first, the laboratory was so structured that it separated and highlighted each. Then, by design of the program and because of the growth of the individuals, these two were integrated in a way that both levels of competence could be brought to bear upon the problem as the situation required. It is interesting to note, however, that when tempers flared and emotions ran high, the individuals tended to return to their original state of emphasizing intellectual competence and rational arguments and de-emphasizing interpersonal competence. This was examined by the group members and they concluded that under extreme pressure they would probably "regress." They also suggested that if it were possible, one of the parties should do his best to point up the "regression." Perhaps both sides would "pull back" and "start all even again." This suggestion proved successful on several occasions at the laboratory and, as we shall see later on, back at the company. They all agreed that the best approach was to strive to reduce the pressures and crises in the first place. Moreover, they reminded one another that this was not simply an interpersonal problem. Eventually there might have to be changes in the nature of organization and controls, in the very structure of their business life. Finally, they also agreed that it would be extremely important if the people at corporate headquarters were exposed to this type of program and the values that it implied for managing people.

BACK-HOME PLANS

I think my guys are trembling with curiosity to see what, if anything, has happened to me. Just before I left they said to me, "This is your last chance to rip us apart because when you go up, you're going to come back nice!"

I guess I'm worried. Will we let them down if we don't say anything to them?

These two comments typify some of the major concerns that the group had about returning to their back-home situation after an absence of seven days. The problems were carefully analyzed and discussed at length. The group arrived at the following conclusions:

1. The most important learnings that we received was increased awareness in ourselves and others. This new awareness has started a chain of events which can help each one to increase his self-confidence in human relationships and to increase the confidence that he has in others.

2. There is nothing in the learning we received that tells us we must go out and do something to people, to change them. There should not be, therefore, attempts "to sell" the laboratory values in a didactic, intellectual manner. The best advice that they could give is to *be* themselves and to behave as best as they can with what they have learned.

The group recalled that no one remembered the educator's beginning lecture of a week ago describing the laboratory approach. "If we do not remember his remarks, what chance is there that the subordinates will remember ours?" Moreover, added another individual, "I think that I have learned there is a big difference from knowing a principle of human relations up here in my mind and actually behaving it."

3. The best that we can probably do is struggle to create conditions under which individuals can express themselves more freely, see the situation more accurately, be less im-

patient with its complexity, and, hopefully, thereby helping ourselves and others to learn continuously.

There were no illusions that these objectives could be achieved easily. No one could lecture about these objectives; indeed, no one could require them of others. If we can only take home our newly developed skills to listen and to see more accurately, we would be doing well.

One executive smiled and said, "It's interesting that we are all saying that the people back home are waiting to hear from us; that they are ready to listen. And now we have nothing we want to sell!"

No. 4: No one has said, "Let's have everyone take this. Let's give people religion." This is excellent.

No. 6: If there are certain things about ourselves that we cannot change, at least we can alert our people that this is us. We're not apologizing for it, just letting them know.

No. 3: When I did this once, I found they already knew it all along. Now they were more comfortable because they didn't have to beat around the bush.

No. 7: I am now more aware that in needling I only created difficulties rather than motivated people. I wonder how I can help my people to see this, since they're probably expecting the old me?

No. 11: Let's not say or imply, "Now hear this, I'm going to be T-groupish."

No. 8: One thing that we've done that has helped is that we have created a more relaxed atmosphere. I no longer feel that I have to race through a conclusion for fear I'll be cut off. I guess I feel more respected.

No. 7: I hope that we can spend more time diagnosing our groups and situations that we get into and see them differently.

PRESIDENT: I'm going to have a problem when we get back. I just looked at my first day's schedule, and it's full of meetings. This means we can't have all the time that we wish. I suspect that I'll have to learn how to cut things off.

No. 1: I feel now it's as much our responsibility to help keep these meetings short.

No. 2: I've always had a guilty feeling if I would say I only have 25 minutes; I feel this is uncomplimentary and degrading. This is why I don't say it.

(The group responded that it would be helpful to know the time limits.)

No. 7: I hear you say that it would be easier if there was an understanding.

No. 8: One of the first things we might do is question the agenda. Are all of these meetings necessary?

I believe that in addition to the above, many of the men left the laboratory with a wish which they probably doubted they could fulfill as much as they desired, but which they would strive continuously to fulfill. As one man said:

"I believe that I should like to develop in my little group the same degree of openness and trust that we have developed here."

PART FOUR

□□

EVALUATION AND CONCLUSIONS

10

The Impact of the Laboratory on the Organization

Understanding and measuring the impact of a laboratory program upon the participants is an extremely difficult task. To understand its impact upon the remainder of the organization seems almost impossible. However difficult the task and however knotty the methodological issues, we decided to try. At least it would be a beginning, and the attempt would help us to understand some of the issues involved, as well as the degree of their complexity.

The basic strategy was simple. Since we had not been able to develop validated instruments, and since, to our knowledge, none was available to understand and measure changes in an organization that may occur from a laboratory, we decided to use as many methods as possible to gather as much data as possible. We attempted to use questionnaires, interviews, and observations.

I. EXPERIMENTAL VERSUS CONTROL GROUP BEFORE THE LABORATORY

When the program was begun, the reader may recall that the executives suggested that one group go through the experience of being diagnosed and then (if they wished) of attending a laboratory. If the results were, in the eyes of the executives, positive, then the other group would be invited to go through the same process. The second group was utilized as a control group.

The objective of the control group was to help us to ascertain if the changes in values and competence that may occur at the laboratory would not tend to occur within the organization in the natural course of events. If it could be shown that the control group's values before and after the laboratory were substantially the same, then it would give us some indication that the changes in the experimental group would not have occurred if they had remained at home and had not experienced the program.

At the outset of the research the group that was brought together to consider the entire experiment numbered 20. These were the top 20 housed in, and operating from, the headquarters. When they decided that only one group (of 11) should go through the laboratory, the remainder (nine) became the control group. However, because of personnel shifts two left the headquarters after the research began. Thus, at the end of the laboratory there were only seven in the control group.

This is a small group. It should have been larger. The same may be said for the experimental group. Here again we see a difference between action research and research. If our objectives were primarily to develop knowledge, we would have asked for larger experimental and control groups. Parenthetically, I might add that I doubted if I would be given them, because the executives wanted to proceed cautiously. Their attitude was understandable and illustrated their high degree of responsibility for the organization, as well as one of the problems a field researcher faces. He may know what is ideal for research design, but he may not be able to obtain necessary approval. Even if somehow one could have coerced the organization to create larger experimental and control groups, the entire experiment could have been placed in jeopardy.

The experimental and control groups were matched for (1) the values that they held regarding effective human relationships (the inputs in our model), (2) the degree of perceived conformity in the organization, and (3) the degree of interpersonal competence.

The members in the control group differed in terms of position in the firm with those in the experimental group. They were all immediate subordinates of the executives in the experimental group. One may wonder, as we did initially, if this difference in position was an important one. The conclusion seemed to be that it was not for certain purposes and it was for others. The research focuses on the changing of values of executives. The control group serves its purpose in that the members hold the same values (and almost with the identical strength) as do the members of the experimental group. The difference in position, therefore, does not tend to influence the values held by the executives. However, as we shall see in the next chapter, the difference in position does have a significant impact upon the degree of freedom the executives feel they have to change their values. There appears to be, therefore, two different but important dimensions. The first is the degree to which the executives hold similar values with similar potencies. The groups are matched in terms of this dimension. The second is the degree of freedom the executives feel they have to change. The groups are not matched in terms of this dimension. The experimental group, which was also the top group, reported greater freedom to change than did the control group.

Before we present the data comparing both groups along these dimensions, it is important to point out that all experienced the diagnosis and none of them knew who was to be in the control group until the diagnosis was almost completed.

COMPARING THE EXPERIMENTAL GROUP AND THE CONTROL GROUPS BEFORE THE LABORATORY

Let us now turn to a comparison between the experimental and control groups *before* the laboratory. In Table 14 the groups are compared in terms of six dimensions.

Another way to compare the groups is to ascertain if they differ in the kinds of satisfactions that they experience on the job. Nine out of 10 of the experimental group reported their satisfactions come from intellective, rational activities. In the control group six out of seven reported that they received their deepest satisfactions from rational intellective activities and only one from interpersonal activities.

Another important comparison would be to rate the reported degree of rational and interpersonal disagreements that

TABLE 14

ATTITUDES OF EXPERIMENTAL AND CONTROL
GROUPS BEFORE THE LABORATORY

(Per Cent)

In any administrative situation whenever possible:	Total Group (N = 18)		Experimental Group (N = 11)		Control Group (N = 7)	
	n	%	n	%	n	%
1a) The leader should translate interpersonal problems into rational, intellective ones......	18	100	11	100	7	100
1b) The leader should deal with the interpersonal problems openly and directly..........	0	0	0	0	0	0
2a) The leader should stop emotional disagreement by redefining the rational purpose of the meeting..................	16	87	10	90	7	100
2b) The leader should bring out emotional disagreements, help them to be understood and resolved....................	1	6	1	9	0	0
3a) When strong emotions erupt, the leader should require himself and others to leave them alone and not deal with them..	18	100	11	100	7	100
3b) When strong emotions erupt, the leader should require himself and others the opportunity to deal with them........	0	0	0	0	0	0
4a) If it becomes absolutely necessary to deal with feelings, the leader should do it, even if he believes he is not the most capable person in the group.....	18	100	11	100	7	100
4b) If it becomes necessary to deal with feelings, the leader should encourage the most competent member in the group.........	0	0	0	0	0	0
5a) The leader is completely responsible for keeping the group "on the track" during a meeting.......................	18	100	11	100	7	100
5b) The group members as well as the leader are responsible for keeping the group "on the track."....................	0	0	0	0	0	0

each group experiences. Although both groups seem to have similar attitudes toward intellective and interpersonal problems, it would be important to see if they experienced each of these in about the same proportion. In Table 15 we note that both groups reported that they experienced about the same frequency of intellective and interpersonal conflicts. The control group, however, tended to report a greater probability for the interpersonal clashes to come out into the open.

A fourth dimension with which the two groups were compared was the degree to which they perceived that conformity exists in the organization regarding the nature of effective leadership. If conformity exists, it should be in terms of an emphasis on intellective technical competence and a de-emphasis of interpersonal competence. If one analyzes the comments the men made regarding "effective leadership," 100 per cent of them in both groups emphasized intellective, technical compe-

TABLE 15

RELATIVE FREQUENCY OF INTELLECTUAL AND
INTERPERSONAL CLASHES

	($N = 18$)		($N = 11$)		($N = 7$)	
	n	%	n	%	n	%
1a) Intellectual, rational disagreements are "frequent" and "happen all the time."	14	78	8	73	6	86
1b) Intellectual, rational disagreements never occur or seldom occur.	4	22	3	27	1	14
2a) Interpersonal clashes rarely erupt out into the open.	13	72	9	81	4	43
2b) Interpersonal clashes do erupt out into the open.	4	22	1	9	3	43

tence. The same results were obtained in "leadership factors that influence promotions," and the same in response to the question "those factors that should be emphasized in executive development programs."

Finally, we turn to the scores on interpersonal competence. Although the results are in the expected direction, they are not as one would have wished. Again the training needs overrode the research requirements. Ideally, I should have observed individuals in both groups with the same frequency. However, since time was limited, I made many more observations of those men that I believed should be in the experimental group. I did so for two reasons. First, it was important to obtain as valid a diagnosis as possible to make some inferences regarding the degree of threat that the laboratory experience would have on the experimental group. If it would probably be too great, then, for the sake of the people and the organization, I would not have recommended the program. Second, I needed to have as much data as I could obtain for the feedback sessions in order to optimize the need on the part of the executives for the laboratory.

Of the total number of observations scored (which the reader may recall was 199) 40 were of the control group. Seventy per cent of these represented failures and 30 per cent successes. The proportion of failures to success is in the same direction as the experimental group, which was 67 per cent failures and 33 per cent successes.

THE CONTROL GROUP JUST BEFORE AND IMMEDIATELY AFTER THE LABORATORY

Since most of the interviews were held several months before the laboratory was scheduled to begin, it seemed appropriate to reinterview the control group one week before the laboratory to see if any changes occurred along the dimension above. From my observations, which were still going on, I inferred that their interpersonal competence scores had not changed. However, it seemed important to obtain their perceptions. Another important reason for the reinterview was the possibility that the very research processes of interviewing and observation plus the inevitable discussions between both groups and myself might have made significant change.

The analysis of the interviews showed that not one individual in the control group changed his opinion in terms of the dimensions above. His satisfactions continued to come from the intellective technical activities. He also tended to suppress interpersonal problems and translate them into intellective problems. He also held the same images of "effective leadership" and of "who gets ahead." Finally, he still felt that the leader should be completely responsible for the success of a group during a meeting. It is fair to conclude, therefore, that time and the research process did not have a significant impact on the dimensions above.[1]

Two days after the laboratory, I interviewed the control group once more, because it might be argued that the absence

---

[1] Later on we shall show this to be the case for the experimental group.

of the experimental group (or some other unknown factor) could have influenced them to change their values. In all cases the control group reported similar responses.

I also interviewed at least one co-worker of each member in the control group. I asked them if they noticed any differences in their department during the past few weeks (while the experimental group was away). During the discussion I was able to ascertain that there were some differences, but all of the differences were related to the experimental group's being away. None reported any changes in the behavior of the control group.

We may conclude, therefore, that at the time of the return of the experimental group from the laboratory, the control group, in terms of our dimension, had not changed. This leads us to the next question. Did the experimental group upon returning "infect" the control group with or attempt to influence them toward, the values that they learned at the laboratory? If not, why not? If so, why so?

II. EXPERIMENTAL AND CONTROL GROUPS AFTER THE LABORATORY

The data collected to evaluate the impact of the laboratory will be presented in chronological order. First will be the data obtained during the first two weeks after the laboratory. The second set of data came from two group sessions held during the third week, one with the control group and the other with the experimental group. The third set of data came from interviews with subordinates of the experimental group held about four weeks after the laboratory. Next, we will present interviews and observational data obtained nearly three months after the laboratory. Finally, there are data from interviews with the experimental group about six months after the laboratory.

First Two Weeks: Comments of Subordinates and Peers not Attending Laboratory

Six subordinates of the experimental group were approached by the researcher. In five cases they remarked about the changes they had observed in their superiors. All were in the direction that their superiors were more patient, better listeners, and more sensitive to their feelings. For example:

1. This morning I was at a meeting, and the pressure was on me as usual. Suddenly Mr. ———— said, "Seems to me that we're pressuring the hell out of you." I was so surprised to hear this. It was how I felt, but no one had ever said anything like that before. I guess I goofed, but it came out. "That's right, and you've been doing it for years!"

2. Interesting thing happened in two different meetings today. Both of them had been chaired by fellows who had been at the program. Both of these men commented to the effect that recently they've become more aware of how they might stifle people at the meetings. They asked for the group to let them know, because it wasn't intended.

Subordinate in (2) also emphasized that there was not "anywheres near the usual amount of table pounding. Also, there was a devil of a lot more listening. But I'm not sure how to take this. Do you think those guys really can change?"

As two secretaries said to the researcher, "Say, what's happened to our bosses? They're human!" a third, who overheard them, came up and said, "Don't worry honey, just relax. They've been on vacation, and it'll wear off in a few weeks."

These questions imply that the subordinates are cautious and do not know how to trust the superior's new behavior. This seems to make much sense. Why should they trust the behavior at this early stage, especially when the men who are manifesting it have probably not internalized it? As we shall see in a moment, this problem is a major barrier to be overcome if change is to radiate throughout the organization.

First Two Weeks: Observations Made by the Writer

The following are excerpts taken from my notes, which were made while I was observing various members of the experimental group "in action."

1. I observed a meeting between No. 7 and No. 10[2] which dealt with a difficult topic of conflict of interest between two departments. Instead of attempting to develop their own points of view and sharpen the differences, the individuals also at-

---

[2] May I again remind the reader that the numbers are systematically scrambled.

tempted to explore the communalities of the points of view. No. 10 privately came into a meeting with a predisposition "to fight," to make the issue a "black or white" one, thereby creating a "win-lose" situation. Of the 11 contributions that he made during the meeting, only two could be interpreted as continuing this pattern. The remaining nine contributions were of the nature that did not place others and, therefore, eventually himself in a defensive position.

2. In another meeting No. 3 and No. 8 were discussing how to develop programs that will help the first line understand the importance of cost cutting and raising production standards.

No. 8: My God, when I think of what we used to do to these fellows to sell them our ideas. God, [smiles] we didn't really want to hear them. Remember, No. 3, the program that we set up last year. We brought the first line managers into a room and gave them 19 reasons why they should like the "improvement program." Bing, bing, bing, we'd go through each one. "Do you [to the foreman] understand No. 1?" They'd shake their heads, and we'd go on to No. 2, and so on.

No. 3 (smiles): I know.

No. 8: What I would like now is to really try to create a program in which the foreman can develop his own sense of commitment to the importance of the program. This means that we ought not to get these consultants with gimmicks and gadgets. We ought to get people who can help create a climate in which the foreman can express himself, can really tell us his point of view and feelings and hopefully could even develop the program by which the objectives could be really accepted.

No. 3 then reminded No. 8 that a researcher was conducting a study that might provide the jumping off point for the program. He asked No. 8 to be patient and wait. This was the first time that I had seen No. 8 agree to place a diagnosis before action.

3. I attended a meeting which No. 9 was chairing. He made 14 contributions throughout the meeting. In 10 of these he behaved in such a way as to minimize one of his leadership patterns that caused the subordinates much trouble. They, of course, had never told him, but he found out at the laboratory.

4. Nos. 1 and 2 had a quick meeting on an explosive issue. No. 1 outlined the problem, carefully discussing

its complexity. No. 2 immediately simplified it, made it much more "black and white" than No. 1 wished, and told No. 1 that he would fight to take certain action. In the past, No. 1 would "agree" and leave.

However, No. 1 responded that he was not comfortable with being told how to solve the problem nor with the solution that No. 2 suggested. He ended by saying, "I want to keep the situation more gray and more flexible because. . . ." (Outlines reasons). No. 2 responded "Good, let me back up again. Why don't you go ahead and do it that way?"

5. The final example is taken from observations made at a company-wide meeting which was being administered by Nos. 1, 2, and 5.

Both No. 1 and No. 5 decided that they ought to have diagnostic-type sessions where people were offered the opportunity to talk about the barriers that they faced in getting their jobs done. According to the people at the meeting (none of whom had attended the laboratory), this was the first time any such meeting was ever held. I interviewed all but one of the participants (seven). All but two felt that the meeting was helpful and hoped that there would be more such meetings. Each person gave me his own reasons why he felt the meeting was helpful to him. The reasons could be categorized in terms of each individual's better understanding of the motives and pressures that were acting upon various people to cause them to behave the way they have been behaving. In other words, their behavior became more intelligible. I will provide some illustrations of this later on.

No. 1 began the meeting by saying that he would like to make this a meeting of "no holds barred" where the focus would be on what were some of the basic barriers that faced the company. He warned about the difficulty of the diagnostic process and said it might be helpful if "We tried not to cut each other off." He then leaned back, lit a cigarette, and waited. The silence, I inferred, was quite uncomfortable to all the men except No. 1 who continued to wait. Finally someone started to talk. He helped to get the members to begin to talk about the barriers which the budgets and personnel freezes created. They then turned to a discussion of the meaning and limits of corporate responsibility. The next discussion was the difficulty of living in a world in which they were asked to have both corporate and divisional responsibility. The discussion concluded that the present divisionalization was not the most effective one. They felt that there might be criteria used other than the ones that were used to make a decision on how they would cut up the divisions. Another conclusion was that the presidents of divisions don't really make the decisions; the major ones are still made by the corporation.

(At the beginning of the discussion I felt that No. 1 was becoming quite involved in the content of the discussion and not focusing as much on the process [but, of course, said nothing]. Toward the end he was focusing more on the process.)

There was a discussion on whether people really understood the reason for the manpower curbs. The discussion continued, and finally someone made the point: "Maybe the problem isn't whether we understand them or not. Maybe the problem is that we feel that explicitly we aren't really trusted."

One of the individuals who complained bitterly about the manpower and budget curb was questioned by the group. One of the members finally suggested that perhaps this individual was complaining too much. Previously, I think, No. 1 would have felt it was his responsibility to tell that man that he was complaining too much. But he refrained. Interestingly, members of the group began to feel a responsibility to tell him so. After several hours, the group members were beginning to cope with some of the feelings that were being raised.

No. 3 came into the meeting. Mr. ———— suggested that No. 3 had "really clipped the wings of the group." Usually No. 3's reply would be "No, I didn't" or "That wasn't my intention." This time, however, he asked, "What did I do to clip the wings of the group? Help me to see that, because I didn't intend to do that."

Mr. ———— then replied, and No. 3 said that he could see how that could be clipping the wings of the group. No. 3 started to describe in some detail the pressures that he felt in trying to resolve budget and manpower problems. He described the pressures in personal terms, the barriers that he faced and anxieties that he had. "Budgets are a painful thing. I don't find them something that I enjoy doing. I do make certain of these cuts partially to save myself. I feel all right now that I've cut this thing, and now I know we're not going to have any problem of not making the budget. Also, another reason why I perhaps cut a little low is that I know that I want to have money when a problem is created or mistake is made that we must solve. I just don't feel that any of us wants to say that we can't afford to solve a mistake."

No. 3 then asked, "I wonder whether if one of our problems is that we don't really believe the budget? Each one of us puts our own little padding into it, and I guess people begin to think that there's always room to cut." (The group nodded in agreement and discussed the problem.) I noticed that four people told No. 3 that this was one of the most meaningful experiences that they ever had. They finally felt that they understood a little more clearly some of the pressures that were on him and why he had to do some of the things that he did.

Another observation was that No. 3 kept quiet while they were talking about budgets and pressures. He did not attempt to criticize people or to tell them that they shouldn't think this way or to tell them that they weren't really understanding him. Some of the "old" No. 3 came out when he told some members, "Well, the obvious thing is . . .", and so on, and he said to another, "Well, what you *really* mean . . .", and so on.

Returning to the diagnosis, the group talked about the "policy" of finding bad guys and good guys whenever a mistake was made. They were worried that their world was very complex and many people had an influence in something if it went well or if it went poorly. However, if it went poorly, someone from above wanted some one man to be clobbered, and so there was always the fear of "Who's going to be the bad guy?" "You can be hero, and that's fine, but you can also be a bum."

No. 3 brought out the question of, "Perhaps we basically mistrust one another." There was a dead silence and someone responded, "You said it; we didn't."

The reader may wonder why no interviews are reported at this time of the experimental group. One of the problems in interviewing participants about what they learned from a program is that the very question may influence them to have an answer when (a) they do not or (b) if they do, it is a negative one and they hesitate to say so. In the case of the latter, the question would not be very helpful.

To make matters even more difficult the researcher was also one of the educators. In a group that developed the degree of openness this one did, I doubt if such would be the case. The experimental group would not hesitate to be frank if they had negative comments. They would know that my greatest sense of esteem would come from being in a relationship where the truth would come out. For research purposes, however, I assumed that this was *not* the case. I decided, therefore, not to interview any of the experimental groups immediately after the program. I concentrated on observing them in group meetings as well as interviewing the people with whom they came in contact.[3]

There were five interviews, however, that arose spontaneously. In all cases the members of the experimental group reported positive experiences. Two examples are included.

1. No. 3 reported that he had significantly different perceptions of No. 2. Before he saw him as bright, ambitious, aggressive, and intolerant. Now he understands No. 2 in such a way that he does not make these same inferences. First, No. 2's behavior has altered. Second, his own confidence with No. 2 has increased. Third, even when No. 2 behaves "in the old way, I see this more as his defensiveness rather than a malicious attempt to hit me."

No. 3 then continued:

Today is one of the first meetings that No. 2 and I had a meeting without an impasse. Usually No. 2 comes charging in and wants to solve it in 15 minutes, which of course means his way. I discussed it with him, and he saw my problem. I don't think we've completely resolved it, but we're much farther than we have ever been.

A month ago, I would have kept my mouth shut. Then I'd prepare my ammunition, and he would prepare his. Then we'd both go to the boss. Now I can't tell you we've resolved everything without going to the boss. But so far we've gone farther than we ever have.

---

[3] The first interviewing actually came as a group interview. The experimental group decided to meet about three weeks after the laboratory to discuss their feelings. These data are presented in the next section.

2. No. 3 told me that he and one of his managers sat down and really talked through the problem of employee improvement. They were worried that the program was beginning to have a negative impact and not really providing the positive motivation that they had hoped. No. 3 described how for the first time they were able to work through a program which at least they felt unanimously was a positive step forward. They took this to the personnel director, who also agreed with them. Everybody seemed to be enthusiastic about this new program, and now they're going to try to work it out.

THE THIRD WEEK: THE EXPERIMENTAL GROUP

Perhaps the best way to illustrate the kinds of learning the experimental group reported that it had obtained from the laboratory experience would be to present some of their own conclusions taken from the tape recording made of the meeting held during the third week by the experimental group to discuss their experience.

The first part of the tape contains a discussion of examples of concrete changes which the members felt were due to the laboratory. A sample of the changes reported were:

1. Developed a new program for certain pricing policies that could not be agreed upon before. The men laid part of the success to their ability to sense feelings.

2. No. 1 described a situation where he unknowingly upset someone, but instead of himself becoming defensive, he sensed what he did and tried to express these feelings. This helped the man to really say what he thought.

3. No. 3 gave an example of how he can now see other people's defensiveness. He concluded the other part was always there, but he had never realized it. Now he is more aware of his own defensiveness.

4. No. 9 stated, "We are consciously trying to change our memos. For example, we found a way to decrease the 'win-lose' feelings and 'rivalries.' "

5. The reader may recall that before the laboratory, personnel problems seemed to have a second-class status. The personnel director reported a distinct improvement in the sen-

sitivity of the line managers to the importance of personnel problems. He is especially pleased with the line executives' new awareness of the *complexity* of personnel problems and their willingness to spend more time on solving them.

Perhaps the best way to view some of the richness of the value that the executives believed they developed from the laboratory training can be obtained by turning to an excerpt taken directly from the tape recording made of the meeting. It is important to point out that this excerpt mirrors the tone of the entire meeting. We did not purposely select only a section in which the men praised the laboratory. If the men had criticized the laboratory, such criticism would have been included. As one may see, the researcher actually pushed the group for more negative comments.

6. One of the subordinates reported that he had the "shock of his life." His superior, a member of the experimental group, had made a decision when the subordinate felt he should have made it.

I was really fuming. I was angry as hell. I walked into his office and I said to myself, "No matter what the hell happens, I'm going to tell him that he cannot do that any more." Well, I told him so. I was quite emotional. You know it floored me. He looked at me and said, "You're right; I made a mistake, and I won't do that again." Well, I just don't think he would have done that before.

No. 7: The most important factor in motivating people is not what you say or do, it's giving him the opportunity to express his views and the feeling that one is seriously interested in his views. I do much less selling but it sure takes longer.

No. 2: I've had a problem. I now have a greater need for feedback than before, and I find it difficult to get. The discussion on internal commitment made much sense to me, and I try to see if I can create conditions for it.

The thing that bothers me is that I try to handle it correctly, but I don't get feedback or cues as to how well I'm doing, as I used to at the lab. The meeting is over, and you don't know whether you've scored or not. So after each meeting I've got 10 question marks. The things that before were never questions are now question marks.

For example, in a discussion last week, I was clear about a decision after one hour's discussion. But I decided to wait to see if they would make the decision. It took two days, and the decision was made. That was a sigh of relief.

You don't get feedback. You ask for something, and they responded, "I know what you're trying to do." They think I've got something up my sleeve. All I want is to get feedback. It was obvious to me they were all waiting for me to make the decision. But I wanted them to make it. This was their baby, and I wanted them to make it. Two days later they made it. Fine, in this case I got feedback. The point was that their decision was a severe reversal, and I realize it was difficult for them to make. But they made it. Before, I simply would have pointed out the facts, and they would have "agreed" with the reversal, but down deep inside they would have felt that they could have continued on. As it is now, it's their decision. I think they now have a greater sense of internal commitment. People are now freer to disagree.

No. 11: My list of decisions to be made is longer. I am hoping that they will make some decisions. I now know how much they wait for me.

(No. 11 also told how he wrote a note which in effect damned No. 2 and said that he [No. 11] was correct. After he wrote it, he re-read it, and realized how defensive he [No. 11] was. "Before I wouldn't have even seen this.")

No. 2: One of our most difficult jobs will be to write our feelings and to write in such a way that others can express their feelings.

No. 3: I have some difficulties in evaluating this program. What have we gotten out of this? What are we able to verbalize about what we got out of this? Do others of you have difficulty in verbalizing it?

No. 2: I have the same difficulty. I have been totally ineffective describing the experience.

No. 8: Each time I try I give a different answer.

No. 1: I don't have too much difficulty. One thing that I am certain of is that I see people more as total human beings. I see aspects of them that I had never seen before.

No. 9: I'm frustrated because I now realize the importance of face-to-face communication. I'm so far from the general managers that it is not so hot. Has anyone tried to write memos that really get feelings brought out?

I find myself questioning much more than I ever did before. I have more questioning attitude. I take into account more factors.

No. 4: We've been talking about things as if we've slowed down a bit. We haven't. For example, remember you [No. 1] and I had a problem? I'm sure Arden Hourse was very helpful. If I hadn't been there, my reaction to you would have been different. I would have fought you for hours.

No. 1: I know we can talk to each other more clearly. It's not a conscious way. It's spontaneous.

No. 3: I have to agree we can make some decisions much

faster. For example, with No. 2 I simply used to shut up. But now I can be more open. Before the laboratory, if I had an intuitive feeling that something was wrong, but I wasn't sure, I'd keep quiet until things got so bad then I have a case to go to the boss. Now I feel freer to talk about it sooner and with No. 2.

I now feel that we are going to say exactly how we feel to anyone. You, [President] for example, don't have to worry, and, therefore, question, probe, and draw us out.

PRESIDENT: Yes, and today I found No. 1, who told me that he simply would not agree with me. And I said to myself, "God bless you. He really is open now."

No. 1: I agree. I would not have expressed this feeling before being in this group. It's obvious that one should, but I didn't.

(No. 2 and No. 1 show real insight into how they are being manipulated by people outside and above the group. They are much more aware of the manipulative process. "This kind of manipulation is dynamite. It burns me up.")

No. 1: Yes, it's really horrible to see it and not be able to do anything about it.

No. 7: In this case it seems to me you've got to really hit hard, because you're dealing with an untrained man. [Laugh.]

(Later on.)

No. 7: I think I now have a new understanding of decision making. I am now more keenly aware of the importance of getting a consensus so that the *implementation* is effective. I am not trying to say that I do this in every meeting. But I do strive more to give opportunity for consensus.

No. 1: One of the problems that I feel is that the "initiated" get confused so they don't play the game correctly. Sometimes I feel walked upon, so I get sore. This is difficult. [Many others agree.]

No. 6: Does it help to say, "I trust you?" I think it does.

No. 11: For example, No. 2, you went to a meeting where you admitted you had made a mistake. Boy, you should have heard the reaction. Boy, Mr. ——— admitted a mistake. Well, wonderful; it helped to get these guys to really feel motivated to get the job done.

No. 9: Yes, I heard that many took on a deeper feeling of responsibility to get the program on the right track.

No. 7: I'd like to come back to what No. 6 said. I used to say to people that I trusted them, that I was honest, and so on. But now I wonder if people really believe me, or if they don't begin to think if I'm not covering that I'm not honest.

No. 3: Another example which I am now aware of is the typical way we write memos. We start off: "I have confidence in your judgment to handle this question," and so on. Few more paragraphs. Then fifth paragraph reads, "Please confirm by return mail exactly what you have done and what controls have been set up."

No. 2: I agree. We do an awful lot to control people. Although I think that we're trying.

(No. 7 gave examples where he stopped making a few phone calls to pressure. Others agreed.)

A: Aren't there negative comments?

No. 11: We have one man who has chosen not to be here. I wonder why?

No. 3: Well, really, to me that is a sign of health in the group. He feels he would still be accepted even if he didn't come. It certainly would be easy for him to come and just sit here.

No. 1: Yes, we wouldn't go to the trouble of avoiding a meeting that you didn't think was important.

No. 3: The only negative that I can think is: "What can you tell me that actually increases effectiveness? I am not sure, but I must agree that there is a whale of a different climate.

No. 7: Well, I'd like to develop a list of things that we feel we have gotten out of this program so far. How do others of you feel? (All agree, "Let's try.")

The group members reached the following conclusions:

1. All of us begin to see ourselves as others see us; to me this is a real plus.
2. A degree of greater confidence in oneself in meetings and in interviews. Beginning to be more comfortable with self.
3. Greater confidence in associates. We feel more secure that you're telling what you think. (People in this group.) Greater feeling of freedom of expression to say what you really think.
4. Individuals have a greater understanding and appreciation of viewpoint of associates.
5. Greater appreciation of the opposite viewpoint.
6. An awareness of what I do and others do that inhibits discussion.
7. More effective use of our resources. I am getting more from them, and I think they feel this. Am patient to listen more.
8. Meetings are taking longer but implementation is more effective. Internal commitment is greater.
9. We have had a great realization that being only task-oriented, we will not get the best results. We must not forget worrying about the organization and the people.
10. We get more irritated to infringement of our jobs and unique contributions.
11. Fewer homemade crises.

No. 6: One of the difficult things about the list is that when you look at it, you wake up to the fact that you haven't really been using these principles. When you tell someone else who doesn't realize the gap between knowing something and actually doing it, he doesn't realize.

No. 7: But I think I really did learn and do care. Now when I think what I used to do, because that was the way. Today I realize that I could have had three times as much if I had known what I know now.

To summarize, the experimental group (about a month after the program) feels that they have learned much from the laboratory program. They include a greater awareness of their impact upon others as well as others' impact upon them, the group, and the organization. They report greater success in understanding group behavior. They also report several concrete organizational changes that they have made as a result of the laboratory experience. Finally, they see more clearly the importance of true participation and internal commitment if decisions are to be implemented. Their tolerance for diagnosis and their respect for complexity in administrative situations has, they report, significantly increased.

These are some frustrations. One seems to be their inability to communicate effectively some of the values that they now feel are worthwhile and practical in the business world. Second, is the apparent inability of the subordinates to provide feedback, to respond appropriately, and in short, to add to their business life a new set of values. (More about this below.)

Above all however, are (1) the increased sense of trust and confidence they have and continue to develop about themselves and their group and (2) the awareness that they have experienced and have "jumped into" a way of living—a *process* which has just begun and has no conclusion. Perhaps these two learnings more than any other can help to develop within the organization an attitude for continual growth and development.

THE THIRD WEEK: THE CONTROL GROUP

About three weeks after the laboratory, the control group was convened to give them the feedback of the original research results. The researcher took the opportunity to ask them to make any comments that they might wish to make regarding the behavior of the experimental group.

There was one clear message running through all the responses. The control group members did observe changes in behavior. These changes were especially marked during the first several weeks after the laboratory. However, they reported a "wearing off" phenomenon after that period. I attempted to study the "wearing off" phenomenon as closely as I could. The tentative conclusions are reported immediately following the comments that illustrate the views the control group members expressed regarding the possible behavioral changes in the experimental group.

1. I had never seen my boss and Mr. ——— talk with one another informally. A few days after the lab I saw these two talk informally with a degree of receptivity that I never had seen before.

My own dealings with Mr. ——— is that he is much more patient with me. As far as my own boss and my relationship, there isn't much difference. [Boss had been at a lab.]

2. I can't really say that I have seen any significant change.

3. I think I did see some change, but it was limited to the first few weeks. The first few weeks my boss was more inclined to really listen to me; he was more patient and more searching. But it seems to wear off.

4. I saw Mr. ——— also be more understanding than he had ever been. I can't say that has worn off.

SOMEONE ELSE: No, I think he is different. I saw it in him. He is different.

I agree. I, too, have seen Mr. ——— become much more concerned about others. He now asks how other people will probably react before he makes decisions. Like X, I too think he's a much better listener.

I have seen some of these changes that you are discussing. 'Course, I don't know how lasting they will be.

5. I think my boss is trying real hard. When he came back he told us that he was told that he ———, and he has really tried to change that. He is seriously trying.

6. All I can attribute for sure is the one meeting that I saw with four of them who had been at the program. They were much freer and carefree. It's hard to describe, but there was a significant difference in the degree of tension. I haven't noticed any other differences.

7. Yes, I did notice something that you might call 'brotherly love.' They got along with and understood one another in a way that they had never done before.

RESEARCHER: Do you feel that is wearing off?

No. 1: No, I'm not sure that I'd say they wore off. It may be still there.

No. 2: If I may add a comment, it may be that at the beginning we were all keyed up and listening. Maybe we were concerned to see if there were any changes. Now we're not watching as carefully anymore.

(Four men nod their heads in agreement.)

8. One of the subordinates of an executive in the experimental group stopped me to tell me how changed things were with his boss. He reported his boss "is really trying." He described several meetings in which he participated where people were trying to get the superior to make decisions. He then added, "The boss sure took a lot of guff. If I were in his shoes, I wouldn't have taken that. I would have told him, 'All right, damn it, here is the decision,' and that would be it."

Up to this point the data support the conclusion that the program has had an observable impact upon the executive's behavior in their relationships with one another. There is also some evidence that the executives attempted to utilize their learning to do away with organizational policies and practices that they now realize have consequences that are unintended, in their opinion, undesirable. Finally there is evidence that the executive's attempted to utilize their new learnings in their relationships with others who had not attended the program. For example, the control group reports changes in the "experimental group's" behavior. They described them as "better listeners," "more patient," "more understanding," and "less controlling."

However, the majority of the control group also reported that the impact seemed to "wear off" after several weeks. When asked to describe how they sensed the changes wore off, the control group was unable to do so. They reported an "over-all feel" that things are back to "normal." One of the members suggested that it may be that they are no longer looking for changes with the same degree of intensity that they did during the first weeks. All agreed that this was the case.

This raised the possibility that the changes reported during the first two weeks could have been distorted because of the "set" of the control group. The probability that this is not the case is supported by the observations and tape recording of actual group meetings where members of the experimental group actually did attempt new actions. Moreover, all of the situations described by the control group, from which they made their inferences of change, were upon interview confirmed by the experimental group. That is, the experimental group reported that they had made specific attempts and that they were understood correctly by the control group.

However, there are data to suggest that the impact tends to begin to decrease about two weeks after the laboratory. There seem to be several reasons. First, the control group reports that they are not certain how to understand the new behavior. It is a trick, a gimmick? Those that do understand the changes wonder how lasting and genuine they are. Most of them tend to play it safe and "see if it occurs again." The postponement of an appropriate response has a negative impact upon the members of the experimental group. They now enter administrative situations with caution, trepidation, and a higher degree of expectation of failure in the use of their new values. When they do not tend to receive the feedback they know they would have experienced at the laboratory, their expectation of failure is confirmed. They may make one or two other attempts. If a "positive signal" is not received, they eventually return to their old behavior. Once they do so, it tends to confirm to the subordinate that, indeed, the new behavior was skin-deep if not just an act. He, in turn, begins to become even more defensive. The superior, now much more sensitive, senses that increased defensiveness and, thus, retreats even more.

There is, as the experimental group points out, another difficulty. Even if the members of the control group do trust their (members of the experimental group) behavior, they may be simply ignorant of how to behave according to "the rules of this new way of doing things, which quite frankly is in a totally different ball park."

Below are three illustrations to show how confused many of the subordinates felt.

1. The subordinates (2) and (3) were interviewed after they participated in a diagnostic type meeting. It was the first

such meeting held in their department. It was led by one of the members of the experimental group.

You know, I had the feeling, "What is the object of all these meetings?" "Why do we need a diagnosis of our problems?" So you tell me your feeling and I'll tell you mine. What the hell good does it do?

2. "To be honest with you, I'm a bit confused. I feel we unleashed and opened up a bucket of snakes."

3. A subordinate was interviewed because it was discovered that he happened to participate in a meeting where two members of the experimental group attempted to solve a problem by making some "here and now" analysis of the processes in the meeting.

Well, it's this way. We were having a discussion and going at it hot and heavy. Suddenly those two started talking about what we were doing to one another. I felt like saying, 'What the hell are you doing? What difference does it make what we are doing to one another? We're here to make a decision!'

Apparently none of the subordinates felt free to communicate bewilderment. When asked why, they provided ambivalent answers; on the one hand they felt that this may be "the new look" and if so, instead of questioning it, they had better learn more about it. On the other hand they felt embarrassed to talk about feelings. "It seemed out of place," reported one individual. "Look, all my life I'm told it's a good idea to keep personalities out of business. Now these guys [members of experimental group] are bringing them in!"

Whatever the reason for not "leveling," the impact upon the experimental group was strong. Time and time again the members of the experimental group reported that one of their most persistent frustrations was the lack of "appropriate feedback" from those who had not been to a laboratory. The experimental group kept looking for signs that would help them understand their own impact upon others. It should be made clear that they were not looking for feedback of a positive nature. They were simply trying to find out how effectively they were communicating.

The control group, the reader may recall, held the same

values, with the same degree of tenacity, as did the experimental group. Why should one expect the members of the experimental group to influence significantly the control group if one of the main reasons for the laboratory was the experts' advice that if such learning is to develop quickly, it best be initiated away from the organization in what Lewin called a "cultural island"? He meant the establishment of a setting with its own unique culture so that the entire setting supported growth and development. Clearly, a laboratory at the office situation would have had great difficulty because, as we have shown, the values of the typical industrial culture are different from those evolved at the laboratory.

Another crucial factor inhibiting the "spread of change" is the gap between intellectual learning and emotional understanding. Anyone who experiences a laboratory realizes, perhaps for the first time in his life, the great gap between the knowledge and acceptance of a set of values and the actual implementation of these values. It is possible for men to learn intellectually in one hour the values implicit in the laboratory approach. But, as one participant said, "My God, it takes a hell of a long time, a lot of hard work, and emotional investment to make these values part of me."

This places the members of the experimental group in a very difficult situation. They now know that it makes little sense to tell others that they are behaving in a way that will not tend to achieve their intended consequences. They also know it makes even less sense to attempt to describe how these intended consequences can be achieved. They know these generalizations to be the case, not so much because they read them in material given to them at the laboratory. They know the validity of these generalizations because they have experienced them. They recalled that they had received feedback from the researcher which suggested that they were partially responsible for creating the human problems that they disliked. They also recalled that they hardly remember any of the first theory lectures given by the educators. If evidence from research taken from their own words and inferred from their own behavior does not lead to changes, if then the experts' lecture seem to have similar lack of effect, then how can they hope to communicate effectively to those who have not attended the laboratory, that their behavior isn't achieving what they intend?

One of the participants cited an example of the difficulties involved. He asked his subordinate to tell him what he was attempting to achieve during the meeting. The subordinate replied. Then the superior with "careful questioning" helped the subordinate to see that he was not achieving his objectives. The subordinate, although somewhat defensive for "being caught" by his superior, said that he had found it helpful. He asked the superior what else he had learned at the laboratory. The superior's reply included "how not" (1) to manipulate people, (2) to make them dependent upon him and (3) to become responsible for their learning. After finishing, the subordinate looked confused. Suddenly the superior blushed because he realized that in the incident above he violated all these learnings!

To make matters more difficult, any member of the experimental group is caught up in many complex organizational decisions, each loaded with pressure to resolve, each requiring much work and tension if they are to be resolved. How can one rightly expect an executive relatively inexperienced in training and plagued by the everyday pressures of executive life to also act as an educator? The professional educators have never set such a level of aspiration.

To summarize, the spread of the values implied in the laboratory within the organization is inhibited by several interrelated factors. First, the present organizational culture, structure, and managerial controls that are, as we have seen, characterized by the interpersonal mistrust, conformity, dependence, management by crisis and through details, interdepartmental rivalries, and so on. Second, the lack of time and other pressures that presently characterize the world of the executives studied. Third, the differences in values held by the experimental group regarding effective interpersonal action from these held by the control group on the same subject. These values may be summarized as follows:

INTERPERSONAL VALUES

Control Group (and Most of Organization)	*Experimental Group*
1. Simplification of situations.	1. Respect for complexity.
2. Action is sign of executive strength.	2. Thinking, reflection, and diagnosis are as important as action.
3. "Diplomacy," "flattery," and so on, to cover up ignorance of self and others.	3. Genuineness and openness to increase awareness of self and others.
4. External commitment.	4. Internal commitment.
5. Only rational, intellective, professional aspects of problems are relevant.	5. The emotional and interpersonal aspects of problems should be explored as thoroughly as the rational, professional aspects.

Finally, add the executive's awareness that (*a*) effective changes are difficult, (*b*) ought to be self-initiated and controlled, and (*c*) that they are not as yet effective agents for change. One can readily understand why there may be difficulties to the spread of learning throughout the organization. This does not mean that no changes are occurring. First, we must keep in mind that the learning within the experimental group is constantly increasing. Moreover, some of the executives of the experimental group have held remarkably successful (for this organization) diagnostic meetings where progress was made. For example, one of the interesting developments was the experimental group's decision to focus on making changes, wherever possible, in policies and practices, structure and controls that would sanction and reinforce the values learned at the laboratory. They reasoned that if they have difficulty in inducing change at the interpersonal dimension, they would try at the organizational level.

The changes have just begun to be implemented. In one case, certain meetings held weekly which always created interdepartmental rivalries and hostilities were greatly altered. The objective was changed from one of "briefing the boss" to "helping one another get the job done." This made it less necessary for the President to be present, which in turn decreased even further the subordinates' dependence upon him.

Another change was the diagnostic meetings some of the experimental group members held with their subordinates. The objective was to discuss organizational problems and ways to resolve them. Whenever interpersonal relationships became relevant, they were discussed as openly as possible.

For example, at one meeting one of the members of the experimental group met with his subordinates to discuss ways to increase the effectiveness of their operation. It became apparent to the executive that the subordinates explored the problems but hesitated to make decisions. He felt (and the researcher who observed the meeting concurred) that the subordinates were waiting for him to make the decisions. He reported that he was caught in an internal struggle. On the one hand, he knew that if he were seduced into making the decision, this would mean one further strike against real delegation of authority and responsibility. On the other hand, he honestly felt he had some good ideas on how to solve the problems and was bursting to tell them. The bubble was broken by one of the subordinates who said:

SUBORDINATE: Well, what do you think we ought to do?

SUPERIOR (smiles): I guess I wonder what it would solve if I make this decision.

SUBORDINATE: What has happened to you lately? Ever since the beginning of the year, you've changed. You're not the man I used to know. I used to come into your office, and in seconds I'd know exactly what you were thinking, and you'd make a decision. Now I feel you're playing guessing games with me.

SUBORDINATE No. 3: Maybe he wants us to make the decisions.

SUBORDINATE No. 2: I don't mind making the decisions as long as I know what he [superior] wants!

SUPERIOR: If I made the decision, then it's mine—not yours.

SUBORDINATE No. 2: Sure—but I bet you have an idea exactly what you want me to do. I feel you're holding back on me, and that burns me up because I don't feel trusted.

SUPERIOR (nods affirmatively): Yes, you are correct. I am holding back. I do it because I believe it is important that you make the decisions. I guess this is new for me, and I'm still not completely sure. Yes, I agree that I am holding back. But I wish I didn't have to. . . .

SUBORDINATE No. 3: You know, the more I listen to us, the more that I think that we want you to make our decisions for us. Then, if something goes wrong, it's your fault.

SUBORDINATE No. 2: Maybe you're right. But honestly, I'm not trying to pass the buck. I just want to know what *he* is thinking about—his limits—before I make a decision.

The discussion continued, and the meaning of delegation was explored thoroughly. Interestingly, the experimental group member saw the entire two-day meeting as "just a beginning." He also reported some disappointment in the degree of defending that he and others have caused in the subordinates. He was even more hopeful, however, that changes were possible if one simply had patience.

The data do suggest, however, a number of other tactics that might be explored to enhance organizational development:

1. Each group should attend a laboratory that is longer than seven days so that they can learn to begin to cope with the problems above.

2. Each member should attend two laboratories, one in which he is with the group where he is the formal "back-home" leader. Several weeks later he would attend a laboratory in which he is with the group where he is a peer and/or a subordinate. (The sequence of these may well be reversible.) In this image, each executive would be required to undergo two weeks of training broken down into two one-week periods and spaced so organizational activity is not jeopardized.

3. A third possibility is for the organization to develop "booster shots." This could be in the form of one-day laboratories where the participants deal with actual problems, away from the pressures of the office, and with the help of a professional. Blake and Shepard have found these to be quite helpful.

Another possibility (and one which is a personal choice of the writer) is for the professional to attend actual meetings at the headquarters. Specimen meetings can be selected by the executives which they will want to analyze in terms of their effectiveness. In this way, the laboratory values are reinforced at the home location and in the natural sequence of events. More of this in the conclusion and recommendations.

III. INTERVIEW OF EXPERIMENTAL GROUP: SIX MONTHS AFTER

In addition to the observations made during the six-month period after the laboratory, at the end of the period an interview was held with each man. No detailed interview schedule was developed. The objective was to provide the experimental group with one final opportunity to say anything they wished about the total experience. The interview lasted from 20 minutes to one and a half hours. Some of the major conclusions were:

1. All the men at the headquarters felt strongly about the learnings that they obtained while at the laboratory. They emphasized the increasing degree of trust, mutual confidence, openness, leveling and the decreasing degree of conformity, fear, and unnecessary "politicking."

2. They all felt that the degree of learning within the experimental group was increasing with every opportunity available to put into use the values learned at the laboratory. Also, the men reported many instances when their ability to work with one another had continued to increase. Each experience became a learning experience for further growth.

Each executive also reported that there was at least one man with whom he had not significantly enhanced his interpersonal relationships. But in all but three cases, they attributed this to the lack of contact. In the three cases where the contact was frequent but positive changes were not occurring, the executives discussed the relationships with me on a diagnostic basis with minimal attempts to condemn the other. In all cases, they reported that the other party was aware of the difficulties. After some discussions they had agreed that, at this time, they were going to have these difficulties. Hopefully, through further experience they could solve their problems. At the end of the six-month period one of the executives reported that his relationship with another was becoming more effective. The other executives and three others (all from the experimental group) confirmed the trend.

3. As was pointed out above, the biggest difficulties encountered by the experimental group was in their relationship with their peers (who had not attended the laboratory) and subordinates (who also had not attended the laboratory) as well as the pressures from "above" and "outside."

Regarding the relationship with the peers and subordinates, the first weeks showed decreasing effectiveness and increasing mistrust. They tended to perceive the experimental group's behavior as composed of "gimmicks" and "techniques."

The final interviews and observations indicate, however, a new trend in these relationships, reversing the old one. At least half of the experimental group reported new progress in their relationships with those who had not attended the laboratory. The analysis of the data suggests at least two reasons for his new change. First, the persistence of some of those in the experimental group "to try again and again." Apparently, the very "failure" in relationships tended to prove to the experimental group that they must try harder. As one man said, "Damn it, when you see yourself succumbing to be the old boss again, where they all nod their heads appropriately, you say 'To hell with it. I'm not going to work that way if I can help it.' And you start again."

This seems to me to be an important phenomenon. It shows the degree to which half of the experimental group had internalized the laboratory values. The "failure" to them was proof that they, as leaders, were creating dependencies and conformity that in the long run would help no one or the company.

The second reason is related to the changes in policies and practices that have begun to occur. These have done much to "prove" to the organization that the experimental group means to develop and use the new values. The changes in the way control systems are used, control meetings are held (in some cases abolished), objectives are set, and budgets prepared, have all had an important influence on the organization. This point cannot be overemphasized. Important changes in values can occur in an organization if the policies, practices, structure, and control systems are modified. However, as many subordinates pointed out, such organizational changes would have been hollow and lead to utter confusion if the superior did not seem to be struggling to behave in accordance with these values.

I do hope that conclusions such as these put an end to the senseless discussions of changing organizational structure *versus* interpersonal relationships. Both go hand in hand. One without the other could eventually lead to deep schism within the organization.[4]

---

[4] For a discussion that unfortunately uses this "straw man" argument see Elliot Chapple and Leonard Sayles, *Measure of Management* (New York: The Macmillan Co., 1961).

With respect to the pressures from above, the men report that they had a problem. For example, they reported that they experienced numerous occasions when they were ready to truly delegate to the subordinates, only to be pressured from above to get a quick answer or make an immediate decision. Also, the top corporate executives persisted in their use of such practices as "management by crisis and through detail." This, of course, coerced the divisional officers to do likewise.

Finally, at certain times, the executive's own impatience or lack of skill in a particular situation acted to coerce them to pressure, to make decisions, and, in general, to favor the traditional values.

They reported that because of these reasons they found it difficult to behave in accordance with their newly learned values as often as they wished. However, they were equally quick to report that now they were at least aware of what they were truly doing to others when they behaved according to the old values. The following excerpt may help to illustrate the point:

Mr. ——— came up to me to tell me that he finds that his learning is increasing. More and more he is beginning to feel comfortable in the new role that he's playing. He pointed out that this new role was not a substitution of the old one but an addition to the old one. He said that he found, and so did others that when they were placed under tremendous pressure, they had to respond with pressure on the people below. However, they were quite aware of when they were creating the pressure and weren't expecting the kinds of results that they had expected previously. He said that he felt that the proportion of times when he could behave according to the laboratory values was definitely increasing. This was especially true if he counted the situations over which he had complete control. He said he felt that the same thing was true with the president, even though, at times, he might be quite directive for a week or two; as soon as the pressures are off, he might go back to developing the values that he felt were more valid in administrating people.

Eight of the executives reported programs in developing competence in the new values as well as finding increasing opportunities to use them. Two reported that they were using them, but not as often as they wished or could.

No. 1:[5]

a) I have a strong feeling that it's easier to talk with one another. We're much more open, much more leveling with our own group. I'm much more conscious of problems than I have ever been before and aware of how other people probably feel. In my estimation, I think there's a significant difference with my relationship with No. 9 and No. 2. It's really open. We're calling a spade a spade. We're trying to resolve some of these issues. I can't honestly tell you that we have resolved all these issues, but we're certainly more open and tackling them in a way in which we have never tackled them before.

b) I think I have not only learned to cope with feelings more openly with the experimental group but with other people. I think I've learned this. I find myself doing it rather spontaneously. If I sense someone is upset, I try to deal with it. I try to explore it rather than ignore it. Previously I would suppress it. If I found myself when there was some disagreement and it was small, I would forget about it. Now I find myself very spontaneously encouraging disagreement to come out, so that we can really discuss it. I think I'm spending much more time in this, and I can't tell you I have arrived or it may not even be worthwhile, but I certainly am trying.

No. 2:

a) Oh, I would say that the laboratory has helped me very much. Not only with my own group but with outside groups. I find that I say what I think, and I say it much more effectively, much more open, much more leveling not only with the experimental group but with other groups. And I find that people respond very well.

b) I think that I see much more clearly now that it doesn't make sense not to cope with feelings. These are important and central to our business. I think that, before, I would not deal with emotionality. Now I try to. I think I find I'm trying to ascertain what is the rational, what is the rationality of emotions. But, before, I just wasn't even aware of this.

No. 3:

a) My feelings about our experience have become increasingly clear and less confused. I am surprised as to how I have to think through the experience every time I am asked to explain it to someone. I now think I know what made this a very valuable experience for me.

---

[5] May I again remind the reader that the numbers representing the individuals are purposely shuffled.

First, I was with the people I normally dealt with. It seems to me it would have been much less valuable if it were in the abstract, that is with people who were not in my working group.

Another valuable asset has been that I can now understand the behavior of my own and others much better. I don't think that I'm saying that my behavior or others' has necessarily and significantly changed. But I am saying that it doesn't matter as much anymore. I understand more clearly why people behave the way they do, and what is the meaning of their behavior.

b) Actually, there are things that I'm doing differently. Things that I hadn't done before. But the most important one from my point of view is that I understand myself better, and I understand others better and they can go ahead and be themselves without it, without my misinterpreting it. Also, I think I can go ahead and be myself with my mistakes and my weaknesses without the fellows' misinterpreting it.

No. 4:

a) I would say things are changing. Everyone in our group is really trying to change things. Even if they get upset, and in a crisis situation you see them saying sometimes, "God damn it, this isn't the way we planned this at all. Let's start all over again."

But I think the changes are small and it's going to take a long time before they get into effect.

No. 5:

a) I think we are getting to where we want to go much faster; we've given up sparring, politicking. We save an awful lot of time. It used to be if I want to get something from No. 3, I'd plan two or three weeks how I would do it. Now I think I can go directly to him and work it out with him.

b) We also feel much more comfortable in making short cuts without worrying how they will be perceived. It used to be before that any short cut could be easily interpreted as trying to hurt the other fellow, and now the trust is great enough that we know that if there was a short cut that should be discussed, we would; if not, we just go right on ahead.

c) I would disagree with those who feel that there has not been a positive learning with the other people. I hope that there has been in my case; at least I think there has been. I find that I am much more dedicated to do a lot more listening than I ever have, much more dedicated to be aware of their feelings. I don't say to you that I know how to handle them the way I would like to completely, but I think I am learning.

No. 7:

a) Well, I noticed signs of change in most of the people. Interestingly enough, I think that the least change is the change in me. I can't say that I tried to behave differently with anyone except, perhaps, with one person. I guess what I really mean, however, is that I see an awful lot of changes in others, but I haven't seen as many changes as I could myself. I think my principal change has been my relationship with No. 7. It's been much easier, and I think I understand him much better. I think he understands me much better.

TABLE 16

BEGINNING AND "END" MEASUREMENTS OF EXPERIMENTAL GROUP
(N = 11)

	Beginning	Six Months After
In an administrative situation whenever possible:		
1a) The leader should translate interpersonal problems into rational intellective ones.	100	10
1b) The leader should deal with the interpersonal problems.	0	81
2a) The leader should stop emotional disagreement by re-defining the rational purpose of the meeting.	90	10
2b) The leader should bring out emotional disagreements and help them to be understood and resolved.	6	81
3a) When strong emotions erupt, the leader should require himself and others to leave them alone and not deal with them.	100	18
3b) When strong emotions erupt, the leader should require himself and offer others the opportunity to deal with them.	0	82
4a) If it becomes necessary to deal with feelings, the leader should do it even if he feels he is not the best qualified.	100	9
4b) The leader should encourage the most competent member.	0	90
5a) The leader is completely responsible for keeping the group "on the track" during a meeting.	100	0
5b) The group members as well as the leader are responsible for keeping the group "on the track."	0	100

Another way to evaluate the change within the experimental group is to compare their answers to certain questions asked at the outset of the program and at the end.

It should be emphasized that these changes are in the values held by the members of the experimental group. It does *not* follow that they are free to or that they actually behave according to these values. As we have seen (1) pressures from above outside the organization, (2) legitimate but unexpected emergencies, and (3) the subordinates' desire to continue in their submissive role make it difficult for these values to be manifested in actual leadership behavior. Apparently the difficulty was greatest during the first six months. After six months, because of persistence and appropriate changes in the organization, it became easier for half of the executives to begin to apply these values.

It is interesting to note that these changes in half of the group have begun to create an organizational norm which now helps to sanction the new values. This seems to have had the impact of loosening up the subordinates as well as those members of the experimental group who have been less persistent.

Another significant change in the experimental group is that 64 per cent of them now report that their deepest satisfactions come from interpersonal *as well as* intellective problems. Thus, the men have *not* substituted the interpersonal base for the intellective. Rather, they have added and thereby enlarged their base for emotional satisfaction.

Let us now turn to a brief examination of the changes in interpersonal scores of the experimental group. Because of personnel changes, one individual in the experimental group was not observed. Also, because of time limitations only half as many sessions were observed as before the laboratory.

Of the total possible score (116), the group scored 86. If one compares it with the scores developed before the laboratory, there is a definite improvement in interpersonal competence. If one analyzes the scores, one finds that the executives achieved almost a perfect score in terms of (1) being aware of their impact and (2) being aware of others' view of the situation. They lost most of their points in terms of the dimension, "being able to solve problems in such a way that they remained solved." This is understandable since, as we have seen, many of the individuals who did not attend the laboratory actually resisted and resented the changes that they were observing and experiencing. As one man told one of the members of the experimental group, "You have changed. You are *not* the person I used to know. I used to be able to come into your office, and you'd tell me exactly what you thought and how you would decide something. Now, I play a guessing game. I can't figure out what you would want me to do."

With such attitudes of dependence it will be a long time before the organization is going to be able to solve its problems in such a way that they remain resolved. If for no other reason than that the subordinates will tend to want to keep the important ones "alive" in order that they can take them "upstairs" for solution.

We conclude with the thought that although the data are very encouraging, much more methodological research is required. Instruments are needed to obtain much "harder" data than the ones that we have presented in this chapter. We are in the process of developing such instruments.

A CLOSING NOTE—NINE MONTHS LATER*

The experimental group held a meeting approximately nine months after the laboratory. There was no fixed agenda. The objective was to freely discuss any and all feeling about and experiences related to the laboratory.

The discussion began with one executive evaluating the over-all impact of the laboratory experience upon his working life. This led others to present their evaluations. One hundred per cent ($N = 10$) of the executives felt that the laboratory experience had a positive impact upon their work life. When I pressed for concrete examples, the men had no difficulty in presenting numerous illustrations.

First, some illustrative examples of the evaluations made.

No. 1: Well, I would say that my job has been made easier by a magnitude of five. One way that I see the impact is to compare my relations with the individuals outside the division. Gad, what a mess! I feel completely frustrated. I go to meetings, and it is clear that no one is leveling. Finally, I decide to say what I believe all of us are feeling. Well, it falls flat on its face. It is as if they say, "Look, we're in a swamp, and we want to stay here."

No. 2: Yes, I agree with you. Most of the meetings I go to outside this division are so task-oriented that they never stop to ask what is really going on in the group.

No. 3: I would say that I have changed a lot with my human relations with myself. I've learned that in the past I had created an environment where I didn't dare to reveal myself. You know this

---

* These observations were obtained while the report was being published.

creates a lot of tension. . . . This feeling that you have to be on your guard. It is a wonderful feeling when you no longer have to be on guard.

No. 4: I would agree with much that has been said up to now. However, one danger that I have found is that in an attempt to be sensitive and empathetic with people who don't really understand, they interpret my behavior as being indecisive.

No. 5: You know, funny thing, if you ask me if I have changed, I guess I would say, "I hope so." I feel much less tense with this group around the table. My answer would be that I believe all of you have made great improvements!

The final quotation illustrates the possibility that the laboratory might be of help to an individual who has not made any significant changes in his own behavior if the others around him have changed. When asked this question, one individual felt that this applied in his case.

I asked for concrete examples of changes other than in their perceptions of their own or someone else's behavior. The group members had little difficulty in citing examples. As an illustration, let us consider the discussion that the men had about budgets. They agreed that budgets are now introduced in a way that greater internal commitment is possible on the part of the subordinates. "The men feel more nearly that this is their budget." "Not that we have solved all our problems, mind you," said another. "We have a long way to go," he concluded.

In an attempt to press further, I asked if the annual budget meetings were significantly different. The majority of the replies were that the meetings were not very much different. However, they quickly pointed out that there were significant differences in the preparations of budgets before the meetings. The managers at the lower levels are apparently given much greater opportunity to participate in the definition of their budgets and greater control in their use. However, the actual formal meetings are not much different.

I purposely attempted to push the men to discuss possible "negative" impacts by saying, "I predicted that by this time there would be a fade-out effect and most learning would begin to become extinct due to pressures from above, and so on." Not one executive confirmed my hypothesis that the learning was, or was on the way to becoming, extinct. Indeed, many gave examples to show that the learnings and trust developed continued strongly within the experimental group. They also reported that they were operating much more effectively with those subordinates with whom they worked most closely. There was also very strong agreement that they experienced great frustration with executives outside their division.

However, some of the men did report a degree of fade-out. The degree of fade-out varied with each individual and varied with the same individual under different conditions. In no case did the men feel that the fade-out was significant enough to have returned the group to its original (prelaboratory) state. From the discussion on fade-out, I surmised that its measurement has to be considered in terms of two dimensions. There is fade-out in terms of the frequency of use of the new learnings. Also, there is fade-out in terms of the potential or capability of each person to practice what he has learned. The use of the new learnings has decreased much more than the capability. For example, in meetings with corporate officials and with peers from other divisions, the executives find it difficult to be as open as they believe they are capable. Apparently, this lack of use of the new values has *not* led to a proportional deterioration of the individual's potential or capability to use these values when the opportunity presents itself. It seems up to the nine-month period at least, that the values learned do not fade away. The individual feels that he is still capable of behaving in accordance with these values even though the frequency with which he is permitted to do so is low and/or is decreasing. One may hypothesize that the values can be dormant without their fading away. If this hypothesis is confirmed, it may be that an important causal factor for this phenomenon is that the values were learned in a laboratory with one's natural group. Thus, the men can feel psychologically supported by each other. Also, their learnings may be reinforced when they hold their own meetings. The executives' comments above suggest that these hypotheses have some degree of plausability.

Another small validity test that could be made of the executives' evaluation was to observe their impact upon each other during the evaluation meeting. How open were they?

How free were they in talking about interpersonal problems that were relevant to the organization's problems?

Admittedly, the answers to such questions must be drawn from highly subjective inferences and consequently must be viewed with extreme caution. The meeting lasted nearly five hours. The discussion on the evaluation of the laboratory continued for about an hour. The remaining four hours were spent in a session that was reminiscent of the quality of the meetings at the end of the laboratory. The session was primarily a combination of a T-group and an organizational diagnosis. That is, as the men discussed their organizational problem, they also felt free to discuss the interpersonal problems, whenever they were relevant. For example, one individual discussed how he felt when he discovered a computing error that could cost the division hundreds of thousands of dollars. He remarked that he could have hidden it for several months, but he felt free to go up to the president and discuss the matter thoroughly. Another example was when the group discussed in detail the impact of pressures on manufacturing, engineering, and so on. There were significant disagreements. These disagreements were discussed on the intellectual level but also on the emotional and interpersonal level. Thus, when one individual discussed the possible positive impact of pressure, he was helped to relate this hypothesis to his own personal way of operating. One executive discussed the conditions under which the behavior of some of his fellow executives creates difficulties for the organization *and* feelings of alarm within that particular executive. Still another executive openly explored how the way he was measured by the control systems influenced him to think and act in particular ways, some of which might not be in the best interests of the organization. The discussion led him to consider new behavior.

To summarize, if the data presented by the executives and if the inferences made from their behavior during the meeting are valid, then one may conclude that the positive impact of the laboratory is still in existence within the experimental group. The men suggest that the next steps should be to attempt a similar program with the corporate officials and with their counterparts in the other divisions.

AUTHOR'S NOTE

Although the data suggest that the executives believe the laboratory was of value and that their evaluation is not unduly influenced by the positive relationship established with myself as the educator, there remains the possibility that factors beyond the control of either party did influence the evaluation. For example, the executives may have been influenced to report positive evaluations by relatively unconscious motives not to hurt me. Also, I could have been influenced by motives, of which I was similarly unaware, to interpret their replies to be more positive than the executives intended them to be.

In anticipation of such possibilities, Dr. Roger Harrison, a colleague who conducts laboratories and is a T-group educator, was asked to plan and execute a separate study to evaluate the impact of the laboratory program on the executives. We agreed not to exchange data until our analyses and conclusions were complete. Thus, the following chapter by Dr. Harrison is the description of an attempt to conduct an independent and objective validity check of the effects of the training.

11

Impact of the Laboratory on Perceptions of Others by the Experimental Group

by ROGER HARRISON, *Yale University*

The design of the procedures reported in this chapter was based on the proposition that change in behavior toward others depends on corresponding changes in values and perceptions. Thus, the training experience is intended to increase the value attached by participants to interpersonal and emotional aspects of organizational relationships. If participants do come to value these aspects more, we expect that they will come to see one another more in terms of emotional and interpersonal characteristics, and proportionately less in terms of intellective, rational capacities or technical competence. Further, we would not expect a significant change in participants' behavior toward others to take place without this corresponding change in ways of perceiving others.

We reasoned that as a person attaches increased value to interpersonal relations in the organization, he will become more sensitive and responsive to others' emotions, feelings, and interpersonal needs. That is, a person's values determine in large part the events of which he can be aware. If an individual sets a high positive (or negative) value on a trait or behavior of others, he will tend to describe them in terms of these strongly valued characteristics. Thus, if one result of a laboratory is that a member changes his values about the kinds of behavior that are important to deal with in his organizational life, he should then begin to see and respond to others in new ways, and he should begin to use a changed vocabulary to describe other people.

The preceding chapters have detailed the extent to which

261

these managers tended initially to define the important human relationships as those related to getting the job done. They tended to see effectiveness in relationships in terms of rationality and technical competence, and they tended to be less aware of the emotional impact of their behavior on others than they later learned to be.

The values of the laboratory, on the other hand, lie in helping participants to become aware of feelings and emotions and to deal with them in open discussion as important and valued parts of human relationships in the organization.

Our point of view is that changes in values and changes in perceptions go together. As one becomes more aware of behavior in the interpersonal area, he comes to feel more strongly about it; as he feels more strongly, he becomes more sensitive to its occurrence.

We expected, then, if the training experience was successful, that the executives in the laboratory would come to see one another more in terms of interpersonal and emotional characteristics, and proportionately less in terms of rationality and technical competence. Also, we expected that as the experimental group moved back into the organization and attempted to act there in accordance with new values, their success in applying the values in their organizational lives would be mirrored in an increased tendency to see their other colleagues more in terms of interpersonal and emotional characteristics.

In this application to the organizational situation the values of the laboratory undergo a confirmation or a refutation. As the new ways of seeing and responding to others lead to successful resolution of organizational problems, we would expect interpersonal-emotional concepts to be used more frequently in describing others in the organization. In the reverse situation, where seeing and responding to others in interpersonal-emotional ways leads to frustration rather than solutions to problems, then we would expect no increase in the use of such concepts to describe others.

The basic instrument used in this part of the study was a modification of Kelly's Role Repertory instrument.[1] The instru-

---

[1] G. A. Kelly, *The Psychology of Personal Constructs* (New York: W. W. Norton & Co., Inc., 1955).

ment presented the respondent with the names of 11 people, including himself. The names were arranged in 20 sets of three, so that each person was in one set with each other person at least once. In responding to the instrument, a member was asked to give an important way in which one of the three persons in each set differed from the other two. He then gave the logical opposite of this characteristic. Below are some sample responses.

Persons Compared			Characteristic	Opposite
No. 3	No. 5	No. 7	Mentally alert	Dull
No. 1	No. 4	No. 7	Warm in personal relationships	Cool in relations with others
No. 2	No. 6	No. 8	High status	Low status

The Person Description Instrument was administered to three different groups:

Two separate studies were made of the original experimental group of 11 managers, using the instrument. In the first they described one another before the laboratory, and again on the next to last day of the training. Thus, we had a measure of change with training in the ways they perceived each other.

Each member also described 10 associates chosen by himself according to criteria which specified that he select people with a variety of personal characteristics, who were well-known to himself but who were not attending the laboratory. These descriptions were made once before the laboratory, and again three months after it. We hypothesized that this form of the instrument would provide a measure of the extent to which new ways of perceiving others were actually used back on the job after the training.

A control group consisting of 12 managers in the division who did not attend a laboratory program during the period of the study also described 10 associates chosen by each respondent as having a variety of personal characteristics and as being well-known to him. The control group completed the Person Description Instrument once before the laboratory and again three months later.

A second experimental group consisted of eight men who

had originally been selected to be in the control group and who had participated in that group's first administration of the Person Description Instrument. Six weeks later, these men participated in a second training laboratory, similar to the one held for the experimental group.

Their data thus became unsuitable for the control group, but rather than eliminate them from the study, we decided to include them as a second experimental group, for which we would predict the same changes in perceptions of others as we expected the experimental group to show. Accordingly, they completed their second Person Description administration at the same time as the 12-man control group, but the data for this second experimental group were treated separately.

The control group and the second experimental group were close to equivalent in organizational level and function. They included men from roughly the third and fourth levels of the division. The original experimental group's 11 men were from the first, second, and third levels.

To avoid confusion it should be emphasized that the control group is *not* identical to the control group described previously by Chris Argyris, though there may have been a few men who were members of both groups.

We predicted that if the members of the experimental groups came to value the interpersonal and emotional aspects of behavior more highly, then they would use more terms referring to such characteristics when describing one another and their colleagues after the training than they had before.

We also considered the possibility that the first experimental group might find the new values applicable to their relations with each other but would find it difficult to apply them successfully with subordinates and associates, because the demands of the organizational structure and the expectations of associates would coerce them to return to previous patterns of relationship. Under these conditions, we expected an increase in their use of interpersonal terms to describe members of the training group, but no significant increase in the use of such terms to describe colleagues who did not attend the laboratory.

A coding scheme was devised to separate the descriptions of interpersonal and emotional characteristics from those referring to intellective, technical characteristics or the organizational function of the person described. Each description (a characteristic and its opposite) was transferred to an IBM card, along with a code number indicating its origin. The 1,572 cards (a few members did not describe all sets of three persons) were then classified according to a scheme which provided six broad categories and two levels within these categories. The assignment of each description to a category was done "blind," that is, without knowledge of whether the description was made before or after training or whether it came from an experimental or control group.

CATEGORY I

Descriptions specifically concerned with the ways a person relates to others. Included would be descriptions of tendencies to dominate or be submissive; to give affection, support, and help or to be critical, destructive and hostile; to participate with others or withdraw from them; to be frank and open or to be reserved or evasive; and to be honest and responsible or to be untrustworthy and irresponsible.

The significant difference between this category and the following one is that the descriptions in Category I specifically refer to a relationship with other persons. They are of the character, "When this person is in relationship to others, he characteristically acts, feels, expresses the following:————"

CATEGORY II

The attitudes, needs and tendencies to act which are described have important consequences for interpersonal relationships, but they can exist outside of such relationships. Included are descriptions of strength of motivation and ambition; confidence, security, and inner comfort; decisiveness, willingness to take risks, and speed of reaction to situations; tendencies to be optimistic and enthusiastic or pessimistic and apathetic; and tendencies to be stable and predictable versus being excitable and inconsistent.

CATEGORY III

Descriptions of a person's cognitive styles and abilities. This category would include a man's approaches to solving problems, the quality of his decisions and judgment, and his possession of important job information.

CATEGORY IV

Descriptions of competence or ability on the job or in parts of the job.

CATEGORY V

Descriptions of a person's status or position in the organization. This would include vertical status in terms of success, authority, and advancement; it also includes horizontal position, such as a person's background, functional branch, and time and experience in the company.

CATEGORY VI

Descriptions of a person's physical characteristics.

In addition to the analysis by categories, two levels were classified within Categories I and II, the interpersonal and emotional categories. The division into levels was undertaken to separate for analysis the "deeper" interpersonal descriptions we felt would increase with training.

Level 1 contained "shallower" descriptions. They referred to how good, effective, or socially desirable a person's behavior is; or they dealt with "surface," "skin-deep" interpersonal-emotional characteristics; or they were vague or ambiguous in meaning.

Thus, the remaining descriptions in Level 2 imply more interest in and understanding of the person described. Only the descriptions at Level 2 were expected to or did in fact increase with training.

The data resulting from the classification were analyzed in two ways. In the first, the changes in Category I, Level 2, were analyzed. These were the descriptions which most specifically dealt with the interpersonal area. Another analysis compared the proportions before and after the training in Categories I and II combined, Level 2. By combining these categories, a measure was obtained which included all the Level 2 descriptions dealing with interpersonal and emotional characteristics of others.

In addition to the initial coding, a second coding of a random sample of 250 descriptions was done by another person, using a detailed outline of each category provided by the author. The results of this reliability check are shown in Table 17 and indicate that the coding process is repeatable.

Table 18 shows the percentages of the total person descriptions in each group which fell in Level 2, Categories I and II, the interpersonal and emotional categories. We had predicted that in every case but that of the control group, there would be a significant shift after training toward the use of more Category I and II descriptions at the deeper Level 2.

This prediction was confirmed for all conditions except that in which the first experimental group described 10 associates who did not participate in the training, before and three months after the laboratory. Under this condition there was no increase in the use of interpersonal and emotional descriptions. The reader will remember that we had expected these results to test the success of the experimental group in applying laboratory values and learning in their relations with others who had not participated with them in training.

This negative finding may be explained in two ways. One explanation is that in solving problems of relationship posed by the laboratory situation and by the educators, members of the experimental group learned to see one another in new ways. These new perceptions were not, however, accompanied by lasting changes in values; hence, on returning to their jobs, the executives had no particular motivation to develop new ways of seeing and relating to associates.

Another explanation would hold that significant change in values did occur at the laboratory. On their return, however, the pressures on the executives from the organizational structure and the expectations of associates to behave according to accustomed patterns were so great that failure and frustration were experienced in applying new values to back-home relationships. A climate did not exist in which the executives could readily apply new perceptions of interpersonal and emotional characteristics to the solution of job problems.

If we knew that the second experimental group had not chosen to describe people who later participated in their laboratory training, we would choose the second explanation, since this would be evidence of one group's having developed new perceptions outside the setting in which they were acquired.

TABLE 17

RELIABILITY OF CODING PERSON DESCRIPTIONS

Proportion of 250 Cards Coded the Same by Independent Coders

Category I versus all others.................................... .96
Categories I and II versus all others......................... .94
Level 1 versus Level 2 in Categories I and II.................. .94

TABLE 18

PER CENT INTERPERSONAL DESCRIPTIONS GIVEN BEFORE AND AFTER
LABORATORY TRAINING

LEVEL 2

	Category I			Categories I and II		
	(Before)	*(After)*	*(Change)*	*(Before)*	*(After)*	*(Change)*
Experimental group describing each other (N = 11).............29		43	14*	65	75	10†
Experimental group describing 10 other associates (N = 10)........34		30	−4	65	65	0
Second experimental group describing 10 associates (N = 8).....29		38	9‡	54	65	11‡
Control group describing 10 associates (N = 12)..30		30	0	54	55	1

* Significance of $p < .02$ using one-tailed Mann-Whitney test.
† Significance of $p < .04$ using one-tailed Mann-Whitney test.
‡ Significance of $p < .07$ when second experimental group is compared with control group using one-tailed Mann-Whitney test.

Unfortunately, this group made their choices privately, and we have no way of knowing whom they described. It is not unlikely that they, too, described people with whom they later attended the training laboratory.

Our person-description data do not by themselves determine a choice between the alternative explanations. Chris Argyris' interviews found, however, that the executives reported difficulty and frustration in applying new learning against the expectations and pressures exerted by subordinates, peers, and superiors, to behave in ways the latter were accustomed to. These data tend to support the belief that values did change with laboratory training and that the failure to develop new perceptions of associates who were not trained was not due to low motivation to apply learning, but was instead related to the counterpressures from the organization.

It might be argued that these findings mean that little of lasting value is likely to result from training even a top group of executives in the manner described in this study, since even those high in the organization and most free from its restraints seem to have met with severe difficulties in applying laboratory learnings to their relations with managers who were not trained. Such a conclusion would, however, ignore the observations made of this group in the three months after the final Person Description measures were taken, and during which the members of the experimental group continued to work to extend and practice their newly acquired values. It would also discount the changes in policy and practice that have already occurred in the division, and the persistence and commitment to the new values and to each other which have helped members of the group to withstand the pressures to return to the "old way."

An alternative and more reasonable position would be to regard the findings of this study, both those based on observation and those based on the Person Description Instrument, as consistent evidence in favor of two general conclusions. The first is that real and lasting changes in interpersonal perceptions can occur through laboratory training. The second is that the expectations of others and the demands and restrictions of an organization's structure may pose formidable obstacles to practicing the values and using the new perceptual skills.

Most practically, though our findings are based on a small sample of top executives in one organization, they may serve as a warning to those who would hope to catalyze major change in any organization through modest "human relations training programs" for middle and lower management. Frequently, such programs are undertaken in hopes that higher management will be sufficiently impressed by the results to involve themselves in the training. The network of structural demands and interpersonal expectations existing in the organization would seem to be quite resistant even to the determined efforts of a group of rather powerful men to behave differently with subordinates, peers, and bosses. What hope is there for real change to be initiated from below by men with less freedom and fewer organizational resources to draw upon?

The findings of this study would indicate, rather, the need for planned links between the training of superior, subordinate, and peers. Such links could be provided by the two-session training sequence in which each executive attends once as peer and subordinate, and once as formal leader.

SUMMARY OF FINDINGS USING THE PERSON DESCRIPTION INSTRUMENT

The Person Description Instrument was administered to both experimental and control groups before and after laboratory training. Its purpose was to assess the extent to which participants saw others in the organization in interpersonal and emotional terms, as against seeing them in terms of rational and intellective competence or in terms of their function in the organization.

It was expected that members of the experimental group would increase their use of interpersonal terms, while the control group would remain constant. This prediction was confirmed, both for the original experimental group describing each other, and for a second experimental group describing 10 associates selected by themselves. However, the increased use of interpersonal terms did not carry over to the experimental group's descriptions of 10 of their associates not attending the laboratory.

These findings are interpreted as further evidence of the effectiveness of the laboratory training in increasing the desire and ability to perceive and respond to interpersonal and emotional aspects of behavior. The lack of transfer, however, underscores the difficulties experienced even by persons of relatively high status and power in changing the demands of the organizational structure and the expectations of others in the organization from a more rational-intellective emphasis to one in which interpersonal and emotional behavior are dealt with effectively and openly.

12

Conclusions

The objectives of the research were (1) to explore the potential scientific pay-off of a model (2) to help a group of executives increase their interpersonal competence and the effectiveness of their executive system (3) by the use of an organizational diagnosis and (4) a specially planned laboratory followed up by (5) efforts "back home" to maintain and wherever possible to increase the learnings obtained at the laboratory.

Although we have achieved all these objectives in varying degrees, the conclusions must be stated with extreme caution because (1) of the small number of cases included in the study (2) the lack of adequate controls, and (3) the loose state of conceptualization of the models.

A. The Use of the Model

The model that was developed attempted to relate the executives' values concerning effective human relations to their interpersonal competence as well as to the effectiveness of the executive system. The model was found to be helpful in four activities:

1. To diagnose the degree of interpersonal competence of the executives as a group and to ascertain its impact upon the executive system and on the organization.

2. To provide an over-all guiding framework for a long-range program of organizational change. The model was found to be especially useful in:

a) Planning the program of the laboratory.
b) Carrying out the laboratory.
c) Guiding the author as a T-group leader.

3. To evaluate the changes, if any, after the program was finished.

4. To guide the executive and the behavioral scientist in his consulting activities after the laboratory was finished.

B. THE DIAGNOSTIC VALIDITY OF THE MODEL

1. We found, as the model predicted, that the top executives tended to hold the following values (personal commands) about effective human relationships within organization:

a) The important human relationships are those that are achieving the organization's objective (getting the job done).
b) Effectiveness in human relationships increases as behavior is rational, logical, and clearly communicated. Effectiveness decreases as emotionality increases.
c) Human relationships are most effectively influenced through direction, coercion, and control as well as a set of rewards and penalties that serve to emphasize the rational behavior and getting the job done.

2. We also found, as the model predicted, that the more the executive adhered to and emphasized these values, the greater the probability that the following would tend to *decrease:*

a) Receiving and giving of nonevaluative feedback.
b) Owning and permitting others to own their ideas, feelings, and values.
c) Openness to view ideas, feelings, and values.
d) Experimentation and risk taking with new ideas and values.

3. As anyone of the above decreased, it tended to influence the others to decrease which, in turn, served to reinforce, in the executive minds, the importance of the original values (rationality, controls, direction, and so on).

4. As (2) and (3) occurred, the probability increased that the interpersonal competence of the executive group would tend to decrease.

5. As interpersonal competence decreased, it reinforced (2) and (3). Simultaneously it *increased* within the organization, conformity, mistrust, external commitment, organizational defensiveness, interdepartmental rivalries, and *decreased* the effectiveness of many human and personnel decisions.

6. All these states of affairs, served to "convince" the executives to be wary of the interpersonal and emotional dimensions of life. This, in turn, acted to cause them to reinforce the original values of rationality, control, and directiveness. The loop is closed to form a self-maintaining system slowly but surely becoming less and less effective along its human and some of its technical dimensions.

7. The predictions above are thought to be applicable to this organization and to all others following the same formal organizational values. Our hypothesis is that the same basic finding will tend to hold in other formal organizations with variations primarily in degree (for example, churches, hospitals, schools, governmental bureaus, as well as other industrial organizations).

8. Although in this study the model was used to evaluate *interpersonal* competence, if one wanted to, the same model might be adapted to diagnose intellective, rational competence. Much research is required to make explicit how the model can be used in the study of intellective variables. The general strategy might be to measure the giving and receiving of technical information, owning technical ideas, experimenting and taking risks with new technical ideas, and so on. According to our model, executives who adhere to the values of formal organization would tend to score higher along these dimensions. This was found to be the case in this company. The executives' technical competence was extremely high. Indeed, this study implies that major increases in the technical competence in this company will probably be made by increasing interpersonal competence. In other words, the organization has available even more technical potential but, because of the lower interpersonal competence and associated human problems, it was not able to use it. An excellent example was the time that technical people reported that they used to perform tasks that resulted from the defensiveness of the system

and ironically served primarily to reinforce the very same defensiveness. Some called it "windmilling." Others simply stated that they spent "a hell of a lot of time doing nothing that moves things forward." Still others described it as, "Spending time keeping someone happy but not getting the job done." Estimates of how much time was spent "windmilling" ranged from a minimum of 20 per cent to 50 per cent of one's time.

The emphasis upon interpersonal competence should not be interpreted to mean that intellective competence is not important in the functioning of T-groups and the laboratory. Indeed, the research has been conducted with a group of individuals with relatively high intelligence. Although empirical research is necessary to document the view, it is probably true that intelligence played an important part in the success of the experience. The men seemed to be able to grasp quickly the cognitive material presented in the lectures. Also, they developed cognitive maps with which to organize their thinking and to develop new learnings.

In the writer's opinion, laboratory training, in the past, has neglected and unduly de-emphasized the importance of intellective competence to the development of interpersonal competence.[1] Mann's conclusion that intelligence is an important predicter of behavior in small groups probably applies equally to T-groups.[2] The time has arrived when the relationship of the intellective and interpersonal factors must be studied systematically. For example, there is probably a minimum amount of interpersonal and intellective competence needed in the participants if laboratory education is to succeed. Also, studies are needed to help us understand the co-impact of various combinations of intellective and interpersonal competence upon one another. Such studies could make important contributions to our understanding of human competence. Also,

---

[1] Gouldner correctly suggests this is a criticism that can be leveled against many of the emerging social science theories of organization. Alvin W. Gouldner, "Organizational Analyses," in Robert K. Merton, and Leonard Broom, Jr., *Sociology Today* (New York: Basic Books, Inc., 1959) p. 408.

[2] Richard D. Mann, "A Review of the Relationships Between Personality and Performance in Small Groups," *Psychology Bulletin,* Vol. LVI, No. 4 (July, 1959), pp. 241–70.

it may help to restore cognitive material to its rightful position in the laboratory.

The "rationalists" have, on the other hand, neglected the importance of interpersonal factors. Some, like March, once they go out into the field, are faced with the importance of nonrational behavior (for example, intergroup conflict, fear of major innovative searching, and so on) although unfortunately, up to this time, deal with it as a given rather than something that is changeable.

During this study I asked the executives to compare the difficulty of interpersonal with rational decisions. In all cases they quickly and unequivocally emphasized that for them the human decisions were much more difficult. When pushed to be more concrete, all said that it is easier to make decisions running into the millions ($150,000,000 was the highest figure volunteered) than to deal with interpersonal problems. If one studies executive decision making, in real life, this finding should not be too startling. For example, we have seen how these executives personally disliked dealing with interpersonal issues and how the executive system sanctioned this avoidance. Secondly, decisions running into the millions of dollars are carefully studied by teams of men, spending countless hours, aided by computers, consultants, research, and any other help that is available. It may be, as some suggest, that these decision-making processes are still quite ineffective. However, within the present executive world, if a decision turns out to be incorrect, *after the best possible study* is made, the executive tends to feel, and to be supported in this feeling, that he did his best. This does not mean that executives do not feel badly, are not criticized and at times discharged or demoted when they make wrong decisions. It simply suggests that one of the main functions of the increasingly bigger staff role with its adjunct technology exists to make rational decision making more effective.

Perhaps in the future an organization will strive to increase its effectiveness in coping with the "rationality of interpersonal relations" and their impact on organizational effectiveness as it is striving to increase its effectiveness in the more rational aspects of decision making.

C. THE LABORATORY: ONLY A PART OF THE CHANGE PROCESS

It is important to keep in mind that the change process was *not* limited to the laboratory program. It had the following steps or stages:

1. The change process began with the research interviews and observations to diagnose the executive system. Although the early diagnostic phase did not by itself change behavior or values, it did help to unfreeze the executives to consider the necessity for change. Moreover, the diagnostic research was especially useful in helping the researcher and the executives determine if they and the organization could withstand a laboratory and related change activities. The change process we have considered could cause harm to certain kinds of organizations, or create more problems in others. In some it could create even greater crises. In short, although the change program can be valuable, it should be applied with caution.

2. After the diagnostic research was completed, the results were fed back to the executives. The research results helped the executives to see their system and its impact upon the organization more clearly and accurately.

3. The next step was a laboratory composed of the president and his immediate subordinates plus a small number of top executives to act as a control group.

4. Briefly, the objectives of the laboratory program were (*a*) to help the executives modify their values about effective human relations in such a way that (*b*) they increase the frequency and quality of feedback, of owning feelings and ideas, openness, experimentation, and risk taking, (*c*) leading to an increase in interpersonal competence and (*d*) a decrease in mistrust, dependence, conformity, organizational defenses, interdepartmental rivalries, thereby (*e*) increasing the effectiveness of problem solving as well as the organization as a whole.

The laboratory is a total (intellectual and emotional) educational experience whose entire makeup is planned to mirror the very values that it hopes the executives learn. It is composed of learning experiences that tend to emphasize trust, openness, internal commitment, minimum of conformity, dependence, and so on.

The proper composition of a laboratory is also very much open to debate and requires more experimentation. At this time, only a suggestion can be offered based upon this and other experiences to date. The composition with the greatest probable pay-off is the "natural group"; that is, a given executive and his immediate subordinates. However, the "natural group" is also fraught with many dangers. If the group or senior executive is too defensive, then the chances for success are greatly decreased and the probability of danger to the organization significantly increased. In this experiment, if the president and/or the group were so defensive that they could not learn from one another, the experience would not only have failed to achieve the objectives, it could have left important barriers and created new problems within the executive system as well as the organization. This is one reason why a diagnostic research phase is absolutely necessary. Laboratory training is education in which human beings are deeply affected. The least that can be done is a diagnosis be made to estimate the degree of defensiveness of the executive system and the chief executive which, in turn, would lead to an estimate of the probability of success, failure, and/or harm to the organization.

In spite of all their difficulties, the "natural group" is recommended as the first step. Needless to say, it should be started at the top. (More of this later.) One can help increase the probability of success by having some of the executives attend a laboratory experience outside the organization.[3] When the time came for the organization to have its own laboratory, one would have several executives with whom to "seed" the natural group. This was done in our experiment, and it seemed to have very positive effects.

After all the members of a given unit have been through

---

[3] The author recommends great caution in selecting a laboratory experience. The popularity of such training has caused a great number of individuals to set up laboratories. Many of them are composed with ill-equipped faculty members. The oldest and most reliable organization (in the author's opinion) is the National Training Laboratories, plus their regional affiliates (for example, the Western, South Western, and Rocky Mountain Laboratories).

a laboratory experience with their own group, then they may be mixed up in any combination necessary for further training or for problem-solving and action-taking conferences.

A possible useful model is for president and vice-presidents to go through a 10-day laboratory experience. Then each vice-president (after appropriate passage of time and in some sequence satisfactory to the organization) can attend a second laboratory with his subordinates. This would mean, for example, that in one year's time each executive would have about two weeks of laboratory training.

The length of the laboratory was, and still is, very much an open question. It depends, too, upon the defensiveness of the participants, compounded by the defensiveness of the organization. Some have suggested that a *minimum* of 10 days is necessary, not including the time necessary for the feedback of the diagnoses. In our case, the time was less, but we were fortunate in having an extremely strong management that was able to capitalize upon its potential. Although 10 days is less than the time typically found necessary for a laboratory composed of "strangers," it may be that a laboratory for a "natural group" with a diagnosed low level of defensiveness can be expected to move faster than a group composed of strangers. For example, French found that in comparing groups composed of people who knew one another versus groups composed of strangers, the former showed definitely more social freedom, "we-feeling," motivation, interdependence, which led to greater freedom of expressed aggression and hostility while, at the same time, manifesting equality of participation.[4]

The learnings developed by the experimental group surpassed ours, as well as the executives' expectations. They reported, and we observed, within the experimental group increases in such qualities as openness, trust, confidence, and decreases in conformity, management by detail, crises, fear, and conflict. However, we found that initially the experimental group faced important difficulties in communicating their newly learned values to, and using them with, the control group

---

[4] John R. P. French, "Organized and Unorganized Groups under Fear and Frustration," *University of Iowa Studies in Child Welfare*, Vol. XX (1944), pp. 229–308.

and others who had not participated in the laboratory. The experimental group turned more to changing policies and practices to influence the subordinates rather than through interpersonal relationships. This seemed to have a positive effect. The subordinates perceived these changes as proof that the superiors were in earnest.

It should not be interpreted that the executives were able to utilize their values as frequently as they wished. There were many factors preventing them from doing so. Not the least were the continuing use of the "old" values by corporate head-quarters, the resulting crises, as well as the confusion and lack of skill on the part of the subordinates to understand and work within the framework of the new values. Also, many routines are more effectively carried out by using the traditional values. I estimate that during the everyday activities the executives were able to use their "new" values from 25 to 50 per cent of the time. However, when they used the "old" values, they were aware of their true impact. The unintended quality of the impact was greatly decreased. Consequently, the executives had to take on responsibility for the "negative" outcomes.

The experimental group did invite the control group to go through their own laboratory. The results were extremely interesting and hopefully may be published in a separate document. Suffice it to say that their laboratory was not as successful as the first (by the standards of a laboratory composed of "strangers," it was about a little below average). Apparently, the problems discussed above had taken their toll at the lower levels. For example, there seemed to be greater feelings of dependence and helplessness and a concomitant expectation that somehow the laboratory staff (Dr. Bradford and myself) would tell them *what to* learn, and guide them through the unstructured program. There was also greater resistance to the laboratory when it became clear that they had to face these feelings of dependence.

This is not to imply that important learnings were not developed. All men returned home with a greater understanding of the complexities of human relationships, of the great gap between believing in "good human relations" and actually behaving them, of their lack of awareness of their impact upon others, of their difficulties in telling others what their impact has been upon them, and of the relatively low sense of inter-personal trust and competence.

These are important learnings. Where the control group "missed" was that it did not go beyond these learnings to establish the climate of trust, openness, and leveling which could help them grow even more, especially when they re-turned home. However, some did increase their development after returning, because they and their superiors (members of the experimental group) held short sessions in which these problems were discussed.

It is interesting to note that upon conclusion the control group reported some sadness that they were not able to learn as much as they believed their superiors did. Perhaps even more important was the reaction of the superiors upon receiv-ing some (officially released) feedback. They decided that this was proof that they and the organization were creating too much dependency at the lower levels and they had to do some-thing about it.

5. One may conclude from this and other experiences that it would not be wise to start laboratory training in a given organizational unit at the middle or lower levels.[5] One may imagine what would have happened if the control group had gone first. The top would probably never have considered the program. But, even if the laboratory had been a greater suc-cess, it would have been difficult for a subordinate to attempt to explain the experience to the superiors. Compounding this problem would be the fact that the subordinates would realize that their superiors held the traditional values and, therefore, would naturally raise serious questions about the validity of the change program. Under these conditions, the probability for communicating and influencing the top would be very low. Unless the top could be influenced, changes made at the middle or lower levels could create even greater problems and at best would remain encapsulated in that particular unit.

Another important lesson learned was the value of the

---

[5] Professor Edward Schein of M.I.T. informs me that he and a group of colleagues have successfully completed laboratory education by beginning at the lower level.

research. At least half of the men, in the second laboratory, had not been interviewed or observed in action. Many asked why they had not been studied. They felt that they would have learned much from the feedback of the results. The lack of research at their level was interpreted by many of the sub-ordinates as evidence that they were not as important as the superiors.

It also became evident that the research had the positive impact of "getting people accustomed to being studied," "to be asked questions," and to have introduced in their life an increased attention to the interpersonal dimensions. Finally, the research was extremely helpful during the laboratory to inhibit the executives from resisting the laboratory by "ganging up" on the staff and insisting that they did not have any problems, such as lack of openness. In the experimental group whenever a man asked, "Is that what *really* happened at the meetings?" the researcher was able to help by presenting an organized picture of the meeting. This also helped the others to unfreeze and to add details and points that the researcher had missed.

6. It is important to re-emphasize that the values regarding effective human relations were not only "caused by" interpersonal relationships. They were a part of the "bone and fabric" of the formal organizational structure, its technology, and managerial controls. Consequently, if change was to remain and become permanent in the organization, these factors must also be altered so they will reinforce and sanction the new values. Changes at any interpersonal level would be doomed to eventual extinction if they were not reinforced by the organization structure, technology, managerial policies, and controls.

7. However, the change process should begin by focusing on interpersonal competence as well as on the degree to which the executives create mistrust, conformity, organizational defenses, and so on. Unless the executives first see themselves and their impact accurately, they will not tend to be able to make effective changes throughout the organization. It may be that changes at the lower levels can be begun by instituting changes in structure, policies, practices, and so on.

8. It is hoped that this study will help to dispel the notion that all laboratory training is aimed at getting people to like one another, to "get along," and to suppress conflict. As the model makes implicit, the values of laboratory are openness, experimentation, risk taking, and owning one's feelings. Conformity and dependence and "diplomatic maneuvering" are not consonant with the values of laboratory education. It is difficult to understand how anyone can attach a "sweetness and light" philosophy to such values. If they are correlated with anything, it is to hard work, pain, discomfort, conflict, tension, and frustration. If anyone doubts this, let him join a T-group. To repeat, the values underlying the laboratory education, known to the writer, are to help individuals become aware of and own their feelings, values, and ideas; to experiment and take risks with new feelings, values, and ideas; to increase their individuality, nonconformity, self-responsibility, and internal commitment.

D. THE BEHAVIORAL SCIENCE CONSULTANT OR CHANGE AGENT

Finally, there was the period of "trying out," "fitting in," the new values into "back-home" executive relationships as well as into the organization. This phase was the longest and from the company's view one of the most important. Its early months were crucial. It was during this stage that the learnings would be placed into action.

The problems of back-home application even for (if not especially for) a group composed of the president and vice-presidents were so complex, that a "change agent," "catalyst," "behavioral science consultant" (or whatever other name one would want to use) could have been used even more frequently than was the case in the study.[6]

a) The job of such a person would be to help the group to continue their own training and growth and to introduce their learnings throughout the organization. This is a relatively little understood area, and much research is required. For

---

[6] See the work by Robert Blake. Also, the recent book by Cyril Sofer, *The Organization from Within* (Tavestock Publications, 1961).

example, little is known about the "proper" time for the behavioral scientist consultant to leave the organization. How much learning must a group have before it can be "put on its own"? How can a group be helped to meet such crisis situations as the departure of old or the introduction of new members? What organizational pressures would tend to require the help of a consultant, and what pressures are not significant? What kinds of "booster" education can be provided, and at what time should they be offered?

Ideally, such an individual should be a competent field researcher, laboratory planner, T-group educator, organizational or small-group theorist who is personally capable of establishing authentic relationships. Admittedly, such an individual is extremely hard to find.

b) However, they can be developed. If industry (or any other sector of our society) wished, training programs could be created. Although there are no systematic data from which to recommend minimum training, one might consider the minimum to be at least one year for an individual perhaps with a Ph. D. in some behavioral science. This amount of time may seem long, especially because of the scarcity of such individuals. However, it is not if we keep in mind the tremendous complexity as well as dangers involved in the kinds of change programs that we have described. For example, in this study there was the constant danger of unintentionally hurting people and decreasing the already existing effectiveness of the groups. There was also a danger of increasing individual and organizational defensiveness. The temporary confusion, anxiety, and dependence could have significant impacts if they were not handled properly.

It should be clear that we are no longer talking about training programs that can be developed by an individual who has industry experience, common sense, and likes people. Indeed, if people would really learn from their experience alone, these programs would not be needed. Nor can they be developed by educators well-trained in the traditional forms of educating. (However, some of these men could probably be re-trained.) If a recent experience is at all representative, these programs may not even be made the direct responsibility of even some of the "best" directors of executive development.[7]

The activities of research, training, and consulting form a new and important role for developing the organization. The men who develop skills in these activities can become extremely useful in helping to increase and make more secure the health of an organization. It is hoped that this role-cluster will be the future responsibility of personnel administration.[8]

E. OLD VALUES SUPPLEMENTED, NOT OVERTHROWN

1. In closing, we should emphasize that the values of the formal organization did, and still do, have utility in specific administrative situations. The difficulty is that, in the past, they had been used to guide the executives' behavior in all situations. The values of formal organization are especially useful in emergencies, in coping with routine decisions, in making decisions where crucial organizational policies are not affected, and when the development of people is not important.

2. The new values learned at the laboratory can be used to *supplement* the old values in different administrative situations. They are especially useful when one wants to decrease mistrust, conformity, dependence, organizational defensiveness, and to increase internal commitment, creativity, organizational flexibility, and interdepartmental co-operation.

The final word of caution is that the entire change program cannot be conceived as having a beginning and an end. If the new values of growth and self-development are inculcated in the organization, then the change actually has added a new way of life to the system. The emphasis then becomes one of continually diagnosing, modifying, and making more effective the new *processes* of work relationships.

Therein lies a tremendous challenge to management, indeed, to any administrator. We are suggesting nothing less than that the basic values which emphasize the dignity and importance of the individual can be integrated with the fury and pressure of everyday administrative life to the benefit of the individual and the organization.

---

[7] Chris Argyris, "Puzzle and Perplexity in Executive Development," *Personnel Journal*, April, 1961.

[8] Chris Argyris, "Explorations in Consulting-Client Relationships," *Human Organization*, Vol. XX, No. 3 (Fall, 1961), pp. 122–33.

INDEXES

Author Index

Subject Index

291